Praise for *Ali vs. Inoki*

"It's only fitting that Josh Gross—an early MMA adopter and as fine a writer/reporter as the sport has—gives us this dispatch of an original boxer-versus-grappler contest. Our only question: When's the movie coming out?"

—L. JON WERTHEIM, *executive editor,* Sports Illustrated

D0645376

ALI VS. INOKI

The Forgotten Fight That Inspired Mixed Martial Arts and Launched Sports Entertainment

JOSH GROSS

BENBELLA

BenBella Books, Inc.
Dallas, Texas

BenBella

BenBella Books, Inc.
PO Box 572028
Dallas, TX 75357-2028
www.benbellabooks.com
Send feedback to feedback@benbellabooks.com

Printed in the United States of America
10 9 8 7 6 5 4 3 2 1

Library of Congress Cataloging-in-Publication Data is available upon request.

ISBN 978-1-942952-19-0

Editing by Erin Kelley
Copyediting by Scott Calamar
Proofreading by Brittney Martinez
    and Lisa Story
Front cover design by Pete Garceau
Full cover design by Sarah
    Dombrowsky

Indexing by Debra Bowman
Text design and composition by
    Aaron Edmiston
Author photo courtesy of Eva Napp
    / © www.evanapp.com
Printed by Lake Book
    Manufacturing

Distributed by Perseus Distribution
perseusdistribution.com

To place orders through Perseus Distribution:
Tel: (800) 343-4499
Fax: (800) 351-5073
E-mail: orderentry@perseusbooks.com

Special discounts for bulk sales (minimum of 25 copies) are available.
Please contact Aida Herrera at aida@benbellabooks.com.

For my mom, who gave me the chance to tell this story

TABLE of CONTENTS

FOREWORD

I was a kid, all of eleven years old, when the fight between Muhammad Ali and Antonio Inoki took place in 1976. At that time, the two biggest names in martial arts were Bruce Lee and Ali. As a kid who got bullied because I suffered from a skin disease, severe asthma attacks, and being very skinny, I often dreamt: "If I only had skills like them, the bullies would be in trouble!"

Several years later, having beaten my childhood bullies, I watched the documentary *Kings of the Square Ring*. That was when I saw the match between Ali and Inoki, which took place in the Nippon Budokan in Tokyo. I would have never guessed that many years later I'd successfully defend my Pancrase world title in that same arena by stopping Frank Shamrock.

Crazy how life goes, right?

Still to this day one of my biggest wishes is to meet the legend Muhammad Ali. This guy had it all: looks, charisma, skill, and he could walk the walk. Later in life, when I knew what pro wrestling was—we don't have pro wrestling in the

Netherlands—I realized that Ali took a lot of notes from that art to promote himself. Getting everybody riled up, you either wanted to see him win or lose. Love him or hate him, he sold tickets.

The other great thing about the way he talked was that he made opponents really angry. And, when competing, anger is not something that belongs in the martial arts world because it clouds your mind.

I really liked Ali's nonchalant way of approaching a bout, so I did it as well when I was fighting. Training and competing would be the serious part, so why not have fun in between? Plus this way fans could also connect with me and see a "person" not just a "fighter," because let's face it, many people still perceive fighters as being angry all the time. I didn't want to be as outspoken as Ali was, though. Just being colorful was enough for me.

During my time competing in Japan, the name "Antonio Inoki" was mentioned in a conversation on many occasions. Everybody I talked to told me that he was not only a great pro wrestler but had real fighting skills as well. And, of course, the match between him and Ali would always come up.

Pro wrestling in Japan is called *puroresu*—that's just the way they say "pro wrestling"—and it's considered a "strong style," meaning they use real submission holds and prefer to connect with hard strikes or not at all.

Many great wrestlers like Yoshiaki Fujiwara, Karl Gotch, Masakatsu Funaki, and Minoru Suzuki are considered strong-style wrestlers. And all these guys tie into Inoki. Inoki was Fujiwara's *shisho* (teacher). Fujiwara and Gotch were Funaki and Suzuki's teachers.

I competed in Japan for the Pancrase organization from 1993 until 1998, and that organization was founded by Suzuki and Funaki. There were different rules than the ones we have in modern MMA. Open-hand strikes to the head, closed fist to the body; you wore shoes and shin protection—it looked like pro wrestling, only it's real. Unfortunately, we didn't use foreign objects like chairs to hit each other.

I was a striker. Growing up I studied karate, taekwondo, and Thai boxing. I always thought that "strikers" were the baddest dudes on the planet until I had my first submission class. For people who don't know how submissions work, let's just say that it's about manipulating pretty much any limb in the direction it's not supposed to go.

I was a good "striker," but that submission class showed me that I wasn't a badass in "fighting." They tore me up and I had no chance whatsoever. I got choked. Leg locked, arm-barred. Neck cranked. You name it. I realized I needed to learn this art because if I were to miss a strike to an opponent and he was able take me to the ground, I would be in major trouble.

Chris Dolman was my first "submission coach," but since his gym in Amsterdam was a two-hour drive from my home in Eindhoven, I didn't spend a lot of time there. When I was competing in Japan I would train at the official Pancrase Dojo. I would come in a few days earlier for the fight so I could hone my submission skills. It took me three losses by way of submission to finally make the decision that I needed steady training partners in Holland; otherwise this "losing" would keep happening. And that was it—after I found a training partner I never lost again and ended my career with an unbeaten streak of twenty-two.

I'll give you one story so you can understand why there were some rules changes just before the Ali and Inoki fight.

I was walking in Tokyo with a group of fighters the day before a match in 1994. We heard this big loud voice saying, "Hybrid wrestling, Pancrase." We looked to the side and saw the biggest TV screen we had ever seen. When I say at least forty feet wide, I am not exaggerating. We were looking at the promo for our fight the next day; it was a compilation of KO's and submissions from previous events.

In that promo I saw a fighter sitting in a certain position and he went for an inverted heel hook on his opponent. An inverted heel hook is a move that enables you to twist the lower leg from your opponent while his upper leg stays in the same position. You can actually twist it about 180 degrees. Needless to say, that's not good for your knee since you can twist it out of the socket. Anyway, I was still "green," only had four fights over there, so when I saw that technique I thought, "Hey, that's a cool move, I should remember that."

The next day I am fighting and what do you know? I am in that position! So I figured, "Let's try that thing I saw yesterday." Now since I had never trained for this, I had no clue what would happen; I just did what I had seen the day before on the big screen.

It resulted in me snapping my opponent's shinbone in half—apparently his knee was stronger than his shinbone. It freaked me out. That was the moment when I realized that "submission fighting" might be even worse than "striking." I mean, you can break or dislocate pretty much anything in the human body when you are well-versed at submissions.

Back to Inoki! So I had heard about "Inoki-san" many times and apparently he had heard about me as well, because in 2000 I was asked if I wanted to join his company, New Japan Pro Wrestling. To talk about this new deal I was asked to come and meet the great Inoki at his gym in Santa Monica.

When I walked in the first thing I noticed was somebody stretching on the wrestling mat, doing full splits as his upper body and face were flat on the ground. When he sat up I saw it was Inoki, then fifty-eight years old and still in great shape. He immediately stood and came over to shake my hand, a very friendly and charismatic person. You knew instantly why people are drawn to him.

It was an easy conversation, like I knew him already. We talked, shook hands, and the deal was done.

When Inoki left I talked a little bit more to his son-in-law, Simon Inoki. We talked about the company and what other things his father-in-law had done, and almost immediately the fight with Ali came up. Now I was always under the impression that the fight he was talking about was a "worked" fight, just like in pro wrestling, but Simon assured me that it was a real fight and he went over all the details.

Talking later to Don Frye, a superstar at New Japan and an early killer in the UFC, he assured me as well that it was indeed a real fight. All the other pro wrestlers that I came in contact with told me the same.

I was also working for the Pride Fighting Championships (PrideFC) as a commentator and in 2002 we had the biggest show ever, called Pride "Shockwave." Over 91,000 people were in the attendance. It was an outdoor event and when the show started Mr. Inoki came parachuting in to ringside. It was crazy, because first of all it was dark, but there was also a very strong wind coming into the arena. No problem for him. The sixty-year-old adrenaline junkie wanted to make an entrance, which he did.

Oh, and just so that you know, apparently Inoki was known for the ability to drink a beer superfast. It was funny, they told me that they heard I could drink a beer really fast as well, and that Inoki was the "champion." So would I like to compete against him? I said: "No thank you, I don't want to beat the great Inoki-san," and laughed. And yes, of course the supercompetitive Inoki now had to have the contest. End result? He lost that title when he challenged me at an after-party for PrideFC! Haha!

I am telling this story because on New Year's Eve Mr. Inoki had a tradition where people would get up in the ring and he would slap them across the face with a "good luck slap" that was meant to transfer some of his energy to you. It was amazing how many people would line up. Stupid me, I was one of them, and man did he slap me—hard! That's why I am telling this "beer story"—it's my payback!

So this book is about a striker versus a submission artist, both at the top level of their respective fields. Ali connects with a punch, the fight is over; when he doesn't connect and Inoki gets ahold of him, the fight is over—no room for mistakes on either side.

In the end, I think the fight between Ali and Inoki was an important one for the history books. Ali took a huge risk, because nowadays when a boxer says he's the best fighter in the world, I always say, "You're not. You are the best 'boxer' in the world." The best fighter is good everywhere the fight goes, standing or on the ground, so if Ali would have missed a punch and Inoki would get him on the ground, that would have been big trouble.

Godspeed, enjoy!

—Bas Rutten

ROUND ONE

The southern coast of Honshu, the largest and most populous of Japan's four main islands, trembled at 10:19 P.M. local time, Friday, June 18, 1976.

Thirty-eight miles away in Tokyo, the most famous man on the planet and some of the troop that followed him everywhere he went had just settled into their rooms on the forty-fourth floor at the upscale Keio Plaza Hotel. This marked the end of the first full day of fight week promotion building to a spectacle in Tokyo pitting a boxer, the one and only Muhammad Ali, against a professional wrestler, Japan's *puroresu* star Antonio Inoki.

Gene Kilroy, an Ali confidant, one of many people to claim close ties to the man during his iconic twenty-one-year boxing career, was shaving when the 4.4-magnitude quake rumbled through. Kilroy heard a bang and, through the reflection of a bathroom mirror, saw his clothes swinging in the closet. Later, he learned that structures in the area were built on rollers to cope with city life along the Ring of Fire, the seismic-heavy zone of volcanic activity surrounding the Pacific Ocean.

The evening jolt apparently did nothing to faze the world heavyweight champion boxer. One time, a plane carrying Ali and his entourage ran out of gas. The pilots initiated an emergency landing, and as the plane shook during its descent, Ali, staring at Kilroy, said calmly, "Allah has too much work for me to do to die like this." According to many of the people who occupied space around Ali for long stretches of his professional life, this was how it was. Very little bothered the man, which partly explains his great success as a prizefighter. Ali navigated scares on the earth and in the air just like he did in the ring: with a sense of invincibility.

By the summer of 1976, eight months after the boxer's heated rival Joe Frazier didn't answer the bell for Round 15 of the "Thrilla in Manila," Ali had hit the peak of his worldwide fame. The timing made sense for New Japan Pro Wrestling, Inoki's promotional company, to find a way to lure Ali to Japan. That meant financing the match, which included spending nearly $24,000 (more than $100,000 in 2015 values) over eleven nights in lodging and food costs for the heavyweight champion and his sizable entourage.

Less than a week before Ali arrived in Tokyo, Inoki gave the press a guided tour of the penthouse where The Greatest was booked to stay. Ali's "imperial" suite, priced at a princely $400 a night, boasted seven rooms. "I don't have to do this, but I will, as I consider Ali to be the greatest boxer in the world," said Japan's most famous grappler. The layout "befits a personality of his standing." Then, with cameras clicking, Inoki punched the bed Ali would sleep in.

Even after Ali's arrival, and with the event mere days away, few people interested in watching knew whether the match would be a lighthearted pro wrestling exhibition or a true mixed-rules competition. Ali's camp operated as if the match was a "shoot"—a legitimate contest—and late into fight week still attempted to negotiate as favorable a set of rules as possible for their guy. The general consensus was that it was crazy for Ali to step away from boxing to tangle up with a wrestler. Everyone from trainer Angelo Dundee to doctor Ferdie Pacheco to promoter Bob Arum thought it was stupid for the most famous boxer of all time to meet a grappler skilled enough to twist arms or slam heads—who, more to the point, was empowered to do so.

"I didn't want him to do it," Kilroy said. "Ali was going into his sport, Inoki wasn't going into Ali's sport."

Still, Ali did what he wanted and agreed to compete against a grappler, thus fulfilling a long-held desire to know what it was to take on a "rassler." Only notorious hypeman Drew "Bundini" Brown, convinced the boxer could easily finish Inoki, egged Ali on.

As the June 26th bout neared (thanks to the international date line, it aired live Friday night, June 25th, in North America), hardcore pro wrestling and boxing fans, Ali supporters, and martial arts aficionados, in small passionate pockets, speculated about the matchup and its legitimacy. Even though the boxer held some hope that the whole thing would end up a "work"—in pro wrestling parlance, a match with a predetermined outcome—talk of that evaporated months earlier after Vince McMahon Sr., a patriarch of American pro wrestling, approached Ali's camp with the idea.

"McMahon wanted Ali to throw the fight," Kilroy said. "Ali wouldn't do it. That's the truth. That never got out."

"Throw" is a sports term that connotes corruption. In sumo, for example, match fixing is called *yaochō*. For an assortment of crooked reasons it continues to happen everywhere. While pro wrestling could be thought of as a sort of con because of the faux competition, by the mid-1970s money wasn't being waged on outcomes rooted in performance art instead of legerdemain. McMahon told Ali he should take the fall and get pinned. The boxer responded that he went down for no man who couldn't make him. The fact that at the apex of his popularity Ali preferred the risk of a real fight over scripted outcomes spoke to his state of mind as a competitor. The industrial influence of Jabir Herbert Muhammad, who managed Ali starting in 1966 after the boxer's conversion to Islam, helped create the right financial picture, including sealing the deal on a live broadcast from Tokyo with the help of his partner at Top Rank, Inc., Bob Arum.

A potential audience of 1.4 billion people in 134 countries was able to partake in the events from Tokyo thanks to the advent of the closed-circuit telecast. Through a groundbreaking satellite-age technology that let audiences congregate and experience far-flung events in real time, more than 150 sites in the United States showed the fight. When the hybrid-rules bout was officially announced at a press conference in New York City on May 5, 1976, Arum proclaimed that the match would "sell more closed-TV seats than any fight event in history. It will be bigger than the Foreman-Joe Frazier fight and all three of the Ali-Frazier bouts."

Two nights before arriving in Tokyo, Ali asserted on *The Tonight Show* how serious this fight was to him. Actor

McLean Stevenson spent the final of four consecutive guest-hosting spots fawning over Ali in a way that must have made his previous visitors—Sonny Bono, Harvey Korman, Suzanne Somers, Kreskin, Bernadette Peters, Phyllis Diller, and Rip Taylor—feel like nobodies.

"I have no idea what to say," Stevenson murmured once Ali sat down. "I suppose we could start with, 'How did you get started boxing?' Now if you find any of these questions stupid, just punch Ed in the mouth."

As the studio laughter subsided, Ali said, indeed, it was "a stupid question."

"I've been asked that so much," he replied. "I thought you were going to ask me how I got started rasslin'. Boxing is old news. We're in a new field now. We're going to Japan to take on this Antonio Inoki, the world's heavyweight karate wrestling champion. This is a whole new thing. People have always wondered how would a boxer do with a wrestler. I've always wanted to fight a wrestler. I've seen them grabbing each other. Throwing each other down and twisting each other's arm. And I said, 'Boy I could whoop him. All you gotta do is hit him, hit him really fast and hard and move off of him.' And now I'm going to get a chance to do it. This will be something. I predict this will outsell all of my fights, and I'm the biggest draw in the world. Everybody should watch this fight.

"Listen, I'm going to play the ropes. We're going fifteen rounds, three-minute rounds. He's allowed to use his bare fists. He's allowed to use karate. No punching in the eyes and no hitting below the belt. If I can grab the ropes when I'm down he's going to have to turn me loose, and you saw a sample on *Wide World of Sports* a few days ago when I beat these rasslers to bloody messes. That's right. And that's what I'm gonna get. Plus he's starting to talk. He's talking about, I better bring a sling and crutches with me, and I don't like fighters or wrestlers who talk too much."

The Carson stand-in and the audience howled with laughter. Stevenson noted that Inoki, whom he called "Hokey Finoki," causing Ali to turn and poorly conceal his snickering from the crowd, was willingly taking kicks to the face in preparation for the impending onslaught.

"He got two or three teeth knocked out, I understand, accidentally," Ali said. "People jumping on his face because he don't do this for rasslin'. He's trying to get ready for shock, but the shock he's taking isn't like my punches." Ali then showed a little bit of humility, considering what he was facing. "I'm a little nervous, I must admit. If this man grabs my arm, or gets in behind me and gets one of those body-snatchers or those backbreakers on me, I'm in trouble. But I'm counting on my speed and my reflexes, because if I hit him right and he don't fall, then he can do what he wanna do."

Charged with protecting Ali from body-snatchers, backbreakers, and everything else he wasn't used to was a man the champ had long admired: beguiling retired pro wrestler "Classy" Freddie Blassie, who, at fifty-eight, still cut an imposing figure. Blassie emerged from behind the multicolored *The Tonight Show* curtain without his cane, a staple of his pro wrestling gimmick after becoming a "manager" in the sunset years of his fondly remembered career. The cane, he liked to say, wasn't a tool to lean on. A man of his distinction simply required a walking stick—not to mention a respectable weapon should the need arise. The blond Blassie strode towards Carson's occupied desk draped in his usual getup—a Hawaiian shirt and khaki slacks—and Ali gladly made space for his "new trainer" by sliding over next to Ed McMahon on the couch. Using catchphrases cultivated over four decades of working every pro wrestling territory worth knowing, Blassie plowed over that "pencil-neck geek" Stevenson. As it was, Ali was attempting to sell a legitimate fight, not a pro wrestling bonanza, and he sensed Blassie's over-the-top shtick would confuse the audience. So the boxer cut him off.

Ali leaned forward.

"There's $10 million involved," he said, which was an exaggeration since he had agreed to a purse of $6.1 million while Inoki was set to take home in the neighborhood of $2 million. "I wouldn't take the sport of boxing and disgrace it. I wouldn't pull a fraud on the public. This is real. There's no plan. The blood. The holds. The pain. Everything is going to be real. I'm not here in this time of my life to come out with some phony action."

The next night Charlton Heston and comedian Kelly Monteith had the pleasure of welcoming Johnny Carson back to Burbank, Calif. After hearing Ed McMahon describe a wacky time at a bicentennial gathering in the West Chicago suburb of Wheaton, Ill.—"You told me never to play a fairgrounds, and I made a mistake," McMahon admitted to Carson. "I didn't listen to you."—the late-night king lamented his days touring the Midwest.

Professional wrestlers knew as well as anyone what it was like to play in front of fairgrounds fans. The tradition of wrestling tours, like America, is long and vast, and in significant ways linked to the man Ali signed to fight in Tokyo.

Inoki, a famous disciple of the father of Japanese professional wrestling, better known as Rikidōzan, was the B-side of a contest poised to produce the largest purse and audience for a bout of this type. Ticket prices at the Nippon Budokan arena were exorbitant, yet, with Ali involved, the fight was a sellout. Ringside seats for regular wrestling shows at the Budokan were 5,000 yen (roughly $17 at the time). For the Ali–Inoki rumble, that price put fans in the nosebleeds of a 14,000-seat building. The face value of the most expensive ticket available to the public was $1,000 ($4,100 today). Sponsors could access "royal ringside" seats for three times that price.

"My memory was, 'Oh my God, you're charging how much?'" recalled Dave Meltzer, a sixteen-year-old fanatic with a pro wrestling newsletter who watched the match at the Santa Clara Fairgrounds, one of four Bay Area venues carrying the closed-circuit feed from Tokyo.

"It was announced in Japan long before it was announced in the United States," he said. "And even though it was announced in Japan, I thought the Japanese wrestling people were just making noise because there was no way in hell this was ever going to happen. And they actually announced it and I was stunned. There was always in wrestling historically this idea of a boxer versus a wrestler going back to 'Strangler' Lewis and Jack Dempsey—it never happened, probably because when the boxer started training with real wrestlers it was like, wow, this is a really dumb idea."

At Shea Stadium in Flushing, New York, 32,897 spectators gathered to watch Ali meet Inoki after a World Wide Wrestling Federation extravaganza, "Showdown at Shea," a precursor to modern-day WrestleMania events. For the sake of business that night, a gimpy Bruno Sammartino returned to the squared circle two months after fracturing his neck in a match at Madison Square Garden against Stan Hansen. Anchoring the event before Shea Stadium went dark for the Ali–Inoki contest, Andre the Giant faced Chuck Wepner— Sylvester Stallone's inspiration for Rocky Balboa. (Decades later, most people believe the action at Shea and Tokyo also prompted Stallone to include a boxer-versus-wrestler scene in *Rocky III*. Through his publicist, Stallone denied any truth to that.) Cards like these took place across North America that night, and at the behest of Vince McMahon Sr., were billed as a sort of "Martial Arts Olympics" to support the so-called World Martial Arts Championship.

Whatever trepidation Ali felt ahead of the Inoki bout, it was at least rooted in combat sports reality. Unlike earlier generations of American audiences, fight watchers in the mid-1970s weren't clued into matches that allowed for more than trading punches. Boxing was *the* combat sport, in large part because of Ali, who ably served as its king and jester. Martial arts in the age of Bruce Lee were repurposed as flash for film and television, further eroding the prominence of American grappling arts that had been influenced by Japanese martial arts missionaries and European immigrants during the Industrial Revolution. By the summer of America's 200th birthday, when fans gathered in arenas across the globe to watch Ali fight Inoki, a sense of excitement brewed on all sides. Ali was the best boxer on the planet, The Greatest of All Time, and anything he did received huge attention. But this? This was unique. Something mysterious. And that made it potentially something bigger.

Seven minutes before Ali and Inoki stood in the ring together, the first images from the Nippon Budokan were beamed by satellite to the rest of the world. Closed-circuit sites—predominantly movie houses with stadiums and arenas sprinkled in—filled with people hoping for a great show on a Friday night.

In San Jose, Calif., Meltzer and some high school friends put the finishing touches on a debate that had raged for weeks. "Beforehand we didn't know if it would be real or not," said Meltzer, who, forty years later, is a highly respected pro wrestling and combat sports journalist. "The prevailing view in the media was that it was going to be a fake pro wrestling match."

Was this thing on the up-and-up? Could a boxer, even someone as great as Ali, really beat a wrestler? Oh my God, what if Inoki takes Ali to the ground and hurts him? These discussions played out wherever people congregated to take in the action.

Jeff Wagenheim spent fifteen dollars on a ticket to watch at the Liberty Theater in Elizabeth, New Jersey. Having graduated high school a week before the match, Wagenheim, who went on to cover mixed martial arts as a reporter for *Sports Illustrated*, had mostly matured past the wrestling fandom of his childhood. Yet after hearing of the Ali–Inoki pairing, he and a friend decided to see what the noise was about.

"I remember the air-conditioning wasn't working," Wagenheim said. "As soon as we got in the theater I started feeling a little feverish, a little clammy and sweating, and you're not quite yourself. The place was packed."

Unlike Wagenheim, Kevin Iole continued to love wrestling into his high school days, especially the McMahon-owned WWWF (World Wide Wrestling Federation). And for Ali to insert himself in that world made the closed-circuit event a must-see. Iole took a seat in the small ballroom at Monzo's Howard Johnson's in Monroeville, Pa., as the summer prior to his senior year was getting started. "I didn't think for one second it would be a real thing," recalled the prolific boxing writer who, while working for the *Las Vegas Review-Journal* in 2004, was among the first American newspaper reporters to give the fledgling sport of mixed martial arts his attention. "I thought it'd be a work and we'd get a kick out of it, and who knew what Ali would do or say."

Noted handicapper Jimmy "The Greek" Snyder explained that he was unwilling to post a line on the fight, highlighting the difficulty in guaranteeing the bona fides of such a spectacle. "How do I know it's anything but an exhibition?" he wrote in his newspaper column on June 3. "I've been bombarded by karate lovers who insist Ali doesn't have a chance, that no fighter can beat a wrestler." At the fabled Olympic Auditorium in downtown Los Angeles, bookies ignored history and installed the boxer as a 3-to-1 favorite.

The Olympic, like Shea, hosted a live wrestling undercard the night of the Ali–Inoki dustup. It was one of several venues scattered amongst pro wrestling territories from the Northeast to the Southwest, under the auspices of the National Wrestling Alliance, that held talent-rich cards in support of the closed-circuit broadcast from Tokyo.

By comparison, Saturday's afternoon action at the Budokan offered little attraction outside the main event. Demonstrations of a traditional Iranian martial art as well as Goju Ryu karate preceded a pro wrestling tag-team match for Japanese fans, whose reputation as intelligent, mindful watchers of combat is well earned. If a sense of uncertainty circulated among American audiences, the Japanese were utterly fixated on the enormous event that, courtesy of Inoki, had arrived on their shores.

Hideki Yamamoto, a fourteen-year-old junior high student fond of Coca-Cola packed in 350-milliliter steel cans, was in his second year at Wakasa Junior High School. On Saturday afternoon the left fielder was supposed to be practicing with his baseball club, but he and some of his teammates slipped out of training and found their way to a teachers' lounge.

"There was a TV set, and some teachers, including our baseball coach, surrounded it," recalled Yamamoto, who years later served as an executive for Japan's seminal mixed martial arts promotion, the Pride Fighting Championship, with which Inoki was also affiliated. "I found out it was the live TV broadcast of the fight. The coaches said something but I could not hear what it was. They did not blame my friends and allowed them to keep watching."

Ali's presence in the match made people across Japan stop whatever it was they were doing to watch. This was precisely what Inoki wanted. While the businessmen who put up the money saw fortune, the ambitious wrestler envisioned his name being exposed to the wider world. Up to that point, he had been largely anonymous outside of Japan. Inoki touched fame in Asia, and some diehard stateside pro wrestling fans knew of him, but his ego demanded a larger audience. So he set out to find one.

During final preparations before his ring walk, Ali preened in front of a mirror in his locker room. Padded with white gauze and bandages, Ali's prized hands expertly tied off his white Everlast satin shorts accentuated by a black waistband and black stripes down each side—the same color scheme he wore for so many indelible moments in the ring. Surrounded by members of his boxing entourage—Angelo Dundee, Drew "Bundini" Brown, Dr. Ferdie Pacheco, and Wali Muhammad—and people there just for this night— Freddie Blassie and Korea's Jhoon Rhee, who popularized taekwondo in America—Ali primped before shooing away a Japanese cameraman.

As a rookie reporter for United Press, Andrew Malcolm worked the occasional boxing event from ringside. He had learned the risk of being so close to the action that snot and spit might fly in his direction, so years later as the Tokyo bureau chief of the *New York Times*, Malcolm chose to settle in fifteen rows back from the apron. Ali and Inoki were expected to enter the ring around 11:30 A.M. local time and as the middle of the day approached, Budokan Hall was stifling. The mugginess made Malcolm squirm in his seat, which was set up with a full-service telephone line connected to a recording room in New York that collected reporters' phoned-in stories or notes. As an event unfolded, staff could take those accounts and begin working them into stories. Narrating the blow-by-blow back to New York was Malcolm's first task, though he felt silly talking on a trans-Pacific phone without someone listening on the other side. Next would be arranging time to speak with Ali after the bout for a feature on how smitten Japan was with him and the match.

From his vantage, Malcolm saw the trio of officials chatting as best they could in a neutral corner. Two Japanese judges, hefty grappler Kokichi Endo and boxing official Kou Toyama, joined American referee "Judo" Gene LeBell, who sported red pants to match his ginger hair, a blue shirt, and black bow tie. He had nearly donned a red tie, but opted for a more formal look. LeBell, an influential martial artist and prolific stuntman out of Los Angeles, was set to play a crucial part. He would control the action in the ring and assign a score after each round, based on a five-point must scoring system and heavily negotiated rules.

Concerns about corruption and fighter safety made this judge-referee combination rare after the early 1980s. Each job is difficult enough without having to worry about doing both at the same time. Still, the use of LeBell's services in both areas made good sense. An accomplished grappler who could box? LeBell was literally one of the few people at the time who had intimate knowledge of mixed matches, though he had not refereed one before.

"Ali knew me as a good wrestler, at least he thought so," said LeBell, who for all this expertise was paid $5,000 in crisp new hundred-dollar bills to officiate the contest. "He wanted me to be a referee. Ali saw me working out at Main Street Gym and that was his world. It was very casual. Ali and Inoki said we want you as the referee because all the guys that were up for it, they're either wrestling referees or boxing. And I did both."

Before cameras picked up LeBell communicating with his fellow officials, he was backstage watching the closed-circuit feed out of Flushing, New York. In Ali's locker room LeBell stood with Blassie, a trusted friend, while the seven-foot-four, roughly 500-pound André René Roussimoff (aka Andre the Giant) dumped Chuck Wepner over the top rope to take the WWWF co-feature at Shea Stadium by count out. Of course, the action in Queens was show business.

Watching alongside Blassie and LeBell, Ali was engrossed. He said he pictured Inoki going after him with "a pro wrestling style" and sounded confident that if he was in there with Andre the Giant, he could have won. LeBell's wisdom compelled him to conjure a much different outcome. The first televised bout of this type in the United States ended when LeBell strangled a boxer unconscious on a wild night in Salt Lake City, Utah, in 1963, which is why the referee figured Ali would be forced to the canvas and, if things went really bad, would get something broken or be strangled out cold.

"Inoki was a scary guy. He was always calm and spoke in a casual way, about breaking Ali's arm, or pulling out a bone, or a muscle. Ali would always banter with him, but I think he too was concerned, because of the unknown pieces," said publicist Bobby Goodman, who worked with Ali in Tokyo on behalf of Top Rank. "Bob Arum put this together with Vince McMahon Sr. and it came not too long after the Richard Dunn fight in Munich. So the length of time Ali usually had to prepare for fights didn't really exist, especially for something he hadn't experienced before."

As Ali readied himself to engage in a form of combat that presented challenges he wasn't equipped to handle, the unflappable boxer, the most famous face on earth, grew anxious in a way earthquakes or flying on a plane that had run out of gas could not make him.

Muhammad Ali met Ichiro Hatta, a fellow Olympian and president of the Japanese Amateur Wrestling Association, at a reception in the United States in April 1975. The story goes that Ali nudged Hatta, an instrumental figure in Japan's Olympic movement, with a dare: "Isn't there an Oriental fighter who will challenge me? I'll give him one million dollars if he wins." Respected for, among other things, introducing Western-style wrestling to Japan in 1931, Hatta devoted himself to grappling, in the way that Japanese strive to find and repeat perfection over the long course of their professional lives. Therefore, unbeknownst to Ali, Hatta was quite simply the best person to relay his message to the Japanese press, which predictably played up the remark. As it happened, a professional wrestler responded.

There are numerous examples of great wrestlers chasing fights with great boxers. There are far fewer examples of great boxers chasing great wrestlers, but that's what Ali seemed to have in mind. Ali's interest in Inoki's offer hinged, of course, on a massive payday. But his love of professional wrestling, and the notion that the boxer-versus-wrestler debate had not been settled, were quite compelling to Ali. That was particularly true, he explained, because a boxer of his caliber, in his prime, taking on a top-form "rassler" was rare. The possibility of what might happen wasn't much of a mystery, though. Documented mixed-style fights date as far back as the days of antiquity, when Athens and Rome cradled civilizations, and the results suggested grapplers held a significant edge when allowed to ply their trade.

The influential sport of *pankration*, a Greek term that translates to "all powers," is the ancient version of mixed fighting. Mythologized as the martial art Theseus used to slay the Minotaur in the labyrinth and Hercules employed to subdue the Nemean lion, pankration in the real world during the seventh century B.C. blended a mix of unbridled striking and grappling that left all attacks on the table. The wide-ranging barbarism of pankration, save eye gouging and biting, was only too restrictive for Spartan fighters, who, true to their reputation, boycotted competitions unless no holds were barred. The Greeks, however, were on board—it was said Zeus grappled with his father, the titan Kronos, for control over Mount Olympus. Mere mortals became godlike if they found success among the three wrestling forms that rounded out the combat sports lineup at the ancient Olympiad. A quite vicious form of boxing, known for disfiguring faces with fists wrapped in hard leather straps, was also featured as sport.

Until 393 A.D., when Theodosius I, the last man to rule the entirety of the Roman Empire, abolished gladiatorial combat and pagan festivals including the Olympics, pankration created many star athletes celebrated by the Greeks. Mixed fighting held a prominent place in that part of the world for more than a thousand years, yet at the return of the Olympic games to Greece in 1896, bareknuckle brawlers capable of punching and grappling weren't welcome. Not that it mattered much. These types of fights persisted as humans across a multitude of generations, regardless of the social mores of the day, were compelled to participate in or watch sanctioned violence.

At the turn of the twentieth century, Martin "Farmer" Burns, whose headstone at the St. James Cemetery in Toronto, Iowa, reads "World's Champion Wrestler," was the man to challenge. Shy of 175 pounds yet incredibly strong, Burns was the obligatory bear on the mat during his heyday, boasting a twenty-inch neck that allowed him to perform carnival circuit stunts like dropping six feet off a platform wearing a noose, as if he'd been convicted of a capital crime, while whistling "Yankee Doodle." Burns' power and skill made him an effective enough grappler into his fifties, handling almost anyone with the "catch-as-catch-can" wrestling style—an influential 1870s British creation that made full use of pinning positions and, absorbing what worked from other parts of the world, a menagerie of painful submissions holds.

By 1910, Burns' prestige put him in position to work alongside "Gentleman Jim" Corbett—who famously took the heavyweight boxing title from John L. Sullivan eighteen years earlier. The pair served as conditioning coaches for Jim Jeffries, the "Great White Hope" to the generally reviled blackness that was then boxing heavyweight champion Jack

Johnson. Say this about Jeffries, the 220-pound banger knew how to assemble a training camp. Burns and Corbett, who in his final fight in 1903 failed to regain the title against Jeffries, are regarded as major influences on the increasingly scientific way people trained their bodies.

During Jeffries' camp in Reno, Nevada, middleweight contender Billy Papke, a very capable fighter at the time, mouthed off at Burns that a boxer could handle a wrestler, no sweat. Burns quickly offered stakes and a classic wrestler-versus-boxer confrontation ensued.

Eighteen seconds after they met in the ring, Papke's shoulders were square to the canvas. That wasn't enough for Burns, who, intent on sending a message, dragged a squealing Papke to the ropes, tied the boxer's arms behind him, and jumped out of the ring to collect $2,300. As it turned out, Burns was considerably more successful with Papke than he was at preparing Jeffries for Johnson.

With America consumed by the first sporting event to truly dominate public discourse—much more than a boxing title was on the line—Johnson scored three knockdowns en route to a 15th-round stoppage. Race riots ensued and Congress made the transportation of prizefight films across state lines a criminal offense.

Johnson entertained his share of grapplers who wanted a piece, but they never got one, even if he fancied himself a fairly decent wrestler.

Four years after the fight in Reno, Burns published a widely read mail-order newsletter entitled *The Lessons in Wrestling and Physical Culture*. Ninety-six pages in total, each set of instructions included lessons on body-weight and resistance exercises, as well as wrestling and submission techniques. The pamphlet inspired a new generation of grapplers such as Ed "Strangler" Lewis, who carried on ancient and modern grappling traditions while captivating the public enough to bank at least $4 million over the course of his career.

Such was the strength of the "Strangler" Lewis name that, with a straight face, he attempted during his championship reign to arrange a fight with heavyweight boxing king Jack Dempsey. The public certainly wanted to see it. Lewis' main challenge came March 16, 1922, in Nashville, Tenn., following another successful defense of the heavyweight wrestling title. "I realize that Jack Dempsey is one of the greatest boxers that ever stepped into a ring, and there is no desire whatsoever on my part to minimize his ability," the five-foot-ten, barrel-chested grappler told reporters in Nashville, "but I am fully confident that I can handle him, else I would not agree to the match. It is my contention that the world's heavyweight champion wrestler is superior to the champion boxer at all times, and that wrestling is a more powerful method of self-defense than the boxing art."

Through the media, Dempsey's manager, Jack Kearns, accepted the match, and claimed the "Manassa Mauler" was a "first-rate wrestler himself."

Four days after the challenge was issued, Colonel Joe C. Miller, a rancher near Ponca City, Okla., wired an offer to Dempsey and Lewis for a $200,000 guarantee and split of the receipts if the boxer-wrestler clash was brought to his property, the 101 Ranch, located on the main line of the Santa Fe Railroad. By the end of the year, however, the Oklahoma offer had been cast aside for a $300,000 payday from Wichita, Kans., where wrestling promoter Tom Law, backed by five oilmen, put up money for a bout to take place no later than July 4, 1923. Soon Lewis spoke in the press as if the match had been signed. Dempsey claimed to know nothing of an official contest, even if yet again he suggested he was ready to take on Lewis.

Speaking to the *Rochester American-Journal* on December 10, 1922, Dempsey noted that "if the match ever went through, I think I'd be mighty tempted to try to beat that wrestler at his own game. I've done a lot of wrestling as part of my preliminary training and I think I've got the old toe-hold and headlock down close to perfection. If I can win the first fall from him, I'll begin to use my fists. But I've got a funny little hunch that maybe I can dump him without rapping him on the chin."

A bold claim considering the competition.

As the first week of January 1923 came to a close, a set of ten rules was released to the public. Two of the ten pertained to Dempsey, who was obligated to wrap his hands in soft bandages, wear five-ounce gloves, and refrain from hitting Lewis when he was down.

The rest restricted the wrestler: a common theme as these matches were discussed.

Among the notable instructions, Lewis could not hit with a bare hand or fist, and strangleholds were barred, as were butting and heeling. To win, Lewis had to pin Dempsey for three seconds. If Lewis spent more than ten seconds at a time on the canvas while Dempsey stood, the wrestler would be disqualified.

While talk captured imaginations across America, the spilled newspaper ink failed to manifest into a real contest. Reports of a signed match were labeled "bunk" by the pugilist. Instead Dempsey turned a desire among fans to see the best from boxing meet the best from wrestling into leverage, agreeing to fight for promoter Tex Rickard on the Fourth of July, 1923. But not against a wrestler. The promoters—oilmen from Montana who originally offered Dempsey $200,000 to fight an unknown opponent and put an unknown boomtown on the map—caved and upped their guarantee to $300,000, the same amount of oil money Dempsey ignored to face Lewis in Wichita.

Two days before the fight, reports indicated that the last of three $100,000 payments to Dempsey had not been made, so the event was publicly cancelled. Dempsey's money came through at the last minute, but not before newspaper stories were published and 200 ten-car trains riding the Great Northern Railway, totaling thirty-five miles if someone wanted to connect them all at once, stopped running. A disaster. The city of Shelby, population 400, had spent a reported $1 million (nearly $14 million in 2015's values) to prepare. They laid eleven miles of new track, erected a stadium with sixteen entrances and eighty-five rows of seats on a six-acre plot of land, created a 160-acre automobile tourist camp, issued four hundred building permits, and budgeted city improvements costing $250,000. Grocery merchants within one hundred miles of Shelby were on call to make shipments to a town that now featured more than thirty places to grab food. Drinking booze and beer was legal, and six dance halls were available in the evenings. If anything got out of hand, the governor of Montana, Republican Joseph M. Dixon, was prepared to send in two units of the National Guard.

Since rail was the prime way spectators would have arrived at a newly built octagon-shaped wooden arena scaled for 40,208 seats, ticket sales produced just a small fraction of the expected gate. Dempsey went on to win an uninspired decision over Tommy Gibbons, and the host oil enclave of Shelby, Montana, was forced to endure a historic fiasco. The *New York Times* called the bout "the greatest financial failure of a single sporting event in history." Only Dempsey, his manager Kearns, and Gibbons walked away with cash. Everyone else got wiped out. Three banks connected to the financing of the fight closed their doors within a week—bad mojo, perhaps, for Dempsey avoiding the "Strangler."

Two decades later, Dempsey, then forty-five, stuck his toes in rasslin' waters. Long retired, he mixed it up as a referee and quickly found himself embroiled in a fracas with a wrestler named Cowboy Luttrell. They settled the matter a couple months later, July 1, 1940, in Atlanta. Wearing the lightest gloves that Georgia officials allowed, Dempsey waited for Luttrell on an overturned beer case in his corner between rounds—a sad sight that did not go unnoticed by newspaper columnists. In front of more than 10,000 spectators, the "Manassa Mauler" smashed the wrestler in a round and a half. Exhibitions in which boxers boxed wrestlers usually rendered down to no match at all. This sort of setup wasn't grounds for debate. Under similar circumstances, few people would have given Antonio Inoki a serious shot at lasting as long against Ali as Luttrell did with Dempsey. But that wasn't the paradigm Ali established for his boxer–wrestler foray in Tokyo, and that certainly wasn't what Inoki had in mind as he hustled to get the fight made.

★ ★ ★ ★ ★

Smart promoters played up these conflicts, which is why the August 1963 issue of *Rogue* magazine, an early competitor to *Playboy*, is still spoken of today. Jim Beck's article "The Judo Bums" threw down a well-worn martial arts gauntlet by offering a $1,000 prize to any judoka who could beat a boxer. Kenpo karate legend Ed Parker recruited "Judo" Gene LeBell to answer the challenge. "You're the most sadistic bastard I know," Parker told LeBell at the judo man's hardcore Hollywood dojo. The prospect of walking away with $1,000 was incentive enough for LeBell, who didn't need selling or history lessons to accept Ed Parker's request.

LeBell fit the bill, for sure. Famous for many things, including handing out thousands of patches to people he strangled cold upon request, LeBell will say that Ed "Strangler" Lewis, Lou Thesz, and Karl Gotch—his "hooker" mentors (pro wrestling speak for legitimately skilled tough guys)—were meaner than he ever was.

"These guys were fanatics," he said.

The trio represented grappling at its purest, highest class, and each made it a point to prove themselves against top strikers and wrestlers of their day. The historic implications of a grappler fighting a boxer were certainly not lost on LeBell, and a chance to prove himself while defending the teachings of the men who showed him the way was an incredible opportunity.

LeBell's experience convinced him that competent martial artists should, under pressure, be able to employ a wide variety of striking and grappling techniques. He was ahead of the curve because combining styles wasn't in vogue while Asian martial arts proliferated in popular culture after World War II. Also, among the folks who trained, the vast majority didn't fight. That's why, when LeBell answered Beck's call, the event poster promised "something new for sport fans."

As a point of clarification, it was new in that spectators likely hadn't seen anything like it before, well, at least not for a generation or two.

In the aftermath of the Great War, boxer-grappler and mixed-style skirmishes became popular again, though not to the degree they were when jiu-jitsu competitors travelled from Japan to share their knowledge with the world at the start of the 1900s. The judo practiced by UFC bantam-weight superstar Ronda Rousey in the Octagon is derived from interactions with folks like LeBell, who studied based on the techniques brought to America by the four "guardians of judo" at the behest of their teacher, judo founder Kanō Jigorō, to make Japanese martial arts accessible to the wider world. Kanō's philosophy was that judo benefits everyone. Mitsuyo Maeda was one of Kanō's judo acolytes, and in late 1904 he operated out of a gym in New York, taking on exhibitions in colleges up and down the East Coast. Maeda was ambitious, and when throwing strongmen and football players bored him, he searched out more difficult challengers. In America those came mostly from professional wrestlers, who were open enough to incorporate some of the unique skills people like Maeda offered up.

Men clad in suits may have lined Parisian streets and filled Parisian theaters to catch a mixed-fighting fad as it swept across the continent. Big crowds may have reveled in watching the world's best fighters across any style make front-page news as far away as Hawaii and Australia. But there were periods in which these types of clashes fell out of favor, and by 1963 boxing was *the* combat sport worth caring about in America. Wrestling and grappling, for all its rich history, had fallen on harder times after scandals trivialized it. Proven lessons were largely forgotten by the public, and wrestling became the thing people didn't talk about.

That was soon to change.

Thirteen years before Ali stepped in the ring to fight Inoki, a generation ahead of Art Jimmerson's contest with Royce Gracie at UFC 1, and nearly five decades before James Toney and Randy Couture tangled in the Octagon, the first boxer-grappler showdown broadcast live on American television—LeBell vs. Savage—represented a key moment in the large arc of these events.

At first LeBell angled for the fight to take place in Los Angeles, where for almost forty years his notoriously tough mother, Aileen Eaton, promoted many of the biggest boxing and pro wrestling events on the West Coast at the Olympic Auditorium. Eaton thrived in the promotion business, but she never had the opportunity to promote a mixed-rules bout because the California State Athletic Commission wasn't granted the authority to regulate this kind of hand-to-hand combat until 2006. The commission classified the boxer-grappler contest as an outlawed duel, so the fighters headed instead to Beck's backyard, Salt Lake City, Utah, which placed no restrictions on that sort of thing. Agreeing to five three-minute rounds, the bout was a jacket match, meaning LeBell would wear his judo uniform and the boxer was required to wear a *gi* top with a belt, and, if he preferred, boxing trunks, boxing shoes, and light speed-bag gloves. The winner would be determined when a fighter was counted out for ten seconds or incapacitated, and the referee was the sole judge of that.

When LeBell arrived in Utah, he was surprised to learn that instead of facing Beck under these circumstances, Milo

Savage would stand opposite him on fight night. LeBell was familiar with the former middleweight contender, having seen Savage box in person once at the Legion Auditorium in Hollywood, Calif. After taking his first twenty-five fights in the Pacific Northwest, Savage headed down the coast with a record of fifteen wins, six losses, and four draws. From October 1947 to February 1949, fourteen of Savage's next fifteen bouts occurred in Los Angeles, and throughout his twenty-five-year career he made twenty-nine appearances in the City of Angels. As of the mid-1950s, Savage had matured into a ranked fighter and LeBell was experiencing the peak of his athletic career, earning the reputation of America's best judoka following consecutive Amateur Athletic Union National Judo Championships titles in 1954 and 1955.

The night before the spectacle in Salt Lake City, LeBell, then thirty-one, made an appearance on local television. The host, whom LeBell felt was pro-Savage, implied that chokes don't work and followed up with a grand mistake when he uttered, "show me." LeBell snatched him, choked him out, and dropped him on his head. The newsman didn't even receive a patch. "Judo" Gene picked up the microphone and offered a rant that his pro wrestling buddies back in L.A. would have been proud of. "Our commentator went to sleep," he said. "I guess he's quitting. Now it's the Gene LeBell Show." LeBell peered into the camera and promised to do the same to the thirty-nine-year-old Savage, now a crafty journeyman prone to trick punches and clowning around in the ring. "Come to the arena tomorrow night and watch me annihilate, mutilate, and assassinate your local hero because one martial artist can beat any ten boxers." The exotic nature of the contest combined with LeBell's antics, honed around grand characters in the combat sports worlds, produced a buzzed standing-room-only pro-boxing crowd of around 1,500 at the Fairgrounds Coliseum on a chilly Monday night, December 2, 1963.

Inside LeBell's locker room, final rules were hammered out for the five-round contest. Savage's people agreed to let LeBell grapple as he pleased, but he couldn't strike at all. To confirm what he could or couldn't do, LeBell pulled out a picture-heavy instructional book he penned that sold for $3.95 via mail order in *Black Belt* magazine.

"Can I pick him up over my head like this?" he wondered, pointing to a photo in *The Handbook of Judo*. Savage's handlers were amused. "Can I choke him?" asked LeBell, placing his hands over his throat in "a comical way." An L.A.-based lawyer who travelled with LeBell to Utah, Dewey Lawes Falcone, told him to quit screwing around. But "Judo" Gene couldn't help himself. He was always the type to push buttons. "They're laughing," he remembered. "They're just all happy that he's going to knock me out."

LeBell was familiar with the reaction. In Amarillo, Tex., where he wrestled professionally and took mixed-style fights for cash, most of LeBell's challengers came from a nearby army base or the cow town's dusty bar crowd. Locals received $100. Out-of-towners, $50. They, too, felt good about their chances. Then LeBell's sadistic reality set in as he racked up ring time, an experience that lent him confidence ahead of the match in Salt Lake City.

Prohibited from striking, LeBell had to figure out how to navigate his way past Savage's strikes to get inside and clinch. To make matters more difficult, Savage wore a *gi* top designed for karate, which meant it was constructed of lighter material than the judo uniform and more difficult to grip. And it was slathered in Vaseline, according to LeBell. The grappler's plan to induce Savage to come at him was only reinforced after LeBell felt the boxer's power as a punch to the stomach snapped the judo man's *obi*—the black belt that tied together his kimono. "I towed broken down motorcycles with them. I've never had 'em stretch or break on me, but when this guy hit me it broke right in half," LeBell said. "This guy hit pretty hard. You could do it a thousand times, I don't think it would happen again. He just hit me right." LeBell alleged that underneath Savage's thin gloves he wore metal plates. Arms in tight, Savage was tentative to attack with anything but distance-controlling jabs, and LeBell, willing but unable to trade strikes, bided his time.

Inevitably LeBell found what he was looking for and locked up in a clinch—a result-defining position in any unarmed combat scenario. A modern boxer clinches to avoid getting hit, and referees are tasked to break up fighters, make them take three steps back, and hope they come out swinging. Wrestling is based very simply on tying up an opponent on the inside. Invariably the clinch favors anyone who knows how to grapple, which most successful boxers did quite well before the Marquess of Queensberry rules superseded London Prize Ring rules in 1867, essentially removing wrestling as part of the skill set required to win bouts. No longer did boxers need to know how to grapple above the waist and throw opponents to the floor. Clinching and holding remained relevant, mostly as a defensive mechanism, but the ability to grapple for takedowns, a benefit of going at it bare-knuckle, was engineered out of the sport.

When Jack Johnson operated atop the boxing heap, his clinch game was derived from the grappling techniques of wrestlers like William Muldoon, a famous athlete and fitness nut tasked with whipping into shape the last London Prize Ring rules champion, party boy John L. Sullivan. Part of the straight-laced Muldoon's regimen for Sullivan was wrestling. Between competition and sparring, boxers seemed to get the message. Corbett, who supplanted Sullivan as the sport transitioned to a gloved affair, said as much when asked by a reader of his syndicated column.

"Ninety-nine times out of one hundred the wrestler would win," Corbett wrote in 1919. "About the only chance for victory the fighter would have would be to shoot over a knockout punch before the echo of the first gong handled away. If it landed, he would win. But if he missed, he'd be gone. And every ring fan knows that the scoring of a one-punch knockout is almost a miracle achievement in pugilism. Years ago Bob Fitzsimmons attempted to battle the debate. Fitz was a powerful man, almost a Hercules. His strength was prodigious. And Fitz knew quite a bit about wrestling—and how to avoid holds and how to break them. So he scoffed when someone remarked that in a contest between a wrestler and a boxer that the former would win."

Ernest Roeber, a European and American Greco-Roman heavyweight champion, ended up stretching Fitzsimmons straight.

Rules defining boxing became hyperfocused on one aspect of the discipline—molding the acts of punching and defending punching into the "sweet science." Boxers still use clinch skills traceable to the days of London prizefighting, though so degraded is the notion of boxers maintaining meaningful clinch games, that a modern-day question persists about whether Ronda Rousey would throw Floyd Mayweather Jr.—the best boxer of his time and a stone heavier than the female judoka—on his head in a real confrontation. By the early 1960s, boxers hadn't needed to earnestly practice holds in the clinch for nearly a century. Those tricks managed to survive through grappling-based systems, like judo and catch-as-catch-can, which LeBell practiced at a masterful level.

During the fourth round, despite aggravating an old shoulder injury earlier in the fight when Savage awkwardly shucked him off in the clinch, LeBell set up for the kill. "Judo" Gene dropped his left arm, baited Savage to throw a right cross, deftly maneuvered underneath the punch, and tossed his opponent to canvas. LeBell clung to the boxer's back and Savage, unaware of what else to do, grabbed a thumb to sink his teeth into it. LeBell threatened Savage. If the boxer bit him, LeBell promised, Savage would lose an eye. That's when a rear-naked choke was set and LeBell made good on his promise from the television broadcast the night before. The referee, a local doctor, didn't know how to react when LeBell strangled Savage unconscious. He hadn't worked a fight that included impeding blood circulation to the brain as an option. Media reports indicated the boxer was out cold for almost twenty minutes, an absurd length that these days would require at least a siren-filled ride to the hospital.

Adding insult to injury, LeBell "accidentally" stepped on Savage's chest as he walked away. He winked. This incensed a riled-up crowd, already uncomfortable with the idea that boxing was bested by an Asian martial art. Well before

Savage came to his senses, the Salt Lake City crowd grew spiteful. Chairs and cushions flew. A fan attempted to stab LeBell after he stepped out of the ring. The martial artist half-parried the attack and moved past his assailant, but he got stuck nevertheless. "I kept on going but it went through me," LeBell said. "It was pretty big." Still, the judo man survived, won the day, and martial artists rejoiced.

With LeBell assigned as the referee, and Ali facing Inoki, the martial arts community reacted in 1976 as if a great opportunity to score another big win over boxing was theirs for the taking. "The way it was billed, we were so excited," said William Viola Sr., a martial artist out of Pittsburgh, who bought all-in on the attraction. "The catch wrestler, Inoki, would actually be able to use all his skills. Ali was the boxer and he'd box. The buildup was unbelievable."

Unlike all-time great Jack Dempsey, Ali actually agreed to take on a mixed-style test. He wanted it and so did Inoki, and in the end their rules weren't so different than what Dempsey and Lewis floated to the public during the 1920s. Ali laid down and Inoki accepted a challenge to determine the best fighter in the world. Yet many English-speaking boxing scribes maligned the heavyweight champion for participating in a "farce"—otherwise known as something great boxers have always been connected with.

ROUND THREE

Marcus Griffin, in 1937, authored an apparent attempt to uncover the world of professional wrestling. Whether Griffin acted as a reporter or a flack is up for debate, as are reported events strewn throughout the pages of his book, *Fall Guys: The Barnums of Bounce—The Inside Story of the Wrestling Business, America's Most Profitable and Best Organized Professional Sport*. Sorting fact from fiction in the wrestling world did not come easy then, and it still doesn't. Wrestling is as underhanded and shifty a business as there ever was. Indisputable, however, is that *Fall Guys* exposed the wrestling world to the public in a way it hadn't been before, and that Griffin earned full credit for coining the "Gold Dust Trio."

No one uttered that term prior to Griffin's work being published, but everyone in the pro wrestling world remembered it afterwards. The group nickname stuck because in many ways the Gold Dust Trio bridged pro wrestling's lingering competitive nerve, the roots of catch-as-catch-can, to part-of-an-angle exhibitions indicative of WWE's product in 2016.

"Strangler" Lewis, Billy Sandow, and one of the smartest pro wrestling people that ever lived, Joe "Toots" Mondt—whom Griffin, a newspaperman, was rumored to be on the payroll of from 1933 to 1937, and whose interviews were used as *Fall Guys*' main source—changed pro wrestling. Mondt's shift in ring philosophy and practice, Sandow's approach to consolidating wrestlers under exclusive contracts, and Lewis' star power, when combined, were that meaningful.

Mondt, a young wrestler, booked matches, plotted storylines, and envisioned an open style that blended elements of combat sports without the trouble of sport—an impediment, from time to time, to exciting wrestling action. Body slams and suplexes were mixed in with fisticuffs and grappling, laying the framework for a charged-up, vaudeville-inspired creation: "Slam Bang Western-Style Wrestling." This wasn't dumb luck. Even in his youth, Mondt possessed a wealth of knowledge regarding many forms of competitive combat sports.

Compared to wrestling during the previous decade, when crowds sat through hours-long grappling matches, Mondt's creation was a huge hit with fans, in part because of the finishes he engineered. More than a revamping of the style of wrestling, Mondt, Sandow, and Lewis established a troupe of wrestlers who traveled like the circuses Mondt worked as a teenager, where he crossed paths with the man who taught him how to wrestle, fellow Iowan Martin "Farmer" Burns.

It took some research, according to Griffin's account, before Mondt unearthed the story of James Figg, through which he explained to Sandow and Lewis what he wanted to accomplish. Figg, a fistic nonconformist whom Jack Dempsey called the father of modern boxing, was one of the first cross-trained fighters. During the second decade of the eighteenth century, the Briton was considered the best prizefighter on the planet. He could box a wrestler. Grapple a boxer. He could fight in the clinch. This was the basis for "Figg's Fighting," a style that became well-known throughout the British Isles as his reputation grew.

Sandow and Lewis saw the light, and within a few months the wrestling gates grew as members of the establishment, four promoters in the Northeast known as "The Trust," quickly felt the pinch of hard competition.

Even before being publicly rebuffed by Dempsey, "Strangler" Lewis, the man most Americans accepted as the best heavyweight wrestler at the time, toured the country as the tip of the Gold Dust spear. The best wrestlers, like Lewis, actually knew what they were doing, and sometimes painfully implemented their knowledge against other presumably tough men. Up until the 1920s, the hierarchy of wrestling was based around whoever was perceived to be the best shooter and hooker, because if push came to shove, the guy who knew best how to push and shove was going to walk away with the belt. Choreographed outcomes, which became standard operating procedure as the Gold Dust Trio's influence grew, needed two willing participants. If the guy tabbed to drop the belt didn't follow the plan, or if wrestlers went off script, a price needed to be paid.

Mondt, a legitimate hooker, was brought into Lewis' camp based on the Farmer's recommendation in 1919. The pair sparred and worked out, leaving Lewis to feel that when he needed a "copper," a pro wrestling euphemism for "enforcer," Mondt along with tough guys Stanislaus Zbyszko and "Tiger Man" John Pesek could ably handle the job.

Pesek preferred wrestling for sport over show, but was vicious in defense of the Gold Dust Trio when required. After a match on November 14, 1921, at Madison Square Garden, Pesek and his manager Larney Lichtenstein of Chicago had their licenses revoked by the New York State Athletic Commission, then chaired by William Muldoon. Pesek mauled a reputed "trustbuster," Marin Plestina, who was known for spotty cooperation when it came to laying down to promotions and their champions. Pesek butted and gouged Plestina in his eyes before being disqualified. The big Serbian was laid up in his room at the Hotel Lenox for several days nursing an abrasion of the cornea, and Pesek never wrestled in New York again.

Pesek and many of the wrestlers under contract to Sandow came and went, yet finding a place to work during this time wasn't a problem. If the consolidation of talent was troublesome for anyone, it was promoters used to doing business with their controlling interests and mechanisms in place. As the trio cobbled together a set of wrestlers, booked venues, and promoted across the country, the "Strangler" Lewis business grew strong—though not so much the industry as a whole. Lewis held on to the title that mattered, except when it suited the business not to, and since fans might grow weary of the same man as reigning champion month after month, year after year, it sometimes made sense for him to drop the belt. Everything was predetermined, mostly due to Mondt's handiwork. Groups of promoters got the message, and because fans passed through turnstiles to watch, this new brand of wrestling was widely adopted. Even with Mondt dictating matches and outcomes, and Sandow controlling talent, the trio wouldn't easily own a field that had been crafted by some of the hardest men of the last hundred years. This is the stock folks like Joe Stecher came from. Stecher, a pig farmer who subdued his animals like many of the men he beat, by scissoring them between his legs, was every bit as dangerous as "Strangler" Lewis, and had the backing of entrenched powers the trio sought to overtake.

"Strangler" and Stecher famously wrestled to a five-hour draw during a shoot match in Omaha, Neb., on July 4, 1916. The bout, with Stecher the titleholder, drew great criticism from press who covered the slow, uneventful contest. These were the types of matches Mondt wanted to rid wrestling of, though that would not come without its share of unintended consequences. Mondt wanted the wrestlers to work less, so he established time limits. Extended grappling sessions were all but removed. For the most part, wrestling manifested into pantomime fighting.

Until Griffin's book, most fans and media operated as if the matches were legitimate when for years they weren't. Anyone who said otherwise broke "kayfabe," wrestlespeak for the portrayal of what was real or true, and hookers had an easy remedy for that. Joints were always there for twisting. Arteries always good for pinching. But pro wrestling was shifting from showcasing athletes well versed in the foundation of the game—the damaging catch-as-catch-can stylings of pioneers Lewis, Gotch, and Burns—to those playing off showmanship and characters who could create "heat" with the audience.

★　★　★　★　★

A couple days before Muhammad Ali—technically he was Cassius Clay, and remained so until 1964—made his first ring appearance in Las Vegas, a ten-round decision over Duke Sabedong, the nineteen-year-old from Louisville, Ky., reformatted his mind as to how he wanted people reacting to him.

During a live radio interview to promote Ali's seventh fight, the boxer, sitting beside beloved matchmaker Mel Greb, responded somewhat meekly about himself, considering the reputation he went on to earn. A year removed from winning a gold medal in Rome, Ali was joined in studio by iconic pro wrestler "Gorgeous" George Wagner, a champion at talking, annoying people, and creating headlines, but not much else as it pertained to wrestling. Thankfully for George, he was in a profession that rewarded such abilities.

The night before Ali took to the Convention Center on June 26, 1961, against Sabedong, a six-foot-six Hawaiian, George faced Freddie Blassie in the same building. George and Blassie were two of the best-known wrestlers working out of the Los Angeles territory at the time. Much had changed about pro wrestling since the Gold Dust Trio days, and while Blassie could handle himself some, George was the sort of wrestler who would have been tied in knots had "Strangler" Lewis or Joe Stecher placed their hands on him. "Gorgeous" George represented a consequence of pro wrestling's push to campiness, a true departure from the submission wrestling techniques born out of Greece and Japan and countless corners of the world, to a showy mindless form of entertainment that fills the gap between television commercials. George was primarily a character pushed to the top of cards based on his charisma and drawing power. After pro wrestling prioritized selling and showmanship over honest-to-goodness skills, the conditions were set for wrestlers like George to emerge.

Well past the peak of George's career—when the TV boom during the late 1940s demanded content to draw in viewers, all three networks featured pro wrestling on their airwaves, and business received a surprising boost that jolted it out of a considerable lull—this reformed psychiatrist from New York City, the 220-pound "Human Orchid," still made the most out of getting people to hate him. George was a drunk by the summer of 1961. His liver was shot, and he was two Christmases from dying, broke, of a heart attack. It was coincidence or fate that Mel Greb put the wrestler in the same room with the fresh-faced, smooth-skinned African American Ali.

"I'll kill him; I'll tear his arm off," George ranted about his opponent, the classic Freddie Blassie. "If this bum beats me, I'll crawl across the ring and cut off my hair, but it's not gonna happen because I'm the greatest wrestler in the world."

Ali absorbed what was in front of him and considered how much he wanted to see "Gorgeous" George in action. No matter what happened, the boxer felt as if something unmissable was about to go down and he needed to watch a man who proclaimed he'd win because he was the prettier wrestler.

"That's when I decided I'd never been shy about talking," the boxer said to historian Thomas Hauser in the biography *Muhammad Ali: His Life and Times*. "But if I talked even more, there was no telling how much money people would pay to see me."

Ali was simply playing off his strengths. He was already a poet, creating and reciting lines about his favorite boxers and moments, so it wasn't as if George inspired him to make rhymes. More to the point, this was brashness recognizing itself in an unadulterated, propped-up form. Ali loved the show business side of pro wrestling, and George woke him up to what was possible.

It was a full house for George and Blassie, about double what Ali and Sabedong managed to produce the following night. Angelo Dundee's charge watched the man that captivated him go through his usual shtick. George stepped into the ring on a cutout of a red carpet. "Pomp and Circumstance" played over loudspeakers. He tossed out gold-colored bobby pins that were removed from his hair to a hissing, snarling crowd. "Georgie pins," the 14-karat version, were reserved for friends and well-wishers willing to swear an oath never to confuse regular bobby pins for these. The wrestler's personal valet, whether lady or gentleman, used a super-sized sterling silver atomizer to douse his corner, the referee, the crowd, and, sometimes, his opponent in the sweet-smelling "Chanel No. 10," a concoction that existed only in the fanciful world of "Gorgeous" George. His marcelled platinum locks, courtesy of Hollywood's famous Frank & Joseph Hair Salon, were perfectly suited for the lacy, frilly gowns and sequined satin robes he wore into the ring.

"I don't really think I'm gorgeous," the wrestler, a natural brunette, was known to say. "But what's my opinion against millions?" Once he stepped between the ropes and prepared to put on a show, he delighted in slowly folding his robes, reportedly valued at as much as $2,000 apiece. The slower the fold, he discovered, the more the crowd despised him. Against Blassie, George wore a form-fitting red velvet one. He was absurd, but that was the point. More than a third of his fans were women, and on plenty of occasions George dealt with the threat of having a purse hurled at him. Men were known to stick lit cigars into his calves. They hated him but they watched, especially in Los Angeles, where the Olympic Auditorium was home for "G.G."

"When he got to the ring, everyone booed," Muhammad Ali would later tell Dundee, according to John Capouya in his book *Gorgeous George: The Outrageous Bad-Boy Wrestler Who Created American Pop Culture.* "I looked around and I saw everybody was mad. I was mad! I saw 15,000 people coming to see this man get beat, and his talking did it. And I said, 'This is a gooood idea.'"

Ali needed no gimmicks to attract or repel people. He was a magnet, always; it just depended on the other side's polarity. The public's feelings about the boxer throughout his career were based on tangible things: cockiness born from self-belief and success in real competition; a conversion to Islam; unconventional political views; changing his identity from Cassius Clay to Muhammad Ali; challenging the U.S. government as a conscientious objector during the war in Vietnam; civil rights activism; and dozens of other important stances he took throughout his career. Ali changed the way fighters approached publicity. Unafraid to consider consequences in the ring and out, Ali spoke like no boxer before him, offering statements on serious topics or clownish things as he wished. The man was much more than a lug, but when he incorporated an over-the-top feel to his language, when he harangued opponents for being ugly or looking like a bear or, in Inoki's case, a pelican, or when he began bragging about himself, which he hadn't done much until pro wrestlers changed his perspective, people simply ate it up.

When George Wagner bumped into Ali in Las Vegas, the bright lights had long dimmed on the wrestler's career. Following promotional wars and match-fixing scandals that emerged out of pro wrestling's turbulent 1930s, George's buffoonery was the sort of thing no one watching could be confused about, and the total lack of a sporting attitude actually helped propel him to prominence and rekindled a new kind of interest in pro wrestling in America. Pro wrestling needed to be fake and not many of the boys were less real than "Gorgeous" George.

In a Las Vegas locker room following the "no contest" with Blassie, Greb brought Ali to see George, whose advice served the boxer well. "You got your good looks, a great body, and a lot of people will pay to see somebody shut your big mouth," George is quoted as saying in Capouya's book. "So keep on bragging, keep on sassing, and always be outrageous."

That ability put George in the main event of the first pro wrestling show at Madison Square Garden since a twelve-year ban in New York that was inspired by a historic double cross. The Gold Dust Trio fell apart in 1929 after Mondt walked away following a dispute over control with Billy Sandow's brother. Mondt learned much about the business and carried on as a major player through the rest of his days. Wrestling, meanwhile, became fragmented, and the lack of a true national champion against an emerging reality of various regional championships confused the public and elicited criticism from the press. One of these champions was Danno O'Mahoney, a showman with little shooting gravitas who operated at the mercy of bookers and hookers. He just couldn't protect himself, so it seemed everyone tried to snatch the belt from him no matter what any script said.

A wrestler named Dick Shikat took his chance at O'Mahoney, and while some of the sport's most powerful promoters were aware of what might happen, it was primarily the challenger's call once they stepped in the ring. Shikat hooked the fish in less than twenty minutes, and all hell broke loose. Burned promoters played games, booking Shikat unbeknownst to him in numerous states until he was barred by many commissions for being a no-show. This prompted a trial in Columbus, Ohio, at which all the major promoters were forced to testify. The lid was blown off wrestling: whatever credibility the business had as a sports venture was gone so far as the public was concerned; the media covered it less and less until it didn't at all, and a multimillion-dollar national spectacle devolved into a regional program that allowed basically everyone to claim they were a pro wrestling world champion.

Fifteen of these so-called champions existed when George appeared at Madison Square Garden in 1949. He was not among them at the time, though even he held a title once. Two days after George appeared at the Garden on February 22 of that year, the *New York Times'* Arthur Daley led his column, "Sports of the Times," with this: "If Gorgeous George has not killed wrestling in New York for good and for all, the sport (if you pardon the expression) is hardy enough to survive a direct hit by an atomic bomb." Less than five years after Hiroshima and Nagasaki, that was quite a statement. Daley was wrong both ways. George wouldn't kill pro wrestling in New York or anywhere else, and the business wasn't impenetrable, though, like the proverbial cockroach in a nuclear explosion, it's a reputed survivor. Despite the weeping of newspaper writers, George's peak through the mid-1950s brought him much fame and money. As gimmicks go, yes, George's panache went stale, yet it was captivating enough even at the tawdry end to rope in someone like Ali.

ROUND FOUR

Two hundred forty pounds. Barrel-chested. Serious. No hint of fragrance to be found. In most ways Rikidōzan couldn't have been more different from George Wagner. Yet, as the "Human Orchid" bloomed over American pop culture during the 1950s, retired sumo wrestler Rikidōzan grew to an even greater stature in Japan. An honest-to-goodness icon. How? By capitalizing on anti-Western sentiment and mollifying the depressed spirit of a people decimated by war.

Television, timing, theater, and good ol' jingoism proved more potent for Rikidōzan than "Gorgeous" George's "Chanel No. 10." Then, after he had acted as savior to a people that loved him only because they did not truly know him, the blade of a *yakuza* gangster's six-inch hunting knife plunged into Rikidōzan's battle-hardened abdomen. His untimely demise in 1963 unveiled a face long shrouded in secrecy.

Kim Sin-rak arrived in Japan in 1939 at the age of fifteen after a touring scout signed him to one of the several licensed sumo houses in that country. At Tokyo's Nishinoseki stable, Sin-rak, strapping young man that he was, received the *shikona* (ring name) "Rikidōzan," which fittingly translates to "Rugged Mountain Road." It was decided that this new identity also required an elaborate fiction. The public wasn't considered capable of accepting a nonnative Japanese *rikishi*, let alone a Korean, beating their own in sumo. That's how Kim Sin-rak from the South Hamgyong Province in northeast Korea, a citizen of the Japanese empire, became Mitsuhiro Momota, pure-blooded Japanese son of Minokichi Momota, the Nagasaki-based scout who discovered him. Years later, well into his incredible pro wrestling stardom, Rikidōzan felt his background, if revealed as false, would have cost him much of his fan base—basically halving the country of Japan—such was the breadth of his popularity and the pervasiveness of anti-Korean sentiment among the population following the annexation of Korea in 1910. It wouldn't be officially revealed until 1978, and even then many hagiographies glossed over or ignored the truth of Rikidōzan's heritage and rise to fame.

The same year Rikidōzan began his journey up the difficult sumo ranks, Isamu Takeshita became the third president of the Japan Sumo Association. Fluent in English, Takeshita enjoyed quite a life. A half century before passing away at the age of eighty, Takeshita set up President Theodore Roosevelt with a judo and jiu-jitsu partner, Yamashita Yoshiaki, who at the president's request taught technique at the U.S. Naval Academy, where he interacted with an assortment of styles including catch-as-catch-can wrestlers. In fact, the pinning of Yoshiaki led the Naval Academy to hire a wrestler rather than a jiu-jitsu man to teach young midshipmen.

Still, Takeshita's diplomatic transaction blazed a trail for four Kanō Jigorō students, including the supremely influential Mitsuyo Maeda, throughout the Americas in the early 1900s. Their efforts created the conditions for the proliferation of Japanese submission arts that are essential to the way the world understands and applies martial arts today.

Takeshita made five trips to the United States between the Teddy Roosevelt and Franklin Delano Roosevelt administrations. During a summer radio broadcast from San Francisco in 1935, six years before the attack on Pearl Harbor, he proclaimed, "No Japanese warship has ever crossed the Pacific except on a mission of peace. No Japanese soldier has ever come to these shores except on a similar mission." Yet the retired admiral, who received a Distinguished Service Medal from the United States for his actions in the Japanese Imperial Navy during World War I, played a significant role in militarizing Japanese youth and sports in the ramp-up to war in the Pacific.

Joseph Svinth, for the *Journal of Combative Sport*, noted, "The fascistization of Japanese sport was among [Takeshita's] duties in these positions, and during the late 1930s Takeshita was responsible for organizing regular foreign exchanges with Germany's Hitler Youth."

Takeshita's considerable influence and fondness for sumo helped it grow into a national sport, but even he fell short in shielding the country's indigenous wrestling style from the impact of war. As the empire churned in the years leading up to the attack on Pearl Harbor, Japanese life was essentially co-opted by the military. School-aged children were prescribed a physical education curriculum that translated directly to war fighting. Sporting arts were derided as unnecessary, and *budō*—the martial ways, specifically the Japanese martial arts spirit—was consigned to hand-to-hand fighting. The central authority for Japanese martial arts, the Dai Nippon Butoku Kai, was controlled by the Imperial Army, which promoted boxing because of the belief it engendered the right kind of spirit, while downplaying Kanō Jigorō's Kodokan judo, which was thought to be too sporting. Kendo and sumo were simply impractical. Boxers such as Tsuneo "Piston" Horiguchi remained busy competing, and, like some sumotori, participated in war bond drives. Athletes in the East and West were useful for this sort of thing, as manipulating sports into effective propagandist tools was hardly new.

Dwindling resources, intensifying attacks from American B-29 Superfortress bombers around Tokyo, and a closely guarded military project halted sumo competition ahead of the summer tournament of 1944. Young battering ram Rikidōzan was close to touching its upper echelon before he and his stable were pulled into the war effort, apparently assigned to factory work during this time. Stories exist that he punched American prisoners of war whose output in forced labor camps wasn't sufficient, though the veracity of the reports is unclear. Other *rikishi*, such as members of the Tatsunami stable, provided labor services like digging up pine roots that produced oil used for fighter plane fuel.

As responsible as anything for the abbreviated sumo season was a secret Japanese initiative with the goal of producing 10,000 bomb-dropping balloons, the Fu-Go Weapon, capable of hitting the continental United States directly from Japan or from warships in the Pacific. According to a 1973 report for the Smithsonian Institution by Robert C. Mikesh,

Tokyo's main sumo stadium, the Ryōgoku Kokugikan, was among several sports arenas, music halls, and theaters the military used to inflate and test thirty-three-foot-diameter balloons designed to deliver a payload of four incendiary bombs and one thirty-two-pound antipersonnel bomb. The Japanese hoped after catching strong winds from the west, America's wooded areas would explode in raging forest fires, tying up critical resources and causing a panic among the civilian population.

For logistical, morale, and propaganda reasons, the American military worked with the media to keep information of potential balloon damage from reaching Japan, all the while stunting a potential hysteria on the West Coast. On May 5, 1945, Elsie Mitchell, age twenty-six, and five children from her husband's church—Edward Engen, Jay Gifford, and Joan Patzke, all thirteen years old; Dick Patzke, age fourteen; and Sherman Shoemaker, eleven years old— were killed during a fishing and picnic excursion near Bly, Oreg., when a balloon did as intended. These casualties, the only ones in the United States that were a direct result of foreign enemy action, prompted the U.S. government to cease its censorship on the topic.

The U.S. Army also responded to the balloon threat via the Firefly Project. Conscientious objectors (group CPS-103) and the first all-black battalion of paratroopers, the 555th Parachute Infantry Battalion, better known as the Triple Nickles, were dispatched to the Pacific Northwest in case these fire balloons lived up to their billing. Despite the precaution, the 555th wasn't called to smoke jump into a balloon-produced fire. There was concern among military brass that the Japanese might float germ or chemical warfare to American shores, but from November 4, 1944, to August 8, 1945, two small brush fires and a momentary loss of power at a plant in Hanford, Wash., were the only recorded incidents of property damage, according to the Smithsonian Institution report.

The situation at Hanford Engineering Works, however, could have been catastrophic. Uranium slugs for the atomic bomb that destroyed Nagasaki, Rikidōzan's adopted hometown, were produced there and the balloon bomb triggered the reactor's safety mechanism. The fail-safe system had not been tested, and everyone was relieved when it worked as designed. The reactor remained cool enough not to collapse or explode—ensuring the Fu-Go Weapon would be remembered as no more than a missed Hail Mary attempt by Japan to turn the tide of the war.

The end of hostilities and subsequent allied occupation did not immediately return Japanese life, including the martial arts, to their premilitarized social order. The Supreme Commander for the Allied Powers, General Douglas MacArthur, instituted numerous edicts, among them directives aimed at removing and excluding militaristic and ultranationalist persons from society. Schools that briefly resuscitated martial arts instruction after the end of the war stopped, and the Dai Nippon Butoku Kai was shuttered. The tangled mess resulted in a purge of people apparently sympathetic to the defeated Japanese Empire, many of whom were seemingly connected to the Butokukai that had been corrupted under the fascist regime. This was the crux of the General Headquarters *budō* ban that lasted until 1950—not the shelving of martial arts, per se, just their perversion.

Under Takeshita's leadership, sumo was not targeted by the Allied Powers' *budō* prohibition. Speaking on the seventieth anniversary of the end of the war, Sokichi Kumagai, seventeen years a top-ranking sumo referee, or *gyōji*, told the *Mainichi*, a major daily Japanese newspaper, that he received word to reconvene with his stable and get touring again soon after Japan's surrender. "The biggest problem was securing enough food for the wrestlers, who were all voracious eaters," Kumagai said. The tour was called *komezumo*, or "rice sumo," and in lieu of money, spectators were required to offer a payment of rice. "At the time we toured in groups of related stables," Kumagai told the paper, "and all the groups toured in areas where rice farming was common."

Soon enough the sumo association issued a notice that a Grand Sumo Tournament would be held in Tokyo in November 1945. Though his reputation remained strong and positive, and he was unaffected by the Butoku Kai purge, Takeshita announced plans to step down as the head of sumo when the *honbasho* ended. Rikidōzan had earned a spot in sumo's top division, the *makuuchi*, and reached the sport's third highest rank, *sekiwake*, by the time Takeshita passed away in 1949. He competed until September 1950, and, citing financial reasons, retired.

Rikidōzan's improbably important pro wrestling journey began in construction. According to Robert Whiting's book, *Tokyo Underworld: The Fast Times and Hard Life of an American Gangster in Japan,* a sumo fan, tattooed *yakuza* gambler Shinsasku Nita, maintained "special connections inside the GHQ." Those relationships led to projects at U.S. military camps, some of which Nita hired Rikidōzan to supervise. The wrestler's English improved and he

enjoyed the nightlife in Ginza. One evening, according to
Whiting, Rikidōzan found himself on the wrong side of
an altercation with a Japanese-American Olympic weight-
lifter, Hawaii's Harold Sakata, who earned a silver medal at
the 1948 Games in London, and, later, appeared opposite
Sean Connery's version of James Bond as Auric Goldfinger's
hat-throwing henchman Oddjob. Sakata and Rikidōzan
quickly worked out their differences, and the former sumo
wrestler was integrated into a touring group of American
pro wrestlers who had been sponsored by the Torii Oasis
Shriner's Club of Tokyo. Before heading to the Korean
Peninsula, where fighting was underway between U.S.- and
Chinese-led forces, former heavyweight boxing champion
Joe Louis joined seven wrestlers, including Sakata and Iowan
Bobby Bruns, in entertaining U.S. servicemen while seeking
to raise $50,000 for crippled children during a three-month
tour of Japan.

Like the Imperial Japanese Army, Americans usurped
the old sumo venue, which had been repaired after U.S.
firebombing destroyed its huge iron roof. Rather than
testing weapons, Occupation forces renamed the building
from Ryōgoku Kokugikan to Ryōgoku Memorial Hall and
staged events—the first bits of Americana introduced to the
Japanese that hadn't fallen from the sky. American-style pro
wrestling, the kind "Toots" Mondt had established in the
1920s, was officially introduced to the Japanese on Sunday,
September 30, 1951, the same month the country returned
to the League of Nations after signing a peace treaty in San
Francisco.

Rikidōzan debuted in late October, feeling his way
through a ten-minute time-limit draw against Bruns.

Sergeant Clarkson Crume, for *Stars and Stripes*, noted that Rikidōzan had lost six inches off his waist since meeting Sakata and the boys, and was "surprisingly good for someone who has been wrestling only three weeks." The squat Japanese grappler hung around the tour through December 11, karate chopping and running over the opposition—a sampling of the hard style that became his trademark. Winter's harshness cut the wrestling program short, but the expedition paid off because Bruns had found a twenty-year-old, 265-pound man who would spearhead the rapid expansion of the "sport" in Japan.

The following February, as a naturalized Japanese citizen—important since status as a North Korean would have made travel to the U.S. problematic—Rikidōzan departed in good shape, down thirty pounds, ready to learn the pro wrestling business. He landed in Hawaii, one of the nearly thirty territories encompassing the National Wrestling Association, and was coached by Bobby Bruns. The NWA-affiliated promotion in San Francisco also gave him plenty of opportunities to step into the ring. Rising from the ashes of the Gold Dust Trio, the NWA attempted to control and organize talent, produce strong champions the public would support (despite knowing that wrestling was more show than competition), and seize the larger space of wrestling. NWA representatives in Honolulu (Al Karasick) and San Francisco (Joe Malcewicz) arranged the historic "Shriners" tour of 1951, and envisioned Japan as a place well worth expanding to.

Rikidōzan made them look smart.

Intent on establishing a lasting pro wrestling promotion, Rikidōzan returned to his adopted country after a year and a half on the road. In short order, a pipeline of mostly large white men, presumably Americans but not always, journeyed overseas to lose—delighting Japanese audiences, most of whom remained ignorant that outcomes were predetermined. Rikidōzan's affiliation with the NWA quickly lent credibility to him and his organization, the Japanese Pro Wrestling Alliance.

More important than NWA ties was the timing of his venture. As it had for wrestling and "Gorgeous" George in the States, television became an enormous driver for Rikidōzan and pro wrestling in Japan. Within a month of the JWA starting operations on July 30, 1953, commercial broadcast networks began distributing programming to Japanese households, which, no different than postwar Americans, purchased televisions in increasing numbers.

Rikidōzan's first *puroresu* event hit airwaves on two networks, NHG and NTV, live from Tokyo, on February 19, 1954. Joining forces with Masahiko Kimura—a pioneering judo and mixed-style fighter three years removed from breaking Hélio Gracie's left arm with a joint lock that was later named in his honor in front of 20,000 Brazilians—the pair competed in a tag-team match against the big-and-tall Sharpe brothers of Canada (to the Japanese, Ben and Mike Sharpe passed just fine for Americans). Three days of pro wrestling, all live on television, served as quite an introduction for Rikidōzan, the "ethnic hero" of Japan, whose ring formula evoked memories of the Second World War. With a twist.

"I get phone calls, letters telling me hit back when American wrestlers hit me," he told the United Press during an interview in San Francisco in 1952. "Finally, when [they] hit dirty, I hit dirty, too."

In the U.S., that was easy enough to understand because for years this had been wrestling at its core. The Gold Dust Trio played off stereotypes—religious, ethnic, or nationalist—and casting the likes of Rikidōzan as a villain was simply how it worked. But in Japan? He couldn't accept such humiliation from *gaijin.* Surrender instead of victory meant reminding people of the Empire's failure. Of the Americans' bombs. The sun hadn't set on the Japanese, Rikidōzan intended to say through his karate chops; that's how he wanted to make people feel when he wrestled.

Pro wrestling and television produced prideful and harrowing moments for the Japanese. In the fall of 1955, a couple years after Rikidōzan captured the public's imagination, an eleven-year-old schoolboy was reportedly killed when a fellow student landed a dropkick while imitating the American style of wrestling. Networks, which were saturated with wrestling at the time, created public service announcements essentially telling kids to cool it.

A growing fervor around Rikidōzan, and Kimura's cemented reputation as one of Japan's best fighters, prompted the media to speculate about what might happen if they were matched as opponents instead of teammates. The wrestlers paid attention and agreed it was a good idea to entertain this question. There was money to be made, and for the advancement of Japanese pro wrestling the match needed to happen. So on December 22, 1954, the first pro wrestling heavyweight championship of Japan was contested at the Kuramae Kokugikan, the home of sumo from 1950 until 1985. Without nationalist overtones, the contest between Rikidōzan and Kimura turned out to be a straight power play. Shifting from work to shoot, the former sumo man chopped the judoka to the floor, a double cross apparently justified by an errant kick from Kimura to Rikidōzan's groin.

"The first bout was going to be a draw," Kimura told *Sports Graphic Number*, Japan's *Sports Illustrated*, in 1983. "The winner of the second will be determined by the winner of a rock-paper-scissors. After the second match, we will repeat this process. We came to an agreement on this condition. As for the content of the match, Rikidōzan will let me throw him, and I will let him strike me with a chop. We then rehearsed karate chop and throws. However, once the bout started, Rikidōzan became taken by greed for big money and fame. He lost his mind and became a mad man. When I saw him raise his hand, I opened my arms to invite the chop. He delivered the chop, not to my chest, but to my neck with full force. I fell to the mat. He then kicked me. Neck arteries are so vulnerable that it did not need to be Rikidōzan to cause a knockdown. A junior high school kid could inflict a knockdown this way. I could not forgive his treachery. That night, I received a phone call informing me that several, ten, *yakuza* are on their way to Tokyo to kill Rikidōzan."

A strain of thought exists that suggests Rikidōzan's stabbing death in 1963 was the *yakuza* catching up with him for the betrayal of Kimura, who, to the surprise of no one, never received a chance to wrestle or fight the former sumo stylist again. As with most things having to do with Rikidōzan, who he was and what he did relative to his public perception were very different.

Rikidōzan and American Lou Thesz wrestled to a sixty-minute draw in Tokyo's first-ever "world title match" in 1957, scoring a record 87.0 rating on Japanese television—two of his matches rank in the top ten most-viewed programs in the country's history and tens of thousands of people packed the streets to watch. His matches against Thesz, the only American wrestler Rikidōzan admitted to having respect for, represent the crowning achievements of his enormous ring success.

When Rikidōzan visited Los Angeles a year later to face Thesz—the best shooter in the world, a man chiseled from granite like Ed "Strangler" Lewis—the message was clear: If Rikidōzan could put up a fight against a man like Thesz, if he could beat Thesz and claim the NWA international heavyweight belt, which he did in L.A., well, he could do anything.

So too could the Japanese.

Not only had the face of Japanese strength adopted the American manner of wrestling, he adopted the American way of life and business. In L.A., Rikidōzan asked Gene LeBell, then twenty-six, to hold $15,000 cash in crisp $100 bills. "He said keep it until the match is over," recalled LeBell. "I could've gone down to Mexico." No matter what happened at the Olympic Auditorium that night, a top-of-the line Rolls-Royce was going to be purchased afterwards. Big money. Big cars. Big homes. Big deals. He operated in the legitimate and illegitimate consumerism that permeated Japan following the war. Rikidōzan put his name on nightclubs, hotels, condominiums, and bowling alleys. He also circulated among gangsters, and in some ways was one himself. When he drank too much he could become belligerent, a bully who ignored police summons.

Rikidōzan indulged in money, power, and influence. He was not who he was portrayed to be, and after his sudden death ten days before "Gorgeous" George Wagner passed away in Los Angeles, the pro wrestling business in Japan was left in shambles. It is testament to Rikidōzan's massive influence that his death didn't bring down pro wrestling altogether. Instead, his protégés rode the tidal wave and established important legacies of their own.

ROUND FIVE

More than a few Cassius Clay watchers suggested that because he moved around the ring so much, the sleek twenty-year-old might not trust his chin.

Due mostly to his locomotion, it's true, the attention-grabbing fighter hadn't been hurt during his first sixteen months as pro. The man's legs, so long as they were strong underneath him, were his first line of defense in that they got him to where he wanted to be faster than he could get touched. And yet this is where some critics conjured questions regarding Ali's potential.

Ali breezed to a 10–0 record and received more than enough press to justify a debut at the old Madison Square Garden to begin his 1962 campaign—but that wasn't successful or quick enough. A hold-the-reins development plan buffered against the Olympic champion's heavy competitive drive. On the subject of his tenth opponent, Munich-born Willi Besmanoff, Ali declared shame at having fought

an "unrated duck." While Ali talked up champions Floyd
Patterson and Sonny Liston he got in rounds with pugs like
the squat Besmanoff, who finished his fifteen-year career
with ninety-three bouts and a ledger of 51–34–8. The fight
with Ali in Louisville was the German's seventy-ninth, and it
marked one of eleven times he was stopped.

No one besides the six-foot-three kid himself—"a
golden-brown young man," A.J. Liebling observed in the
March 1962 edition of the *New Yorker*, "big-chested and
long-legged, whose limbs have the smooth rounded look
that Joe Louis's used to have, and that frequently denotes
fast muscles"—was eager to approach deep waters. Trainer
Angelo Dundee knew superior talent could get a person by in
some fields, but not boxing, not even for a specimen like Ali.

There was much to learn on the arduous road ahead.

The purpose of boxing is to inflict damage with your fists
while avoiding strikes in return. During a career in prizefighting that's nearly impossible. Boxers are expected to be stout
because almost all of them get caught. The game ones respond
to trouble and fight on. The great ones do that then win.

For Ali's doubters it boiled down to, yeah, sure, the
fancy-footed dancer's talent was obvious, but what kind of
fighter was he really?

New York matchmaker Teddy Brenner lived up to his reputation by testing Ali's doggedness in the boxer's Garden debut,
and Sonny Banks, a twenty-one-year-old converted southpaw
puncher from Detroit, got the nod. Midway through the
opening round, Banks snapped off a left hook that put Ali on
the canvas and turned the Miami-based Dundee from tan to
pale. Ali, a 5-to-1 favorite, needed only the count of two to
regroup, shake off the cobwebs, and get to his feet.

"That was my first time knocked down as a professional," Ali told the press on a twelve-degree February night in Manhattan. "I had to get up to take care of things after that because it was rather embarrassing, me on the floor. As you know, I think that I'm the greatest and I'm not supposed to be on the floor, so I had to get up and put him on out, in four as I predicted."

Suckered by the illusion of landing a second money punch, a fight finisher, Banks became a predictable head-hunter with that left hook. As he crumbled under Ali's angular fighting and incessant, buzzing jab, Banks, penned Liebling, "was like a man trying to fight off wasps with a shovel."

Unsure of Ali's recuperative powers until Banks touched his charge's off button, Dundee was encouraged to see the type of pugilist he was dealing with. Critics, meanwhile, had new information to critique regarding the quality of Ali's chin.

For all of the whirlwind dancing and speed that defined so much of Ali's career, Banks showed that perhaps The Greatest's best boxing trait was standing when he had to. Ali did so many things better than most, and determining his "best" is difficult to pin down. The man's energy output in life was preternatural, yet he was as relaxed as any fighter—a fundamental reason for his legendary stamina and pace. A rare few boxers, never mind heavyweights, moved as Ali did. As Liebling noted in his *New Yorker* piece "Poet and Pedagogue," which beautifully described the Banks fight, the "Louisville Lip" needed no help providing the press a quote, making news, or, as the story noted, coming up with rhymes. Less than two years removed from the Rome Olympics, Clay was a business, the full package, well on his way, with financial backers and a support system, to an unparalleled life.

★ ★ ★ ★ ★

Beating Banks set in motion a pivotal stretch for the rising contender. Eighteen days passed between Ali's debut at MSG and the last night in February, a Wednesday, when he stopped another left-hooker, Don Warner, in four rounds in Miami. Ali predicted a finish in five, but because Warner wouldn't shake hands before the fight he said he deducted a round for poor sportsmanship. Highlighted by three bouts in Tinseltown, Ali fought a half dozen times in 1962 and enjoyed the run of L.A. during a period that shaped him as a boxer, showman, and person.

Vice President Richard Nixon dedicated the Los Angeles Memorial Sports Arena on July 4, 1959, barely a year before Senator John F. Kennedy of Massachusetts accepted, inside the same building, the Democratic party's nomination for President of the United States of America. Kennedy bested Nixon in the fall of 1960 after a groundbreaking election that produced another sort of combat sport: televised presidential debates.

By the spring of '62, as Ali checked in to the Alexandria Hotel on 5th and Spring Street in Downtown L.A., Kennedy was entangled in the Bay of Pigs, Vietnam festered, the Cold War frosted, and the Cuban Missile Crisis was mere months away.

On top of everything else, the young president faced the pleas of L.A.-based pro wrestler "Classy" Freddie Blassie, who stood as the dominant West Coast champion after taking the belt from Frenchman Édouard Carpentier at the Sports Arena in June 1961. The following month, Lou Thesz, who put over Japan's Rikidōzan in '58, did the same for Blassie while legendary boxer Jersey Joe Walcott served as the referee.

Blassie drove big television ratings in L.A. on Wednesday nights from 8:00 to 9:30 P.M. on KCOP channel 13. So far as live sports went, boxing (and, ahem, wrestling) were easier and less expensive to broadcast than, say, baseball because they required only a couple cameras to sufficiently cover the action. From the start, TV and pro wrestling went as well together as any two things could, a fact that was partly responsible for Rikidōzan's success in Japan.

On March 28, 1962, within walking distance of Little Tokyo, L.A.'s strong Asian community filled the Olympic Auditorium hoping that the father of *puroresu*, Rikidōzan, would make history as the first Japanese to challenge for and subsequently win an American pro wrestling title.

Despite stomping Masahiko Kimura in Tokyo and possessing a wild-man reputation away from the ring, Rikidōzan wasn't well known in the West. Still, the new hero—such was Rikidōzan's stature at the time—received a far more honorable portrayal than most Japanese wrestlers after the Second World War. While Blassie's old tag team partner, Mr. Moto, played the role as untrustworthy, maybe scheming another Pearl Harbor, Rikidōzan, proud and seemingly forthright, was talked about as the sort of man who wouldn't stoop to hitting another when he was down.

Blassie the villain lost the belt to the pride of Japan when referee Johnny "Red Shoes" Dugan counted out the tanned American. Though many fans reviled Blassie and wanted him to lose, most viewers at home or at the Olympic Auditorium couldn't have imagined him without the World Wrestling Association world heavyweight title. Everyone went wild as Rikidōzan won the first and only fall during an hour of wrestling. The time limit elapsed and Blassie flipped when famed ring announcer Jimmy Lennon raised Rikidōzan's hand, officially declaring him champion. Blassie hollered that the contest was supposed to be two of three falls, then he ripped the referee's shirt in half down the front.

"I've never seen such injustice in all my life," Blassie howled at KCOP-13's Dick Lane. "I'm going to take this up with the World Wide Wrestling Association president and then I'm going to take it up with the athletic commission. If that isn't far enough I'm going to see my great friend President Kennedy because this was the dirtiest trick that's ever been pulled."

Damaging investigations into pro wrestling during the 1930s forever altered the business on the West Coast, yet the California State Athletic Commission, mainly as a way of collecting fees, continued to treat the scripted stuff like a sport for many years. After going ballistic Blassie was summarily fined for manhandling Dugan, as if the rampage wasn't part of the show. He paid and said not a word. Even on his deathbed Blassie wouldn't break character, so there was no way he'd betray wrestling by stating on the record that the match and his reaction with the referee was an angle.

Born Frederick Kenneth Blassman to German parents in St. Louis, February 8, 1918, Blassie wrestled during World War II under the name "Sailor" Fred Blassie while stationed with the Navy at Port Hueneme, Calif. After the war he ditched the "Sailor" routine and toured the Midwest, but it wasn't until returning to the West Coast's sandy beaches in Venice and Santa Monica that Blassie struck a chord with wrestling fans by playing the antagonist.

On April 23, 1962, the day Ali made his L.A. debut against George Logan, Blassie rematched Rikidōzan in a bout that captivated the Japanese. Even more startling than the nation's hysterical reaction to the contest was its response to Blassie, whose tactics stunned audiences. They simply hadn't seen anyone like him before. Plenty of American wrestlers made similar trips to Japan, gave Rikidōzan a go, then did the job and lost. For having the audacity to challenge Rikidōzan, they were generally well behaved and contrite. Not Blassie. He may as well have been a vampire, so scared were some Japanese.

Combined with a mastery of the televised interview, Blassie's profile as the heel (pro wrestling for "bad guy") grew immensely in the early '60s by doing the kinds of things he did upon landing in Japan for the rematch. Pulling out a file, Blassie appeared to sharpen his teeth in front of cameras. The gimmick worked wonders. Flashes popped, the Japanese ate it up, yet like almost everything else about his profession it was a con. The wrestler had befriended an L.A. dentist who crafted false dentures for Blassie so he could do crazy things like rasp his "teeth" into fangs then bite into stuff.

Rikidōzan's second clash against Blassie in Tokyo made headlines for more than huge television ratings or a win for the local favorite. Several elderly Japanese reportedly died from heart attacks after Blassie appeared to bite Rikidōzan, draw blood, and spit it in the former sumo wrestler's face. This was absurd theater, an example of pro wrestling's proverbial "crimson mask," and, of course, Rikidōzan sawed his head with a razor blade to make it happen. Blassie, true to form, showed no remorse. The dead, he said, had it coming.

Blassie returned to L.A. for the final contest in his three-match series with Rikidōzan. Since the July 25 bout was held off television at the Olympic Auditorium, Rich Marotta, a wrestling-crazed kid from Burbank, Calif., pleaded with his father to take him. Marotta got his wish and the young fan's first sensory memories of the Olympic were born on a mild summer day.

Seated with his father in the top row of the 10,400-seat-capacity arena, Marotta was as far from ringside as he could have been, but he was there and being in the building watching from the nosebleeds was a far better proposition than sitting at home in the dark.

"It didn't smell good in the place," remembered the L.A. native who made his way in life via boxing as a media personality. "It certainly wasn't a modern arena. I remember going into the bathroom and they had about two stalls and three urinals. And guys would just be peeing in the sinks. I had never seen anything like that. Guys just peeing in the sinks. It was dirty in there."

The Olympic Auditorium, unlike today's arenas, was a fairly intimate setup. People in the building focused on the action in the ring, not big screens, so for twenty minutes Marotta excitedly watched through binoculars as the Japanese hero beat up the blond, tan American.

Because Marotta despised Blassie he screamed for Rikidōzan. After slamming Blassie hard into a turnbuckle, Rikidōzan charged, missed, and tumbled through the ropes into the steel ringpost. Blassie snapped off a necktwister and mauled Rikidōzan until "there was blood everywhere," said Marotta. "Johnny 'Red Shoes' Dugan was the referee again. And finally 'Red Shoes' Dugan stopped the match and awarded it to Blassie. So my first trip to the Olympic Auditorium turned out to be a terrible disappointment that way."

Blassie's matches were less a choreographed wrestling match than a straight brawl, yet his series of matches with Rikidōzan proved important because they signified that Blassie's belt, the WWA title, was prestigious enough to attract challengers from faraway locales and was also worth hunting after. Therefore the Southern California wrestling territory run by Aileen Eaton and her son Mike LeBell was an entity to be reckoned with.

★ ★ ★ ★ ★

The Olympic Auditorium opened on August 5, 1925.

Los Angeles was in the midst of establishing entertainment as its industry and silver-screen legends Charlie Chaplin, Douglas Fairbanks, Mary Pickford, and D.W. Griffith created United Artists to push back against the entrenched studio caste system.

A mile from the location of the United Artists Building and its ornate Spanish Gothic theater that depicts studio executives as demons, the "Auditorium blazed with glory on its opening night, the light of many electric lights surpassed only by the sparkling jewels that adorned the persons of several of our well-known citizens and citizenesses," the *Los Angeles Times* published the following day. "Hollywood and the moving picture colony slipped into their tuxedos and formal apparel and blessed the ringside by their presence."

During the 1932 Los Angeles Olympic Games, the venue hosted boxing, wrestling, and weightlifting events. This was its intended purpose, and even from its least desired seats, the views of the action were good. With a capacity of 15,300, the Olympic—the so-called Madison Square Garden of the West Coast—registered as the largest indoor venue in the U.S. at the time.

Lou Daro, a carnival strongman who left home when he was ten to join a flying trapeze act with the Barnum & Bailey circus, took the money he earned from almost being ripped apart in a game of tug-and-war with eight Clydesdales and secured the rights to promote pro wrestling and boxing at the Olympic Auditorium from its opening through the end of '30s. The shift in pro wrestling from legitimate to show business was swift under the direction of "Carnation Lou," who spoke eight languages by the time he moved to L.A. from New York. Daro was known for managing Ed "Strangler" Lewis and pinning a white carnation to the lapel of his dapper suits.

While wrestling across the U.S. in the '30s suffered under the weight of controversies, entrenched battles between the industry's power brokers, and the public's shifting tastes, Los Angeles remained a hotbed. Daro was far more successful at selling wrestling than boxing, and with the help of Joe "Toots" Mondt, one third of the Gold Dust Trio, a bridge was built between the wrestling business on both coasts. Then misdeeds caught up to Mondt, Daro, and his brother Jack after a special investigation by the California State Assembly found financial irregularities, including more than $200,000 paid over a four-year period to politicians, media, and public relations firms in an attempt to maintain their alleged wrestling monopoly.

Crowds soon dwindled at the Olympic, and pressure from the California State Athletic Commission prompted the arena's owner, one of the city's richest men, Frank A. Garbutt, to briefly pass the Olympic business off to George Zaharias, a former wrestler and bodybuilder who married perhaps the best female athlete of all time, Babe Didrikson, in 1939.

Three years later, the irrepressible Aileen Eaton began her thirty-eight-year run at the helm of the Olympic. The fight business revealed itself to Eaton, a widowed mother of two. In 1941, Eaton worked as the private secretary for Garbutt, the president of the Los Angeles Athletic Club, whose net worth was $91 million (nearly $1.5 billion in 2016). Garbutt instructed Eaton to report back why the arena was operating in the red. Within days, she found bookkeeping irregularities, cleaned house, and recommended hiring boxing inspector Alvah "Cal" Eaton as the venue's promoter. Garbutt empowered Eaton to run the building, and on the business of fight promotion, she was hooked. Ten years later, she and Cal married.

Left to her own devices, the first female fight promoter in the country transformed a block of downtown real estate into a combat sports cathedral. Four decades after discovering the fight business, Eaton received a written tribute from famed *Los Angeles Times* sports columnist Jim Murray while she recovered from successful quadruple bypass heart surgery. "Red-haired, blue-eyed, pound for pound, she was as tough as any welterweight who ever came down the aisle," Murray wrote. The diminutive Eaton was liable to chew out a handful of managers one hour, and fit in fine at a fancy tea party the next.

Before passing away on a Saturday night in the fall of 1987, Eaton claimed to have seen more than 10,000 professional fights, including 100 world championship bouts she promoted; a few of them had needed more seats than the Olympic could offer so she had booked dates at the Los Angeles Memorial Coliseum or Dodger Stadium.

★ ★ ★ ★ ★

Wrestling crowds were wild and noticeably different from the more affluent boxing set. For untelevised wrestling on Friday nights, lines assembled around the block before lunch. Wrestling matches at the Olympic housed more of the crazies, the purse-swinging grandmas. Popular boxing nights felt subdued by comparison, even if the arena still buzzed. If regular boxing patrons missed two weeks of action without notifying the box office, they lost their seats. Folks located in the row behind moved up, which made everyone else happy because they bumped forward too.

Gamblers on boxing nights flashed signs at each other regarding who or what they wanted to wager on. There was a whole section of them near Aisle 10 employing a well-established system that included odds on much more than the outcome of a fight. One regular bet centered on which unsuspecting patron might slip down a slick metal ramp that should have been cordoned off with caution tape. Another famous Olympic wager centered on the fighters' corners, which were determined when legendary ring announcer Jimmy Lennon flipped a large disk. Black or white, blue or red, it was one more game to play for the bettors.

"I just remember through my life my dad flipping the disk and claiming he could make it come up any color," said

Jimmy Lennon Jr., the youngest of five kids who followed in his father's footsteps and became a beloved ring announcer.

On both boxing and wrestling nights, Lennon handled the PA. Because of the acoustics inside an enclosed concrete box, sound echoed and reverberated everywhere inside the Olympic Auditorium.

"When the crowd was on, it would be the loudest place," said Lennon Jr., who as a kid enjoyed the run of the building and the closest views in the house. Boxing and pro wrestling in Los Angeles remained solid business and though competition existed between promoters, especially for Latino boxers, Eaton and her sons, Gene and Mike LeBell, loomed large.

While Eaton worked for Garbutt at the L.A.A.C., Gene stumbled into mat-covered rooms full of tough guys. Even as a kid, he fit right in amongst a crew of war-torn men wearing scarred faces and cauliflower ears. LeBell had a chance to learn grappling, a combination of everything from pins to joint locks and strangle holds. He was eager to participate, and the famous Ed "Strangler" Lewis provided LeBell his first lesson: the double wristlock (i.e., downward arm crank or Kimura).

Literally and figuratively, "Judo" LeBell bumped up against the best in the combat sports world for the rest of his days, in part because he is so colorfully classified as one of these folks himself. So it was no surprise that LeBell got near the Olympic champion when he visited Los Angeles for several months in 1962.

During his initial interaction with Ali, LeBell said his mother handed the boxer a button. "I'm the greatest," it prophesied. According to Gene, Ali balked: "Excuse me Mrs. Eaton, I couldn't wear that. What would people say?"

The hard woman looked into Ali's soul and set him straight. "I don't care what they say. If it sells *boletos* (tickets) that's all that counts." Eaton's logic won the day.

A run from the Grand Olympic Auditorium to Main Street Gym lasted a good two miles. Newspapermen infatuated with the fighter hung from convertibles and snapped photos while the young, handsome man from Louisville pounded the pavement. That button didn't go unnoticed.

This is one of several moments during Ali's Southern California excursion that stuck with him.

Ali's third straight round-four technical knockout in 1962 came when George Logan went down unremarkably at the Sports Arena in the spring. Less than a month later Ali returned to New York to earn his fourth stoppage in as many months by putting away tricky Billy Daniels in seven rounds. Ali returned to L.A., and spent much of his time training all across the boxing-rich city.

Ali mainly concentrated his efforts at the Main Street Gym, a boxing institution on skid row within jogging distance of the Alexandria Hotel and Olympic Auditorium. Along with Stillman's and Gleason's in New York, Main Street Gym, located on the second floor of the old vaudeville venue the Adolphus Theater, a dance hall circa 1911, was, by the 1960s, as classic a boxing dive as America ever produced.

Rudy Hernández first trained there in 1974 when he was twelve years old. A decade later, he was the last boxer to walk out of the doors before the gym was leveled and paved into a parking lot.

"You saw all these fighters and you knew they were good and they were popular, but I didn't realize how great they were until I got older," Hernández said. "Then I understood what it was like to see these guys and how great they were in their time."

The Main Street Gym supplied many fighters to Aileen Eaton, who promoted weekly fights at the Olympic Auditorium. The Hollywood Legion stadium also put on shows every Saturday night. Boxing clubs in Santa Monica, Southgate, and in the valley, near Burbank airport, would go periodically. There was plenty of boxing in Southern California through the 1970s, and many of the top fighters trained out of the Main Street Gym.

Ray Robinson put in enough sweat equity at the Main Street Gym that, when pickings got slim, he sparred the likes of Gene LeBell. Well on his journey to mixing standing and grappling martial arts into its own seamless style, LeBell trained in boxing for free at Main Street Gym. By the time LeBell was old enough to drive he shared the same ring with Robinson—that's to say being punched in the face many times by the best welterweight boxer of all time. This was regular stuff for LeBell, who also had a chance to wrestle and teach moves to "Sugar" Ray and Archie Moore.

Paramount Studios was where LeBell first saw Ali sparring with a stuntman. "When he went to Main Street Gym to work out, there was no fooling around," LeBell said. "He was there to do a job. I would have wet my pants if Ali wanted to wrestle with me. I would have jumped off a building. But I know they wouldn't let me wrestle with him."

Main Street Gym was unique for several reasons, but perhaps none as unique as its racial diversity. Boxers of all backgrounds regularly shared what would have otherwise been cloistered techniques. "That was probably one of the only gyms that had everything," said Hernández, who trained his younger brother Genaro Hernández to a super featherweight championship run in the 1990s.

When Hernández was a sophomore in high school he was picked to spar three rounds with Alexis Argüello, the rangy 130-pound world champion Nicaraguan. Argüello, the first fighter since Henry Armstrong to win belts in three divisions, was impressed with Hernández's effort and offered another $15 to spar a fourth period. They had a deal. Afterwards Argüello produced a good laugh when he learned Hernández was as old as his fee per round. A few close watchers around the gym inquired about the availability of Hernández's contract that day.

"I left the Main Street Gym knowing this is what I wanted to do with my life," Hernández said.

Argüello, Bobby Chacon, Danny "Little Red" Lopez, Albert Dávila, Roberto Durán, Art Aragon, and fighters of various backgrounds had similar epiphanies at the Main Street Gym. All the while other boxing cauldrons turned out quality fighters, too. There was a spot on 108th and Broadway out in Watts. And a gym near the Los Angeles Memorial Coliseum on 78th and Hoover that "takes the absolute, uncontested award as the dirtiest, filthiest gym I've ever seen," said Boxing Hall of Fame publicist Bill Caplan. "It made Main Street look like it was sterilized. The Main Street Gym didn't smell that noxious. They had a lot of windows. They could get fresh air. It smelled like a gym, the sweat. But that locker room was so nasty that I wouldn't even go in there to take a leak."

Showering without a hazmat suit was a risky proposition. It speaks to LeBell's stuntman leanings that he dared to stand under the running water in slippers.

"You could always tell when you got to the second floor," the grappler said. "It smelled like a urinal."

Used as the interior location for "Mighty Mick's Boxing" in the first three *Rocky* films, the gym at 318½ Main Street was filled with characters pulled from central casting. The space offered two fifteen-foot rings, side by side, and always showcased a wide variety of fighters going through their routines. Life-size cutouts of famed champions helped cover the peeling walls.

The pros sparred during the day, and anyone could get upstairs to watch. All they had to do was pay Arthur "Duke" Holloway, the large black man wearing a bowler and smoking a cigar at the top of the staircase, whatever he charged that day. Rarely was it more than a dollar to step inside the gym. From 1960 to 1977, Holloway worked for Howie Steindler, a New York expat, perhaps the Main Street Gym's greatest eccentric, who was killed in an unsolved murder in front of his home in the San Fernando Valley. Steindler's body was found in his Cadillac on the Ventura Freeway.

Steindler didn't take any bullshit, was as profane as anyone, and made boxing his life while laying down the law at a hothouse nestled between burlesque theaters. There are reasons Burgess Meredith's Mickey was modeled after Steindler, who fought as an amateur featherweight before heading west in 1942.

"You'd pass right by where Howie Steindler would have his office," Rich Marotta said. "And you'd see him in there. He was eventually the manager of Danny 'Little Red' Lopez. And when those guys would be training down there, I'd go down and watch. Just as a kid boxing fan. They had a little set of bleachers you could sit in and watch the fighters. It was amazing because you could end up talking to the fighters a little bit. You were right there among them. That was another new experience."

John Hall, a sports columnist with the *LA Times* after the paper absorbed the *Mirror* in May 1962, visited the Main Street Gym two or three afternoons a week just to talk with people. Hall and Steindler became good pals, and they shared a few drinks most afternoons.

"He had a great sense of humor that people didn't know," Hall said of the loud manager and gym owner. "He hustled all the time. He was a hustler but I thought he was terrific. He was not perfect."

Hall took several opportunities to speak with Ali at the Alexandria Hotel, which opened in 1906, and spent several hours chatting with the curious boxer. If Ali wasn't training he was usually standing on the hotel's busy street corner with his brother checking out women, or engaged in some sort of press.

"When Ali came in town the first time I ended up sitting next to him during lunch," Hall recalled. "He asked all kinds of questions about Gorgeous George and Art Aragon—how they perfected the villain routine, got all the publicity and drew so well. There's a lot of Gorgeous George that rubbed off on Ali early on.

"He was really naive and trying to learn about everything. He asked a million questions.

"I didn't think he was a genius. He was street smart. Smart enough. He kept developing that act of his. It took him about three years to really get into it. He was smart enough to recite a poem, that's for sure."

★ ★ ★ ★ ★

Sitting in on a session at the Main Street Gym is how Bill Caplan met Cassius Clay.

Five years after moving with his new wife to L.A. from Des Moines, Iowa, Caplan paid the bills as a frozen food broker for Birds Eye and Ore-Ida Potatoes. Boxing was where he wanted to be, though, and like everyone else Caplan had begun to hear about this heavyweight kid who had won gold at the Olympics. He took the chance to see the boxer in person at the Main Street Gym ahead of Ali's fight with Logan.

"I walk in and Ali is sparring," Caplan said. "He's going backwards around that little ring as fast as most athletes can run forward. I never saw anything like it, his legs, and his speed. I was in awe. I guess he was about twenty years old; he was already famous and already made a mark and getting huge publicity.

"I am carrying a little red Zenith transistor radio. Because I always have been, to this day, a Dodger fanatic. I would always have the radio with me, even when I went to a movie with my wife. I'd be listening to the Dodger game while watching the movie. And transistor radios were new then. And these little red Zeniths were the best transistor radio you could buy. It was my pride and joy.

"And I'm watching Ali spar and the Dodgers had a game on the road. And he sees me listening to that radio. And when sparring was over, he was wiping the sweat off and he said, 'What do you got there?' I said, 'That's a radio.' And he said, 'That little thing's a radio?' Portable radios then were much larger. They had these heavy batteries and probably weighed about 12 pounds, but they felt like they weighed

50 pounds. And this was about half the size of a pack of cigarettes. Yet it had great tone and everything. And he says, 'That's a radio?'

"He comes out of the ring and says, 'Can I see that thing?' I said, 'Sure.' He said, 'Can you get music on this?' I said, 'Sure you can.' We dialed it around and got a music station. He said, 'Man, that's really something. That thing plays nice music.' He said, 'You know what? I've got music at my hotel. It's a recorder.' It was a wire recorder. This was before tape. There were spools of wire and it worked the same way. He said, 'I want to see if I can record music off your radio.' So we walk over to the Alexandria Hotel on 5th and Spring Street. That's where the fighters stayed, and I'm sure the wrestlers, too.

"So we go up to his room, and it's a two-room suite. He said, 'Sit down and make yourself comfortable.' And he brings out this wire recorder. And it's about the size of the cable box on your TV. And said, 'Let's get some music on the radio.' And we recorded it and played it back and he was thrilled to pieces. He said, 'I'm gonna get me one of those so I can record and blah blah blah.' And he asked what I do. I said, 'Well, I represent frozen foods.' And he didn't understand what that was about. I said, 'But what I really want to do is I want to be a boxing publicist. That's what I wanna be.'

"'Ohhhh,' he says. 'Publicity, huh? Let me show you something about publicity.'

"Do you know about *Seinfeld* reruns and Kramer's coffee table book that had legs and became a coffee table? So Ali comes out with a scrapbook that looks like Kramer's coffee-table book. The thing is about ten inches thick. Many pages, and absolutely full. And he puts it down on the coffee table and he starts going through the pages with me. *Sports Illustrated, Sport Magazine, New York Times, LA Times, Chicago Tribune.* This book is full of clippings and cover stories—and this was 1962. He was just a young buck getting started. And he said, 'Now this is publicity.' To say I was impressed, I can see the picture in my mind right now of all the clippings. It was unbelievable for a guy that young who wasn't a champion. It was Muhammad Ali."

Later that year, Bill Caplan was hired as a part-time publicist for his boyhood hero, the long-retired heavyweight champion Joe Louis. Caplan went on to do publicity for virtually every major promoter in the game, including the feared and respected Aileen Eaton.

"In her time, it was so unusual for a woman to be in charge," Caplan said. "Nowadays we'd call it a CEO. It was so unusual for her to be such a factor in a man's business. She had no background in it. She had no training. She just went in there after a very short time of watching those guys and going through the books in a day and a half confirmed that they were cheating the Los Angeles Athletic Club. She suddenly was running the show."

Caplan went to work for George Parnassus, a former matchmaker at the Olympic who moved on to promote boxing once a week for Jack Kent Cooke at the Great Western Forum. In 1970, after two years on the job, Caplan had an altercation with Don Fraser, another publicity man at the Forum, over the truth. Caplan said he slugged Fraser in the chin. Fraser claimed they both got in good licks. Either way, Parnassus, a Greek immigrant, fired Caplan, who immediately dialed Don Chargin's office at the Olympic Auditorium.

"Bill was a heck of a PR guy, so I went to Aileen and said I have a heck of an idea of who we can get," said Chargin, who served as matchmaker for the Olympic from 1963 through 1984. "She always knew what you were thinking and said, 'Don't mention that name.' I said, 'How do you know what I'm talking about?' She said, 'You're talking about Bill Caplan.' I said, 'Aileen, he's got five kids. He can do it.' They ended up being real good friends."

★ ★ ★ ★ ★

Aileen Eaton is not without her critics. Don Fraser, who survived Caplan's haymaker to promote Ali's rematch with Ken Norton at the Forum in 1973, suggested the Boxing Hall of Famer receives more credit than she deserves for driving the sport in L.A. That's the minority opinion.

Eaton was regarded for selling stories, for finding a "hook" that interested people and got them in the building. As a result of Eaton's lost influence, attendance dwindled at the Olympic. The LeBell boys, Gene the fighter and Mike the pro wrestling promoter, eventually ended Friday night pro wrestling showcases in 1982, and Los Angeles no longer ranked near the nation's best wrestling or boxing town like it used to.

"If I needed a mother, she was there, and if I needed a business adviser, she was there," Gene LeBell said around the time Eaton passed at the age of seventy-eight. "What can you say? She's my mother."

Ferdie Pacheco, Ali's longtime physician, recoiled at the mere mention of Eaton's name. "An awful woman," he moaned. "We called her the 'Dragon Queen.'" Eaton, Pacheco said, attempted to dangle Ali around Los Angeles like a jewel among Hollywood's constellation of stars. "As a boxing promoter and a woman: evil," said Ali's doctor. "She controlled a lot of the boxing that went on because she had her tentacles in the mafia in Los Angeles. She ran boxing pretty strong. Some people lost fights they shouldn't have lost. Some people won 'em that shouldn't have won 'em. She wasn't a good person. She wasn't a bad person. She was a boxing person."

The underworld and fight world were well intertwined throughout the U.S., and in L.A. they often intersected at the Olympic Auditorium. The influence of famed gangster Mickey Cohen, who himself participated in underground prizefights in L.A. in the late 1920s, was well known.

Cohen managed several boxers from the shadows, and would often treat LeBell to candy, Cokes, and hotdogs with not one but two dogs per bun. After one gangland altercation the five-foot-five media darling, dubbed "Public Nuisance No. 1," was sent to recover at Cedars Hospital. LeBell happened to be there battling anemia, and, as the story goes, the teenager wandered over to Cohen's guarded room and startled police officers. One of Cohen's bodyguards vouched for the kid, who was allowed inside. LeBell, barely old enough to drive, chatted with the famous Jewish gangster as buckshot wounds soaked through his bandages.

Cohen would disappear for stretches of time, including a fifteen-year prison sentence in 1962 following his second conviction for tax evasion. When Cohen reappeared after ten years, he walked like a man that had suffered a stroke. After a fellow inmate cracked him in the head several times with a lead pipe, the tough guy was never the same. Cohen passed away in Los Angeles at the age of sixty-two, a month after Ali fought Inoki in Tokyo.

"I remember meeting some old man walking with a cane," said Lennon Jr. "My dad would introduce me. Mickey rubbed the top of my head and called me 'Lemon Head.' I saw him periodically at the Olympic. My dad also told the story of having dinner with my mom and Bugsy Siegel, and saying whatever you do don't calling him 'Bugsy.'"

Boxing was in the early stages of working through blowback from the organized crime–supported International Boxing Club of New York era of the 1950s when Ali moved to the pro ranks. Congress, reacting to Supreme Court decisions around the International Boxing Club antitrust suits, spent nearly four decades attempting to establish protections for boxers. The Muhammad Ali Boxing Reform Act of 1998, for instance, focused partly on solving fighters' continued exploitation outside the ring, especially via coercive long-term contracts.

During Eaton's run at the helm of the Olympic, one of the things that made her promotional style unique was that she didn't offer long-term deals to fighters. She believed that multi-fight agreements came with the temptation to protect boxers in easy bouts, thus cheating the fans.

"We lost some good, good fighters by doing that," Don Chargin said. "She would say, 'Look, if they don't want us, we don't want them.' You'll never find that kind of approach again."

There were plenty of big fights, of course, like Ali's return to L.A. in July of '62 against ranked Argentine Alejandro Lavorante. Fighting for the last time at less than 200 pounds, Ali looked tremendous on his way to a fifth-round knockout that set up a graduation of sorts against Archie Moore.

(Lavorante tragically died following injuries sustained in a bout at the Olympic Auditorium two months later.)

Moore, like Ali, could talk. Not as poetic or poignant, but after 217 fights, he had figured out how to promote. He was also smart enough to know he really didn't have a chance against Ali, and took the fight versus his former training partner with that in mind. Moore had previously attempted to mentor Ali, but the young stud had no interest in sweeping floors or doing gym chores like a typical pug. He left Moore in 1960 and signed up with Angelo Dundee.

When they met in 1962, "The Old Mongoose" talked a big game, as he usually did, and came up with fun lines like a "lip buttoner" punch. But Moore really had no intention of fighting enough to risk getting hurt. A paid crowd of 16,200 at the Sports Arena watched the soon-to-be retired boxer try to score hooks to Ali's body, but the aspiring heavyweight's speed was simply too much. Moore's cover-up defense cost him as he went dizzy under a stream of punches that dotted the top of his head. Moore fought once more before retiring, stopping a wrestler no less, Mike DiBiase, who made his only boxing appearance in Phoenix in 1963.

By the time Ali stepped into the ring with Inoki, he had felt enough hard shots to be too familiar with the full-body jar that punctuates a clean hit.

Throughout Ali's career the ability to endure punishment proved to be both a blessing and curse, which is why absorbing punches isn't high on his list of attributes. But it was nonetheless true and tested several times before, during, and after the peak of his fame.

Sonny Banks' fist elucidated answers about the great boxer's recuperative powers, and sixteen months after being floored at the Garden, Ali scared his supporters again. England's Henry Cooper dropped Ali with a vicious left hook at the end of the fourth round, nearly knocking him through the ropes. Ali was saved by the bell and Dundee's guile—lore places the delay at closer to a few minutes, but the trainer actually bought Ali an extra six seconds with some commotion in the corner about his fighter's gloves. Cooper, the British champion, was put away by Ali in the next round.

Just in case critics were onto something and Ali's chin really couldn't hold up under the strain of heavyweight boxing, his handlers figured it was time to put him in front of "The Big Bear" Sonny Liston.

In Miami, on February 25, 1964, Cassius Marcellus Clay Jr., like his father named in honor of a white abolitionist from Kentucky, won the heavyweight championship of the world when Liston, a 7–1 favorite, quit on his stool after six rounds. The following morning in front of reporters and with Malcolm X at his side, Clay, twenty-two, a decendant of African slaves, revealed his conversion to Islam then renounced his surname as a "slave name." The young champ would be known as Cassius X until the Nation of Islam founder, Elijah Muhammad, bestowed him a holy name. On March 6, he became Muhammad Ali.

ROUND
SIX

In wrestling. In business. In politics. In religion. In life. Inoki, the wrestler with a landing strip of a chin who attached himself to Muhammad Ali, almost always broke the rules and found a way to prosper. There are many reasons for fans to celebrate Inoki, not the least of which is one of the most recognizable faces in Japan.

From his days as an apprentice "young boy" under the direct guidance of Rikidōzan through his legendary retirement from *puroresu* thirty-eight years later, Inoki carved out a niche as a mercenary capable of creating and inserting himself into dynamic, sometimes prickly situations while emerging largely unscathed.

Inoki's ambition to face the boxer was born out of his plan to capitalize on the foundational relationship laid down by Rikidōzan that bonds wrestlers and the Japanese people. Meanwhile, Inoki's machinations helped extricate himself from his deceased mentor's murky shadow, even if he sometimes wandered similar paths. Inoki is a complicated man, as difficult to pin down in life as he was in the ring. Even when Inoki appeared to be finished he was not, and his subversive nature helped him become an important sporting and political figure throughout Asia.

Like many Japanese boys of the 1950s, Inoki was infatuated with wrestling and the televised spectacle that Rikidōzan perpetrated before his death in 1963.

Inoki was reportedly born to an affluent family in Yokohama in 1943, the second-youngest of seven boys and four girls. Some people have openly asked if segments of the story of Inoki's life, including where he was born, are fact or fiction. Like Rikidōzan, skeptics wonder if Inoki was also brought into the world in Korea, perhaps even the North.

The official account says Kanji Inoki was five years old when his father Sajiro, a businessman and politician, passed away. As Inoki matured he was a natural athlete and showed ability throughout grade school in various sports, including basketball and track and field.

By 1957, Inoki's family had fallen on hard times and the decision was made to depart Japan for Brazil. The first Japanese settlers had arrived in Brazil a half century earlier, escaping poverty and unemployment to serve as laborers on coffee plantations in the southern part of the country following the abolition of slavery. Conditions were difficult. The cultures were vastly different, and so were illnesses like malaria, which exacted a terrible toll on the immigrants. But in spite of the hardship, the contributions that Japanese immigrants made to Brazilian society are far-reaching. They introduced organized farming to the Amazon, replacing a hunter-gatherer system, and early settlers popularized martial arts, helping create Brazilian jiu-jitsu with the influence of judo men like Mitsuyo Maeda.

Inoki, aged fourteen, joined his grandfather (who died during the trip), mother, and brothers in emigrating to the country with the largest ethnic Japanese population outside of Japan. This is where Inoki's connection with pro wrestling and Rikidōzan took root. During a wrestling tour of Brazil in the spring of 1960, Rikidōzan heard stories of the Japanese boy winning championships in shot put, discus, and javelin. The superstar wrestler sought out Inoki and found a strong young man who had shaped his adolescent frame toiling on coffee bean plantations.

"In those days, it was like living as a slave," Inoki said in interviews. "Now it is good to think I worked on the plantation in 45-degree [Celsius] heat. I struggled to eat, but such a life gave me the spirit to fight."

In the same way that a sumo wrestling scout found Rikidōzan and delivered him to Japan for grooming, the star performer intended to mold a young Inoki, who learned as a "young boy" for six months before stepping into the ring. The mentorship of Rikidōzan instilled in Inoki the principle that a pro wrestler is supposed to be the strongest. The kid learned a great many things from his teacher, and on September 30, 1960, Inoki was part of a trio of debuting Japan Wrestling Association prospects who made it big, including Shohei "Giant" Baba, a six-foot-eight baseball player turned wrestler, and Korean star Kintaro Ohki. Only Inoki was asked to lose, which he did to Ohki in front of 6,000 fans in Tokyo.

Over the next three decades, the two biggest stars in Japan were "Giant" Baba and Inoki. A negative stigma clung to pro wrestling in Japan in light of revelations regarding Rikidōzan, but the emergence of Baba and Inoki led to a second boom from '67 to '71. The pair teamed up for tag-team matches and produced sellouts wherever they went, regardless of the night.

As the audience experienced it, Baba was the sun and Inoki was the moon. Without the light of the sun, the moon isn't visible at night and Inoki could not stand playing second fiddle. Inoki was recognized as Baba's partner when they worked for the JWA until 1972. The Japanese people love watching athletes with size, and Baba, a notably tall man, was immediately captivating to them. His stature worked away from Japan, too. While Inoki failed to develop notoriety away from home, Baba became a big star in the U.S. throughout the 1960s.

Inoki grew frustrated with Baba, who did not have it in him to take risks in business when he secured booking control of the company after the owners of the JWA, businessmen with no real connection to wrestling, went broke gambling. Both of the company's stars wanted to get away, and Inoki left first, insinuating he had been fired. Fans and other wrestlers felt Inoki's impatience as he played the bad guy. With the helpful defections of some of the wrestlers Inoki had groomed alongside Karl Gotch, New Japan Pro Wrestling soon formed. Both Inoki and Baba, who quickly created the rival All Japan Pro Wrestling group, were able to headline on television in primetime in 1972.

After dropping his first wrestling match in 1960, Inoki wanted to beat everyone. But such was Inoki's reverence for

Gotch, who was awarded the title "God of Wrestling" after settling in Japan, that he lost the first NJPW main event to a wrestler in his 40s. "There is one man who is worthy of the belt," Gotch said in the ring. "It's Inoki." They rematched four times, alternating wins and losses, with Gotch taking the lifetime series. Inoki could have done what he did with everyone else—win the last two matches and stand out as superior—but for realism's sake, he couldn't top the catch wrestler.

Gotch's reputation as a Wigan-trained grappler became the backbone of New Japan Pro Wrestling. Matches may not have been real, but the wrestlers were. This is how NJPW and Inoki attempted to convey that pro wrestling, a remnant from the old days, remained a legitimate fighting style.

"The idea was you put in any of our guys against football players, rugby players and the New Japan wrestler is kicking ass," said wrestling scribe Dave Meltzer. "That was what New Japan Wrestling was built on, and Inoki was the king."

Starting in 1972, Gotch was paid $60,000 a year as the head trainer and booker for NJPW. He received the money until passing away at the age of eighty-two in 2007. Months before he died, *Gong*, the Japanese fight sport magazine, sent a reporter to Tampa, Fla., where Gotch had retired to, and asked the no-nonsense trainer to look at fight footage from Josh Barnett's classic 2006 clash with Antônio Rodrigo Nogueira in the Pride Fighting Championships. At the time, it was considered one of the great heavyweight fights in mixed martial arts. Because Barnett trained with Gotch and represented the catch-as-catch-can lineage into the twenty-first century, the concept was for professor and student to discuss—and critique—the Nogueira clash.

Gotch didn't care who you were or what you did. He didn't think much of Brazilians and their jiu-jitsu, according to LeBell, who said Gotch described the practice of fighting from the guard—a neutral position where one fighter is on his or her back and the other sits between their thighs—as spreading legs like a whore. In catch, this position is called "hip-and-leg control," and it was Gotch's contention that anything jiu-jitsu pedaled as new or revolutionary was in truth old and well tested. As far as he was concerned, if he sat in a jiu-jitsu man's "guard" he would simply fall back, take a leg, and give them a half-second to tap or suffer a broken ankle.

In 1948, three years after being interned in a Nazi concentration camp in Poland, Gotch, twenty-three, wrestled in both freestyle and Greco-Roman competition at the London Olympic Games.

Remaining in England, the hard-nosed Belgian shooter born as Karel Istaz made his way to "The Snake Pit," Billy Riley's incubator in the Lancashire mining town of Wigan, near Manchester. He turned to professional wrestling and won several European titles before moving to the United States, where he took on the surname Gotch in honor of American catch-as-catch-can pioneer Frank Gotch.

In Los Angeles, Lou Thesz introduced Gene LeBell to Gotch, who was in town looking for sparring partners. Thesz and Gotch didn't have a meeting of the minds, but "Lou knew who was good and who wasn't," LeBell said. "Lou grappled like a boxer. Karl was a grappler. He grabbed with either hand and had a death grip. He used to snatch parts of bodies and use them as a handle, because everything is a handle."

"He loved wrestling and he didn't like clowns," continued LeBell. "If somebody fooled around in the ring, turned his back to the crowd to get heat, he'd soufflé them—and hard. He didn't pay attention to wins or losses. A lot of people would not work with him."

For the most part Gotch blew off pro wrestlers he didn't respect. And he didn't respect many. He probably hurt more people than he gave the time of day to. Buddy Rogers, the first wrestler to hold the WWWF and NWA heavyweight titles, was confronted by Gotch and another wrestler, Bill Miller, in Columbus, Ohio. In the skirmish, Rogers broke his left hand. Refunds had to be issued for the August 31, 1962, event, and charges were filed. The incident made Gotch's bad reputation worse. There was chatter about Gotch hurting Thesz's ribs, and about Gotch injuring 1972 Olympic wrestler Riki Choshu with a submission.

"They happened enough where everyone knew the stories," said Meltzer.

Gotch's stateside wrestling career, or lack thereof, is a good example of how pro wrestling shifted from shoot to show. He was never much of a draw and couldn't get the crowd to react to him, which confused and frustrated a wrestler who was likely the most dangerous guy in the locker room. Gotch may not have racked up big wins or scored famous matches, but he became a mythical figure and was hired by Inoki to teach New Japan wrestlers how to shoot.

Developing a reputation for strength based on the Indian grappling art *Pehlwani*, Gotch later instilled his work ethic in the men around him. Inoki, for example would often do pushups and squats during airport layovers.

As *Gong's* reporter and photographer sat with Gotch watching Barnett fight Nogueira, the surly old man was clearly unimpressed. "That looks like shit," Gotch said as the video played. Expecting a far different experience, the Japanese pair grew increasingly nervous. When Barnett's exciting split decision win ended, Gotch looked at Barnett. "Does that piss you off?" Gotch said. Barnett, a six-foot-three smart submission artist, replied that it did not. He said all he wanted was an insight into Gotch's mind so he could improve. If there was a possibility to be better, why wouldn't he embrace that? Gotch nodded, and until his death regularly called Barnett to chat.

Barnett also had the occasion to train with Billy Robinson, regarded by most observers of "The Snake Pit" as the top shooter in the gym during the 1960s. Robinson wrestled some in the U.S. and enjoyed better success with crowds and promoters than Gotch, but he never went over big. Robinson ended up in Japan in the late '60s, and for years never lost by pin or submission. He brought a sense of showmanship with the technical sensibilities of scientific wrestling, straddling the line between work and shoot people at that time strived for in pro wrestling.

"Karl was very bright. Him and Billy were incredibly bright when it came to fighting," said Barnett. "Very hard-nosed. Very demanding people. The thing about guys like Karl and Billy, you always hear stories about them yelling at you, but the biggest thing I think was the yelling wasn't so much about you doing wrong, the yelling is about you not doing it with your all and you making things more difficult for yourself than they need to be. You're overthinking things. Getting too caught up in the thought of something rather than existing and doing."

Inoki met Robinson for a famous match at the end of 1975.

Sold in the Japanese press as a contest between the top two technicians in wrestling, they tussled during a classic work that was treated like sport. A sixty-minute draw indicated Inoki was much improved over the green wrestler Gene LeBell saw in Los Angeles in the mid-1960s called "Little Tokyo."

After the tie, "Giant" Baba offered Robinson a hefty fee ($8,000 to $10,000 a week) to wrestle for him in 1976. Seeking to one-up Inoki, the first thing Baba did was pay the man from Manchester, England, a bonus to suffer his only loss in a singles match in Japan.

Still, as a promoter, Baba was considered a more honest broker than Inoki. He forged relationships and contracts with a group of American stars including Terry Funk, Bruno Sammartino, Harley Race, and "Killer" Kowalski. Inoki was effectively frozen out and could only count on himself and ambitions of building a roster of wrestlers to support his business. Tiger Jeet Singh, a wild man from India who literally accosted fans, and Canadian Johnny Powers helped Inoki and NJPW rapidly expand their footprint in the 1970s.

Part of that effort included the idea that Inoki should be matched with outsiders to make the popular Japanese wrestler the new Karl Gotch. With his manager Hisashi Shinma, Inoki set out to create an image of himself as a shooter, the Japanese dragon slayer. By the mid-70s, Inoki fancied himself another Rikidōzan, defending pro wrestling and Japanese honor against foreign invaders and their disciples.

"I think that at his peak Inoki was probably the third most popular athlete in the country," Meltzer said. "As big as wrestling was, it wasn't the biggest sport in the country. For a pro wrestler to be that big culturally, it really was amazing. Americans can't grasp Inoki because most think Hulk Hogan. Hogan was big. The Rock was big. Steve Austin was big. As wrestlers, none of these guys were even close to as big as Inoki was in Japan."

Grit and determination were hallmarks of Inoki's matches. He rallied against the odds and looked good doing so. Inoki never turned heel (became a bad guy, in wrestling speak), but his matches were so heated that even a good guy like him could only take so much abuse. Inoki showed his fist and made a big deal of what he was about to do before doing it. In a lot of ways, Inoki's gimmick was a forerunner to Hulk Hogan's. Charisma and unique facial features, courtesy of that protruding, pointed jaw, certainly helped set Inoki apart.

"He's an incredible performer," Barnett said. "Hearing about his taking on these other practitioners of martial arts and fighting arts. Even seeing pictures of him and his matches, he's a great worker. If you just sit back and watch, he has tons of charisma and appears to be the real deal when he's out there. He's great at being a wrestler and captures your attention right away."

Inoki and his band of wrestlers embraced a "strong style." The closer the action looked to a real fight, the better, because Inoki sought to give audiences the emotion of a real struggle with less song and dance.

"He would end up breaking the rules of wrestling in almost all his matches," Barnett said. "He had a system of getting pushed so far that he couldn't take anymore. He would punch with a closed fist. He was brutal. It would look brutal as hell when he would take out people."

"Whether it was working or shooting, Inoki's mindset was 'real.' You're really doing everything real all the time, in Inoki's mind. It's just whether or not you're actually shooting, having a real fight, or working, doing a predetermined match. If you treat it real, keep it real, keep your mind real, then whatever it is you do out there will come off as real, and the people will be more engrossed and involved in it and they'll feel the emotion of the match more than the moves that you're doing. Trying to keep the suspension of disbelief going, because that will draw the emotional investment out besides just throwing out a bigger and more expensive firework."

ROUND

SEVEN

An American cultural icon out of the turbulent, status quo–challenging 1960s went global by the mid-1970s. This is why throughout the emergence of the jet and satellite ages, Muhammad Ali grew accustomed to working at odd hours.

In 1974, for instance, Ali challenged George Foreman at 4:00 A.M. in Zaire. A year later, he stepped into the ring for a torturous third time with Joe Frazier, not as he had in thier first encounter in primetime on a New York night at Madison Square Garden but at a quarter to eleven in the morning several miles outside of Manila.

More than a decade had passed since Ali took the most popular first name on Earth as his own, and the world champion's traveling carnival was at its craziest when he and Frazier went to war in the "Thrilla in Manila," on October 1, 1975.

"That was one of the great fights of all time, that third fight," Pacheco said. "One of the hardest fights I've ever seen.

I can go back all the way to Jack Dempsey, nobody fought like Ali. When he put on the gloves, you thought, oh, that's the champion. He would beat the shit out of people.

"If there was a fight you were looking to stop boxing, to make them stop it as a sport, that was it. That was so rough, so tough you were looking at death in the ring. When Frazier quit, one more punch could have put him out. And when you were looking for the good stuff, that was the one. Boy those guys were tough, tough, top of the line, toe to toe, and it's me or you. For Ali, it was him. He was giving Frazier everything he could possibly give him to knock him out, and he did."

In the later rounds Ali pummeled Frazier, prompting the proud Philadelphian's trainer, Eddie Futch, to save his fighter from the possibility of a terrible end. Frazier's left eye was completely closed. He couldn't see so well out of his right. Everything Ali threw landed and Frazier spat up blood. When the decision to stop came from Frazier's corner, Ali, who indicated to his camp after the fourteenth round that he was overwhelmed and wanted out, collapsed in his corner.

Later Ali would say the experience was the closest thing to death that he knew of.

"Right after the fight all the press was waiting for us," recalled publicist Bobby Goodman. "I ran up to Ali's dressing room and he was laid out. He was exhausted. Man I never saw him as tired as that. I said, 'Muhammad, the press is waiting outside.' Ali said, 'I just can't do it. I'm too tired. I'm exhausted.' He was shot. I didn't know quite what to do so I ran across the hall to Joe Frazier's room. He was being consoled by Eddie Futch, who had his arm around Frazier.

I think there were some tears. I said, 'Joe, the press is downstairs. You got nothing to be ashamed of. You fought a great fight.' Eddie says, 'OK, let's go Joe. Let's go down.' He said, 'OK' and he toweled himself off. He got his shoes and that was what I needed. He started moving so I ran back across to Ali and I said, 'Champ, Frazier is on his way down.' He said, 'Frazier is going? Frazier is going to the press conference? Where's my comb?' He started picking his hair. He put his shoes on and went down."

Of all the things that made Ali great, the simple yet crucial piece was desire. He needed the rivalry with Frazier to extend himself as far as he could go without breaking. Outside the ropes, though, he sometimes went further than that.

Compelling, charismatic, handsome, and a notorious ladies' man, Ali was in the midst of a torrid love affair with Veronica Porche as he faced Frazier in '75. Ali had met Porche the previous year after the model and actress was one of four women chosen to travel the U.S. promoting the "Rumble in the Jungle" before flying to Kinshasa for the fight with George Foreman. Soon, Ali boldly brought Porche almost everywhere he went while his wife at the time, Belinda Ali, remained home taking care of their four children.

Ferdie Pacheco said one reason Ali took the fight in Manila was to spend time with Porche, which meant getting away from his wife for six weeks. Sometimes Porche was Ali's "cousin." Other times, according to photo captions in *People,* for instance, the "nanny." To no one's chagrin but Belinda's, Porche was also called Ali's better half—which was just about the last straw. In Manila ten days before the fight, the boxers had the occasion to meet with Ferdinand Marcos and his wife, Imelda, the "Steel Butterfly," who became known for her collection of more than one thousand pairs of shoes. As Marcos spoke, he paid respects to Ali and his "beautiful wife." No one corrected the president of the Philippines, who since 1972 had run the country under martial law.

"Your wife is beautiful, too," Ali had the audacity to respond.

Newsweek reporter Pete Bonventre was in Manila covering Ali, and in his piece for the magazine, "The Ali Mystique," he referenced that the "stunning Veronica Porche, sometimes known as 'Ali's other wife,' was touring Manila with the champ."

After the article was published, Belinda, all five-foot-ten 160 pounds of her, flew to Manila. Some insiders looked forward more to Belinda vs. Veronica, the L.A. beauty pageant winner, than Muhammad vs. Joe.

Belinda Ali told her husband that if what she read in *Newsweek* was true, and Porche was sleeping in the same room with him, then she was showing up with divorce papers. According to Pacheco, Ali's wife also arrived with about sixty suitcases. Very costly suitcases. And she told Ali that either Porche goes or each of the bags would be filled with outrageously priced goods from Manila and Tokyo. After giving Ali a piece of her mind for an hour in his hotel suite, one of fifty-two rooms under the champ's umbrella, she flew home.

Porche stayed.

"It wasn't nice but it was deserved," said Pacheco, who claimed Ali felt he'd bought freedom for cheap.

A serious decline in the boxer's ring presence loomed as his physical prowess faded over the next five years. Yet his stardom burned as bright as ever, and that meant there was money to be made. This wasn't the "radical" who conscientiously objected his way to the United States Supreme Court during the Vietnam War. By 1975, in the wake of America's withdrawal and Saigon's fall, Ali was rich, commercialized, and accustomed to being a global star.

Yes, Ali lived lavishly and treated the people around him very well, but he also faced divorce and aimed to keep Porche happy. A significant portion of his money went as quickly as it came, particularly in the direction of the Black Muslim movement the Nation of Islam. While Ali left the Nation in 1975 and converted to the more mainstream Sunni branch of Islam that year, his manager, Herbert Muhammad, the third son of Elijah Muhammad, remained tied to both for years to come. Muhammad was the organization's chief business manager until his father passed away in Chicago in '75, operating several entities, including a newspaper he founded with Malcolm X. With a significant portion of the funds delivered by the champ, Muhammad opened the Masjid Al-Faatir mosque in 1987 in a predominantly black neighborhood of Chicago called Kenwood. The opportunity to build Chicago's most impressive mosque was largely owed to Ali's success.

Despite the intense flame of celebrity and an ability to generate millions of dollars per fight—more than anyone before him by a wide margin—Ali's closest confidants say he was never affected. To the boxers who met Ali in the ring in the mid-1970s, however, his magnetism was always felt. Ali made them the biggest purses of their careers, and when they fought him they became known at least to some degree.

Four months after Manila, Ali weighed 226 pounds when he stepped into the ring in Puerto Rico against the relatively harmless twenty-nine-year-old Belgian champion Jean-Pierre Coopman. "Let me have a little rest in between [hard fights]," Ali said at a New York press conference before the bout. He got away with one—who could hold it against him? Coopman famously drank champagne before and during the fight before staying down in the fifth round.

Resting wasn't something Ali did often and his seemingly boundless supply of energy was tested in 1976. After the Coopman victory, Ali officially announced his participation in the Inoki match at a New York City news conference in late March at the Plaza Hotel.

Under the verbal onslaught of Ali, surrounded by the media, with something to sell, Inoki took the stoic approach.

"When the wind blows, I shall bend but not break," Inoki said through a translator.

Ali played his usual games, and said he "cannot miss" Inoki's protruding jaw. It was then that the boxer dubbed the wrestler "The Pelican."

"When your fist hits my chin, I hope you do not hurt your fist," Inoki replied as he smiled. Inoki then said he hoped Ali would not duck out at the last moment.

"If I ain't afraid of walkin' down a back alley in Harlem, I ain't afraid of you," Ali barked back.

Both men insisted the contest would be real, though the rules had yet to be hammered out. "I think Ali thought it would be more of a show," said Bobby Goodman, whose father, Murray, a Boxing Hall of Fame publicist, worked the New York portion of the June event at Shea Stadium. "But the first time we got together with them about the dos and don'ts and rules of the fight it became very obvious to me that Inoki's people were serious." Discussions to that end were at the preliminary stage, and Ali spoke with excitement about the desire to punch when he was on the ground.

Boxing writers questioned whether or not it was demeaning for an active and defending heavyweight champion of the world to participate in a contest of this sort. Ali, the only three-time lineal world heavyweight champion, said it was not.

"I'll be going outside my speciality," he said, "and I'm drawing the greatest crowds in the history of the world."

Andre the Giant, the ostensible eighth wonder of the world, attended the press conference at the Plaza Hotel and shared the stage with Ali.

"You think you can beat me up?" Ali asked the massive Frenchman.

"I could beat you up and throw you out of this building," said the Giant, whom Gene Kilroy described as incredibly gentle and sweet.

With the Inoki match slated for the summer, Ali ever so slightly turned his attention back to boxing. A similar setup to the Coopman bout was arranged for April 30 in Landover, Md. Tasked with fighting the journeyman Jimmy Young, a bored Ali showed up pudgy—230 pounds, the heaviest of his career until his final bout against Trevor Berbick in 1981.

Newspaper reports before the bout with Young indicated Ali had spent time preparing for Inoki with The Sheik, a famous wrestler and fellow Muslim operating out of Detroit. He made occasional trips to Ali's home outside Chicago, and was said to be training with the boxer a week before Ali headed off to Tokyo.

Ali maintained a target weight for most of his thirty-one fights after returning to the ring in 1970. A couple pounds either way wasn't a big deal, but Ali always liked to come in around 220 pounds. "Ali was a little bit egotistical sometimes about that weight," Goodman said. "It was important to him. He didn't want to seem like he was sloppy." Such that he was against the passive Young. The pair made for an awful heavyweight title fight, one that failed to entertain anyone who watched a slow, undertrained Ali win by unanimous decision.

Acknowledging the poor showing against Young and a let-down public, Ali promised never to look so bad again.

Twenty-three days later Ali stood on a stage in Munich, Germany, to make weight for his next defense against England's Richard Dunn. The bout with Dunn, promoted by Bob Arum and set to air live and free in the U.S. on May 24, 1976, was not selling well. Dunn wasn't considered any kind of threat, and coming off the dud against Young, German fans weren't interested in watching a potentially unmotivated Ali stink up Munich's Olympiahalle. As he said he would, Ali showed up in much better condition, hitting that 220 pound mark.

"I was handling the scale weighing Ali and all of a sudden the stage collapsed," Goodman recalled. "Down went Ali and the scale and everything. I was left standing there on the edge of the platform. Everyone was in a hole. It was odd."

Ali and his team were put up first-class in one of the city's finest old hotels, the Bayerischer Hof. Like in Zaire, Ali travelled with an entourage of more than fifty people at the time. One way or another they served some purpose, but many were also a drain of Ali's precious time and resources and had been for several years. With bills piling up in Munich, Goodman said, the abuse was bad enough that Ali had to call the group together to tell them not to squander their good fortune by looting his.

"Guys you can't keep spending an hour on the phone calling home with your wife or your girlfriend or your kids," Ali told them, according to Goodman. "You can't order anything any time you want."

Typical Ali, he couldn't keep up the bad-guy routine. And the more he spoke, the softer his approach turned.

"If you're hungry and you want another steak you can order it but don't waste it," he said. "If you gotta call home, call but do it once a day."

Said Goodman: "Imagine fifty or sixty people calling from Germany every day. The bills can add up."

Ali wanted everyone around him to enjoy themselves and handle their duties. And while he generally wished the group well, this mostly hinged on his desire to have people near him feel good no matter what. When it came to relationships with friends, strangers, and loved ones, this was his instinct and where he focused his energy.

As for hangers-on, vultures, and sycophants, Ali couldn't move more than three feet without twenty people descending upon his footsteps. Bonventre's story in *Newsweek* described Ali's entourage: "Solemn Muslim guards have given way to streetwise hustlers. Liberals who cherished him as a symbol of pro-black antiwar attitudes have been replaced by wry connoisseurs of pure showmanship."

Jhoon Rhee isn't any of these things and he wasn't at the Dunn fight, but his presence was felt in Munich nonetheless.

The taekwondo grand master met Ali through a mutual friend in Philadelphia, and beginning in March 1975 visited the puncher's training camp in Deer Lake, Pa., several days a month to train for martial arts. Rhee worked with Ali on the so-called "Accu-punch," a name the Korean immigrant coined for a strike that melds thought and action into high-speed data flow. The strike required a screwdriving motion at impact, Rhee said, calling it a lesson from his days training with Bruce Lee. This made sense to Ali, who obsessed over celerity and beating opponents to the punch.

Whenever Ali had the time and Rhee could make the two-hour drive from Washington, D.C., the large boxer and diminutive martial artist shared no-contact sparring sessions that never lasted more than thirty minutes. Other boxers usually showed up so Ali could finish his conditioning routine. Otherwise, Ali and Rhee, a martial arts philosopher and idealist, spoke often in the Pennsylvania country compound about Lee.

Ali took more punches and punishment in the gym than in most of his fights. He would clown around with sparring partners, draping his arms around their shoulders and letting them bang him to the body. This infuriated Angelo Dundee. "Don't do that," the trainer warned. "You'll be pissing yourself ten years from now not knowing why." Instead, Ali sometimes put his hands up around his ears and invited sparring partners to hit him about the head. His personal physician, Dr. Ferdie Pacheco, had already begun to express concern. Pacheco's distaste for many of the people around Ali, and the circumstances of the great fighter's decline, were more prevalent as each fight passed. And the post-Frazier bums like Coopman and Young would only last so long.

Against Dunn, the last of three tune-ups from February through May of '76, Ali scored five knockdowns. Afterwards, speaking to NBC's Dick Enberg, Ali began with a plug for the upcoming contest against Inoki.

"I want to say I will be fighting next month," Ali said. "The wrestling champion of the world."

Enberg ignored the statement and asked Ali about Dunn. The American champion talked up his English challenger as a "young man" who's "gonna be a top-notch contender."

"I'm glad I was in shape for this fight," Ali said. "If I was in the same shape this month like I was last month I would have lost the fight, no doubt, because he's a great fighter. He's better than I thought he was. And I predict you'll hear a lot about Richard Dunn."

Ali was better at prefight prognostication than the post-fight kind. Dunn lasted two more contests before retiring in 1977.

Ali's late-September title defense and rubber match against Ken Norton was mentioned, then the boxer again plugged his pending action against Inoki.

"First I'm going to get the Japanese wrestler," Ali said. "I have great karate teachers. From Washington, D.C., Mr. Jhoon Rhee is his name. He's training me now for the Japanese wrestler."

On the NBC broadcast, replays of Ali pounding the southpaw Dunn with right-hand leads appeared on screen.

"That wasn't a right hand," Ali noted. "That was the unique 'Accu-punch.' It was a karate chop right. If you watch it again."

Enberg giggled: "That's already your 'Accu-punch' you were talking about?"

"That's the 'Accu-punch' I told you about," answered Ali. "Keep watching and you won't hardly see it. It's so fast.'"

Up next, a trip to Tokyo and another odd start time.

ROUND EIGHT

As with any successfully promoted fight—in this case "success" is determined by the amount of money generated—the point is enticing a large enough group of people to spend their hard-earned cash and participate in a moment.

Muhammad Ali had long been a master at inciting crowds to, among other things, do just that. By 1976, selling himself and boxing was old hat to the thirty-four-year-old superstar. In some quarters there was a belief that his act had worn stale, though that didn't change the fact there wasn't anyone who came off as charismatic as Ali. Combined with his sporting pedigree and status as a showman and statesman, basically anything Ali did was picked up by the media. In this way, he was a publicist's dream.

"I worked with many champions," said Bobby Goodman, the flack hired by Top Rank to work with Ali for the Inoki match. "Everyone stuck to the schedule. They'd talk to the press and maybe give you a little leeway with an hour or so a day trying to fit things in. Ali was an open book. There were some times he said, 'Jeez, can't we do a little more?' I would go to Ali when I couldn't come up with another idea or the promotion was going slow."

In November 1971, for example, Ali faced Buster Mathis at the Astrodome in Houston. Mathis offered little to make Ali angry or competitively aroused. Each time Mathis was in Ali's vicinity he giggled like a kid on the way to the toy store. He loved Ali. Affection between boxers had never been an effective marketing ploy, so Goodman, who worked with Ali since 1963, asked the boxer for help in the promotion department.

Ali's eyes grew big and wide. He had an idea to grab front-page headlines around the world. Goodman listened as Ali detailed his thoughts on perpetrating a fake kidnapping. Get a log cabin in the woods, Ali told Goodman. Set him up with a ring and sparring partners, and a few days before the scheduled bout he would miraculously emerge unscathed and ready. Goodman made a fair point. "If you're missing," he told Ali, "no one is going to buy tickets to the fight." Ali agreed and the boxer said they could come up with something else.

Most of the time promoters didn't need a gimmick to sell an Ali fight. The boxer's presence alone was enough to make it a successful venture. But what about when the fight itself was a gimmick? That, after all, is how most people viewed the Inoki contest, which was sandwiched between Ali's day job: title defenses against Richard Dunn in Munich and Ken Norton at Yankee Stadium in the Bronx.

Ali was not above stunts. Clearly. But even for a man reputed to push boundaries, selling the Inoki contest stretched the limits of the imagination. Few people knew what to make of it, and one of the major story lines leading up to the contest centered around the notion that it wasn't on the up-and-up.

Ron Holmes, president of Lincoln National Productions, the California corporation created on March 30, 1976, for the sole purpose of making Ali vs. Inoki, was charged with "promoting" the mixed-rules contest. The week of the match in Japan, amidst swirling rumors and speculation that the matchup was (a) a scripted pro wrestling match, (b) a freak show destined to be a debacle, or (c) a lawless sham, Holmes told Phil Pepe of the New York *Daily News* that, for $6.1 million—the biggest purse ever awarded to a fighter at the time—"it better be on the level. If I wanted an exhibition, I could have had it for one million."

"For six million," said Holmes, who was also described by the media as Inoki's American liaison in Japan, "I want to see blood."

New Japan Pro Wrestling (Inoki's group), through Lincoln National Productions Ltd., guaranteed to deliver $3 million to Ali regardless of how well the bout sold at the gate or on closed circuit. The boxer was then promised the first $3 million that Top Rank banked from broadcast-based revenue. Inoki would receive the next $2 million of Top Rank's television earnings. Presumably, more than enough fans would have bought in that everyone involved could go home happy.

Of course, that was contingent on convincing the public that this was worth watching, regardless of its legitimacy or not. That required a hard sales pitch from Ali, and, beginning the day the bout was officially announced at a press conference in New York City to the final media events in Tokyo, Ali put in his work. In Japan and the U.S., Inoki did too, participating in multiple press tours during the run-up to the fight. Yet the bulk of the promotion, the reason people cared, fell squarely on the boxer's shoulders.

As much as any bout he participated in before or after, this match was Ali's baby. He pushed for it in the press. He contested that the point needed to be proven. Ali used every ounce of his fame to sell the bout. And this was exactly what the promotion's other interested parties hoped for.

New Japan Pro Wrestling was just establishing business ties with the WWWF when Inoki and his manager, Hisashi Shinma, approached Vince McMahon Sr. with the idea for Ali–Inoki. Because of Ali's history on closed circuit, the wrestling folks looked to attach their train to him. McMahon went around convincing promoters in other wrestling territories to participate. A lot of them were skeptical because it was something new. They had their business and were doing all right. Fronting with Inoki was a bit strange since no one in the U.S. knew who he was, but of course Ali was the biggest thing going, and his presence made the night the first wrestling-affiliated closed-circuit that transcended the genre.

"You had Vince Junior saying, 'Wow, I have the most famous person on the planet promoting what I want to do, or at least part of what I want to do,'" said Dan Madigan, a writer for the WWE in the early 2000s.

Wrestling fans tend to stay within wrestling confines, but the rub from the righteous lineage of boxing, a smart guy could do something with that. During the weeks leading up to the fight, Ali and pro wrestling legend Freddie Blassie, Ali's "manager," appeared as guests on numerous talk shows, including *The Tonight Show*. They joined the ubiquitous Howard Cosell on ABC's *Wide World of Sports* and Ali wrestled in scripted showcases in Chicago and Philadelphia.

On June 1, in the City of Brotherly Love, Ali tangled with Robert Marella, aka Gorilla Monsoon. Before a quick victory for Monsoon, Ali was introduced to the crowd as he took a seat in the front row. After the match, Ali entered the ring, took a few shots at Monsoon, and pointed his finger at him. Monsoon picked up Ali, twirled him around, and dumped the boxer to the canvas.

"Monsoon was going to put him down gently but Ali got a little scared, and he fell on his hip," said Gene Kilroy, who joined the boxer at the Philadelphia Arena and witnessed the pre-bit rehearsal. "I saw and said, 'Oh shit.'"

Vince McMahon Jr. called the broadcasts for some WWWF shows and interviewed Monsoon at ringside. Ali was a great boxer, Monsoon said, but a lousy wrestler who didn't know a wristlock from a wristwatch.

On script were two matches in Chicago at the International Amphitheatre on June 10 in conjunction with one of the WWWF's territorial partners, Verne Gagne's American Wrestling Association. Wearing sixteen-ounce gloves, Ali peppered Kenny Jay, thirty-six, a 225-pounder from Cleveland, and curly-haired, twenty-six-year-old Buddy Wolff of St. Cloud, Minn., into bloody wrecks. Ali was tossed around some and even showed a few wrestling maneuvers of his own as 1,000 fans, given free entry into the building, chanted his name for TV cameras from ABC's *Wide World of Sports*.

"I hit him with shots a boxer would fall with," Ali said in the dressing room afterwards. "Just wait 'til I get on those little four-ounce gloves against that Japanese wrestler. He'll really be bleeding."

As newspaper columnists across the country questioned Ali's affiliation with wrestling and reminisced about the days when a boxer fighting a grappler might have meant something, the world champion continued to drum up press for the Inoki match.

Ali joined his trainer, Angelo Dundee, and Freddie Blassie, adorned with an eye-popping diamond ring on his right pinkie, on a red double-decker bus ride around Los Angeles the day after their *The Tonight Show* appearance. The U.S. press tour for the most important mixed match since the turn of the century concluded at Aileen Eaton's Olympic Auditorium, which would host a live wrestling event promoted by Mike LeBell to coincide with the closed-circuit feed from New York and Japan.

Up until the contest was officially signed at a ceremony during fight week in Tokyo, the rules of engagement for the match between Ali and Inoki were under scrutiny and produced a heated debate that seemingly imperiled the whole production. Newspaper reports pegged LeBell as an important figure in the Ali–Inoki rule-making process. According to wire reports, he joined Dundee and Vince McMahon Sr. in drafting the original set that was released a month before the bout.

On May 28, newspaper reports indicated rules had been agreed upon to govern the mixed-style fight. During fifteen three-minute rounds, the wrestler could use tactics common to both karate and wrestling, including chops and elbow strikes. The fight would be scored on a five-point must system with two judges and the referee keeping tabs. The referee could only separate the fighters if they touched the ropes. If a contestant was counted out to ten, or his shoulders were pinned to the mat for a count of three, or a corner conceded or the doctor stepped in, the fight would be called.

Ali and Inoki could wear regular boxing trunks or wrestling tights, with boxing shoes or bare feet. Four-ounce gloves, karate protective gloves, or any reasonable modification of those gloves were allowed. Or they could fight bare fisted. The boxer was able to use regular two-inch gauze and one-inch tape on his hands with the bandaging to be supervised by the Japanese Boxing Commission and a rep of the wrestler.

Oil, grease, or other foreign substances on a fighter's body, fists, hair, or gloves would be prohibited.

Fouls included hitting, kicking, or kneeing below the belt; butting with the head or shoulders; jabbing or thumbing an opponent's eyes with an open glove or hand; tape on the wrestler's wrist or fist; and hitting or attacking after a break by the ref or after the bell.

The boxer was expected to observe customary boxing rules while standing. Ali could continue to throw punches if he went to the canvas, and he had the right to switch at any time to Inoki's style of martial arts.

The wrestler needed to observe customary wrestling rules while standing, kneeling, or on the canvas, but he could punch if both men stood.

★ ★ ★ ★ ★

Despite Mike LeBell's influential role, there weren't many people who would claim to be fans of the L.A. wrestling promoter. Part of the reason wrestling folks disliked Aileen

Eaton's elder son was they felt he had no respect. Eaton put him in a position of privilege and while he cared about making a buck he displayed no loyalty or reverence for the boys or the business. It may be strong to say he was generally despised, but in 2009 no one from wrestling went to his funeral when he died at the age of seventy-nine from respiratory failure. The only calls Gene received were from people who said Mike owed them money.

Freddie Blassie hated Mike LeBell. In his autobiography, Blassie was blunt: "Even during the best of times, I was always waiting for him to put a hatchet in my back. I feel pretty confident saying that every wrestler in the territory felt the same way. Because of all the publicity we got in L.A., you'd wind up with the press clippings while he wound up with the money."

East Coast star Bruno Sammartino was sufficiently put off by LeBell in 1972, and never worked with him again.

Perhaps most telling, into his eighties "Judo" Gene LeBell maintains an intense distaste for his deceased brother. Considered cold and callous by many, some employees at the Olympic took to calling him Mike "LeSmell."

"Mike LeBell was a cold, cold customer. It's hard to believe that Mike and Gene were brothers, because they couldn't possibly be any different," said Bill Caplan. "They looked completely different. Their demeanor was different, their personalities. I'm sure Mike never got into a fight, let alone be a martial arts guy and a stuntman like Gene. I'm certain that he never did what I did, pop Don Fraser in George Parnassus' office. He seemed to be a guy without passion. He had dark black hair, combed straight back, and Gene's this curly red-headed guy. It's unbelievable they were brothers.

"It was rumored that Mike made a lot of money by skimming out of the box office. I don't know if it's true or not. He bought a big mansion. Aileen lived in a big home but Mike's was even bigger and more expensive."

★ ★ ★ ★ ★

Ali's arrival at Haneda Airport in Tokyo on Wednesday, June 16, was an event on its own.

Hundreds of fans greeted The Greatest as he deplaned with Blassie, Rhee, Dundee, Kilroy, and others. Camera flashes popped like an intense lightning storm while the media horde scratched and clawed to get near the boxing champion.

Almost immediately Ali and Blassie, the latter well-known in Japan after his historic matches with Rikidōzan, broke out into their routine.

Blassie: "We're here! Inoki wishes we weren't here. He's lost."

Ali: "He's in trouble."

Blassie: "Right!"

Ali: "He don't stand a chance."

Blassie: "We'll kill him. Annihilate that pencil-neck geek. He's got a neck like a stack of dimes. Like all the rest of you geeks out there. Look at them all. Show 'em that right hand, champ. That's the one!"

Ali raised his right hand: "When I hit him with that it's all over. It will be all over."

Blassie: "He's talking about you guys with the short cocks."

At this, Blassie busted up laughing and Ali looked sheepish.

Ali: "I'm only after Inoki. I like all Japanese people but Inoki."

Ali walked through the swarm behind Blassie, placing his hands on the wrestler's shoulders.

Blassie: "The champ-een's invading Japan. The champ-een's here. The greatest man that's ever stepped in a ring! Muhammad Ali! Ali! Ali! Ali! Ali!"

Ali: "What will we do to Inoki?"

Blassie: "Kill him! Inoki's lost. Take out insurance on Inoki. Inoki, pay his policy. Big funeral for Inoki! Extra! Extra! Read all about it: Inoki sinks. Pearl Harbor, he's through!"

When the bout came together there was plenty of promotional fodder to be found in jingoism. Ali and Blassie, who had retired from wrestling two years earlier and was in the managerial phase of his career, stepped off the plane and greeted fans and media.

Ali's match with Inoki, like Rikidōzan's trilogy versus Freddie Blassie, took place at a time of significant tension between the U.S. and Japan. Before resigning from office in 1974, U.S. President Richard Nixon took the U.S. dollar off the gold standard, causing, in part, massive inflation of the Japanese yen. The U.S. had also recently relinquished post–World War II control of Okinawa to Japan.

When Blassie invoked Pearl Harbor, Ali shushed him. But of course that didn't work.

Blassie: "All you pencil-neck geeks, there shall not be no Pearl Harbor! Muhammad Ali has returned just like MacArthur!"

Ali: "Shall destroy him! Shall. Destroy. Him."

Pandemonium ensued as Ali stepped into a car curbside. Fans surrounded Ali's car, chanted his name, and delayed his ride to the hotel.

Three Japanese Muslims, according to the Associated Press, also met Ali at the airport with signs in English and Arabic: "Indonesian, southern Philippine, and Japanese Moslems welcome our great man and Moslem hero, Muhammad Ali."

Forty-five minutes after reaching the Keio Plaza Hotel in the Shinjuku neighborhood of Tokyo, Ali and Blassie took questions from the press. Ali strode down a red carpet as Japanese musicians beat out a welcome on large drums. He explained, again, that he always wanted to fight a "rassler" and always believed he could destroy a "rassler." A great boxer can defeat a karate man or anyone else, he said.

Ali said he though respected all Japanese people save Inoki, certain training sessions would be private to keep prying, spying eyes away. Again allusions were made to Pearl Harbor, and Ali appeared less embarrassed about mentioning it in conjunction with Inoki's alleged dirty tactics.

"Inoki is the favorite in Japan," Ali said. "He's well-liked wherever he goes. He's been allowed to get away with these things. Worldwide I know I have more fans than Inoki. Worldwide. I am making him famous. There are places he's not known. There's people who don't know Inoki until he meets me."

"They always say that a wrestler can beat a boxer," Blassie said. "Well it might have been a case until Muhammad Ali. We've got a lot of surprises in store for Inoki and none of them are pleasant. Without a doubt this is going to be the greatest fight that Ali's ever had. This is the first time I've seen him so mad, and so angry."

Then Ali predicted a finish in round eight.

"I don't like Inoki because he talks too much," Ali said. "No respect. He has no respect for me whatsoever. I'm gonna give him a beating. I'm going to whip him like a daddy whips his son. Because from the look of his jaw I cannot miss."

On Friday, June 18, a lunch at the Foreign Correspondents Club of Japan put Ali and Inoki face to face for the first time since their press conference in March at the Plaza Hotel in Manhattan. An unofficial weigh-in placed both fighters at 100 kg (220.4 lbs).

Again, Ali was put in the position to comment on the legitimacy of the whole show.

"How can I be wrapped up in a phony event?" he said. "I can't take part in no sham. I'm a world symbol."

For his part, Inoki said he was taking the match seriously—then he presented Ali with a crutch.

Ali took every chance he had to prod Inoki, verbally and physically. He grabbed the Japanese wrestler about the shoulders and neck, sizing up the man who might twist him in knots.

"You're gonna have the whole world watching him this time," Ali said, ramping up the pressure on Inoki. "Not just a rasslin' match, but every country on Earth!"

Inoki remained stoic and from time to time offered a wry smile even as Ali admitted to trying to make him angry.

"I'm nervous," Ali said. "I admit it. Ain't he nervous?"

"I consider it a great honor to talk and speak with the great Ali," Inoki responded.

"He's smarter than I thought he was," said the champ.

"But at the same time the contents are rather ridiculous," Inoki said through an interpreter. "When your fist connects with my chin, take care that your fist is not damaged."

That line got a laugh from the crowd, which seemed to enjoy the show. Ali even gave Inoki a nod. Ali flexed his biceps and said Inoki's weren't bigger than his. The wrestler pointed out that tendon strength counted more than muscles as far as he was concerned.

"If he beats me he'll go down as the greatest boxer [and] rassler of all times," Ali said. "Let's read the rules off. Someone's got the rules. We gotta make the rules?"

The specter of the rules continued to hang over the event. Despite publicly announced criteria, behind the scenes the Ali camp was extremely nervous about what Inoki might do, especially since it seemed he wanted to do anything he could.

The following day, Saturday, June 19, Ali held an impromptu press conference to undercut persistent rumors in the press of a pending fix. A work, really, but the sportswriters didn't seem to know the difference.

Ali called the upcoming fight "100 percent legit."

"This match is serious," he promised. "It's not like your average rassling match. The worst thing I could do would be to involve myself in a public scandal, or fraud, taking $6 million and deceiving the people of the world. That's the worst thing I could do as a religious man. A fixed or rehearsed fight—never. I'm not gonna go out in nothin' like that."

Ali said no one in Japan was after him to rig the fight. Rather, he was warned by people associated with the American broadcast that a real fight with Inoki might result in his death. Ali said he was told that Inoki "could possibly take his fingers and pull my eyes out of my sockets. Or he could take his hands and reach them inside my pants and pull my testicles out.

"These people were trying to deceive me, making me think the fight was fixed," he said. "And then Inoki, not knowing it, he could harm me with me thinking he would go easy and then me get harmed thinking it was fixed.

"To show that this thing is 100 percent legit, is 100 percent serious, I'm here to announce that I will use my bare fists and no gloves. The most I will use, if anything, to protect my hands from being hurt or broken is hand wraps and bag gloves, which we use punchin' the bag, which is real small and just like bare fists. They're about one ounce."

To protect himself, Ali said his hand would be wrapped "real hard—like rocks," and in case Inoki does something illegal he can pull them off and use his fingers.

The next day, Father's Day, Ali sparred with Jimmy Ellis and Rodney Bobick, whom he staggered in front of 1,000 fans during an afternoon at Tokyo's wonderful Korakuen Hall. Ali added rope jumping and shadow boxing tantamount to a ten-round workout.

Speaking to the crowd, Ali said he hoped "Westernization doesn't destroy Japanese morals . . . I don't want to see Japanese people lose their identity . . . Every country I go to I will tell people how wonderful Japan is."

Inoki's turn came next but Ali had to play the showman. Thirty minutes after finishing his open workout, Ali returned to the small, historic venue ready to pounce. He made a bit of noise before leaving Inoki in peace.

Fight week began with Inoki slapping submissions on three wrestlers in front of his countrymen. He also warmed up using Karl Gotch's Indian body-weight routine, skipped rope, and did neck bridges as a 250-pound New Japan Pro Wrestling teammate sat on him. Afterwards Inoki said Japan hadn't seen anything yet. He purposely held back because Ali was lurking, and a smart fighter doesn't reveal his tricks. Inoki said for the past month he'd been working with a Japanese heavyweight boxer and "what I did today is not what I will be doing in the fight. This was just our usual training procedure."

A Monday-morning meeting with members of both camps put a renewed focus back on the rules. The promoters went over, once again, what was permissible in the fight and what was not.

"You wouldn't believe what went on in that meeting," Angelo Dundee told Phil Pepe of the New York *Daily News*. "They talked about Inoki being allowed to punch with a closed fist and whether or not he could kick with his toes, which we decided he couldn't. They gave demonstrations of what Inoki can do and they even wanted him to be allowed to use a karate chop to the Adam's apple. I couldn't believe what was going on at that meeting. The whole thing was making me sick to my stomach, and damn scared."

Ali skipped a workout on Tuesday and took most of the day off inside his plush hotel suite, venturing out only to visit a camera factory. Inoki continued closed training sessions, insisting there was nothing the public could see until the fight.

Dundee touted Ali as being in "fantastic condition, perhaps the best physical condition in all his career. He can beat George Foreman or Ken Norton easily now. What he needs is to keep it up."

Prior to a $175-a-plate dinner for four hundred at the official contract signing on Wednesday evening, both camps continued to hammer out the rules. There were rumors that Ali was considering pulling out, and no one seemed to have a handle on just what the fight would look like.

Following a five-mile morning jog in the Tokyo rain, Ali kept to himself most of the day watching hours and hours of tape on Inoki. His only breaks were to shower, to eat, and to take a phone call from Chuck Wepner, who was days away from wrestling Andre the Giant at Shea Stadium. Ali wished Wepner well but asked who his beneficiaries were just in case Andre fell on him.

"I'm testing fate!" Ali told Shelly Pepper from the Los Angeles *Herald Examiner*, who was in the room when Wepner called. "I'm fighting to uphold a part of boxing and all those great names. I'm fighting for men like Sugar Ray, Joe Louis, Rocky Marciano, Jack Johnson, and so many others. No rassler will beat me."

Meanwhile, Gene Kilroy, Ferdie Pacheco, Angelo Dundee, and Wali Muhammad represented Ali in the final rules negotiations. Inoki's manager, Hisashi Shinma, and his old tag-team partner, Giant Baba, tried to keep the Americans honest as debate raged on as to how the contest would be run.

"I had something to do with shaping the rules, and making sure they didn't screw Ali in the rules meeting," Pacheco said. "I knew about Japanese. I was in the war and dealing with Japanese officers. They're tough. We're in the meeting and we're going through the rules. What rules? It's a wrestler and a boxer. What rules can they have? That Ali doesn't knock him out? If he stands Ali knocks him out."

There were heated moments, though Shinma remained steadfast and classy throughout the process.

"He picked into his pocket and took out his fountain pen, his wallet, had credit cards and everything, and threw it on the table," Pacheco said. "His lump sum of wealth. He said 'There, now you got everything. Keep that until the fight's over.' We said we don't want all your money. He said: 'Just to show we're straight.' We said we're not dealing with your wealth. We're dealing so you can't kill our guy, or twist his arm and break it."

In the original format, certain rules were put in place to protect Ali from any serious physical threat. But when Ali began mouthing off, calling Inoki "that Jap wrestler," casting aspersions on all wrestlers, Inoki's people insisted on changes that would make the rules less restrictive.

"Inoki felt it was an insult," his spokesman Ken Tajima told the press. "I don't know if Americans realize how derogatory this term is to the Japanese people."

Inoki described "Jap" as a racial slur on par with "nigger" and said it was not appropriate. "I don't want to take it personally, but in terms of the Japanese people as a whole, I can't accept it," the wrestler told the press.

That's when things got serious and stories circulated of a supposed double cross. Ali was told to knock off the insults, which he did, and during meetings late Tuesday into Wednesday morning the rules were finalized.

"Inoki's manager, after a lot of arguing—a lot of arguing—threw all the papers on the table," Pacheco recalled. "He said, 'Here, sign whatever you want. I understand what you want. You want to tie his hands. He can't do this. He can't do that. What can we do? We're a wrestler.'

"We had his fucking hands tied. He couldn't do a thing to us but we could kill him.

"Ali didn't care about the rules. All he cared about was getting paid and getting out of there."

At the signing ceremony later that evening, Inoki offered a rebuke of the process, and scolded Ali and his camp. But he said he would accept the rules as negotiated and move forward with the contest.

"I agree to all of the rules as requested by Muhammad Ali such as no dropkicks, no karate chops, no hitting on the mat," Inoki said. "But there's a limit to the requests. It seems that my hands and feet are tied."

Basically that was true.

Kicking was mostly prohibited and would be declared a foul unless the person delivering the blow was kneeling, squatting, or operating down on the canvas. In attempting to bring an opponent to the ground, leg sweeps, leg whips, and leg pulls were allowed using shins or the side or top of the foot.

Other fouls included hitting below the belt with a fist; hitting with the knee or elbow to any part of the body; hitting with any part of the body to the groin; butting with the head; jabbing, gouging, or thumbing the eyes; hitting or attacking after a ref break; any blow to the back, to the neck, or kidneys; and all chops as traditionally used in wrestling, such as chops with the side of the ungloved hand.

Palm or heel strikes were fine, so long as they didn't connect with the throat or Adam's apple.

"To me it wasn't a joke," Pacheco said. "I wasn't laughing. To fight a wrestler? Are you kidding? Is Ali going to get on his knees and fight him? If this guy kicks Ali's legs how are you going to stop that?"

In a publicity stunt, Inoki proposed a winner-take-all $9 million prize.

"Including wives?" Ali asked. "Does that include wives?"

Inoki, who was married to Japanese actress Mitsuko Baisho, shot down Ali: "Don't ask ridiculous questions, please."

After the fighters signed their names to the official contracts, Inoki brought out a plaster cast he had made especially for Ali.

"He prepared what for me?" Ali bellowed. "He prepared what for me?"

*Aileen Eaton chats with Jimmy Lennon Sr. at the Olympic Auditorium
(photo used courtesy of the Lennon family)*

*Bob Hope and "Sugar" Ray Robinson at a charity event at Hope's home
MC'd by Jimmy Lennon Sr. (Photo credit Theo Ehret, and used courtesy of
the Lennon family)*

*Jimmy Lennon Sr. interviews Mike Quarry at the Olympic Auditorium
(photo used courtesy of the Lennon family)*

*Jimmy Lennon Sr. holds a microphone in front of boxers at the Olympic
Auditorium (photo used courtesy of the Lennon family)*

*Jimmy Lennon Sr. poses with his wife, Doris, and son, Jimmy Lennon Jr.,
outside their home (photo used courtesy of the Lennon family)*

*Jayne Mansfield sits ringside at the Olympic Auditorium with then
husband Mickey Hargitay Jr. (photo used courtesy of the Lennon family)*

Jimmy Lennon Sr. stands with pro wrestler Haystacks Calhoun and unnamed wrestler (photo used courtesy of the Lennon family)

Jimmy Lennon Sr. shaves John Tolos' head in the ring at the Olympic Auditorium (photo used courtesy of the Lennon family)

Jimmy Lennon Sr. announces Andre the Giant as the winner (photo used courtesy of the Lennon family)

Freddie Blassie gets his arm raised by Jimmy Lennon Sr. as Olympic wrestling matchmaker Jules Strongbow joins them in the ring (photo used courtesy of the Lennon family)

Muhammad Ali and Jhoon Rhee deplane in Seoul, Korea, the day after Ali fought Antonio Inoki (photo used courtesy of Jhoon Rhee)

Muhammad Ali poses in a taekwondo gi, wearing Jhoon Rhee's patented gloves, at his training camp in Deer Lake, Pa. (photo used courtesy of Jhoon Rhee)

Jhoon Rhee throws a side kick as he trains with Muhammad Ali in Deer Lake, Pa. (photo used courtesy of Jhoon Rhee)

Jhoon Rhee and Muhammad Ali chat (photo used courtesy of Jhoon Rhee)

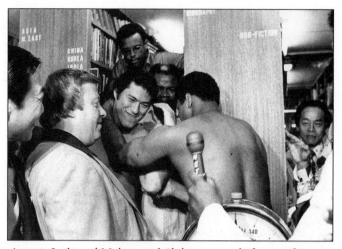

Antonio Inoki and Muhammad Ali horse around after a preliminary weigh-in in Tokyo prior to their fight. From left to right: Bobby Goodman, Antonio Inoki, Drew "Bundini" Brown, Muhammad Ali, Jhoon Rhee (photo used courtesy of Bobby Goodman)

Muhammad Ali stands on the scale as he makes preliminary weight for his match with Antonio Inoki. From left to right: Antonio Inoki, Drew "Bundini" Brown, Bobby Goodman (foreground), Muhammad Ali, Butch Lewis (photo used courtesy of Bobby Goodman)

Scene at Deer Lake, Pa. From left to right: The Greatest *producer*
John Marshall, Bobby Goodman, Gene Kilroy, Richard Harris (actor)
(photo used courtesy of Bobby Goodman)

Bobby Goodman poses at the International Boxing Hall of Fame following
his induction in 2009 (photo used courtesy of Bobby Goodman)

Antonio Inoki stands on the scale as he makes preliminary weight for his match with Muhammad Ali. From left to right: Bobby Goodman, Antonio Inoki, Freddie Blassie, Butch Lewis (photo used courtesy of Bobby Goodman)

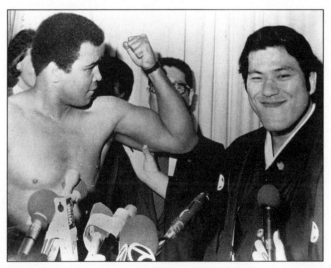

Muhammad Ali flexes for Antonio Inoki and the cameras at their prefight press conference at the Plaza Hotel in March of 1976 (photo used courtesy of Bobby Goodman)

A publicity shot of Muhammad Ali (photo used courtesy of Bobby Goodman)

A publicity shot of Antonio Inoki (photo used courtesy of Bobby Goodman)

Gene Kilroy poses with Muhammad Ali at Ali's wedding with Veronica Porche in 1977 (photo used courtesy of Gene Kilroy)

Gene LeBell poses with Antonio Inoki at a Cauliflower Alley Club event (photo used courtesy of Gene LeBell)

*Gene LeBell poses with Antonio Inoki at a Cauliflower Alley Club event
(photo used courtesy of Gene LeBell)*

*Antonio Inoki barely misses a kick to the face of Muhammad Ali (photo
used courtesy of Bobby Razak and* The History of MMA*)*

*Referee Gene LeBell steps between Muhammad Ali and Antonio Inoki
(photo used courtesy of Bobby Razak and* The History of MMA*)*

*Muhammad Ali taunts Antonio Inoki as the Japanese wrestler asks the
boxer to join him on the ground (photo used courtesy of Bobby Razak and*
The History of MMA*)*

ROUND NINE

Freddie Blassie changed Gene LeBell's life as much as anyone.

In his early twenties, LeBell fawned over motorcycles. Two to three times a week he took his Whizzer motorbike over to the Honda of Hollywood motorcycle dealership to hang out and daydream. He fantasized about what it would mean to have a new bike, even if he wasn't very good at riding yet. He told himself that he could beat everybody if he got his hands on a racing model with a high-backed fender. The problem was affording one.

Honda of Hollywood owner Bill Roberston Sr. enjoyed LeBell's company for obvious reasons, not the least of which was that "Judo" Gene paid him respect and was fun to be around. One day, as they often did, the pair made small talk and Robertson mentioned a customer who came into the dealership and wrote a bad check for $2,000. Robertson said the dealership tracked the customer down over the phone,

and he threatened that if anyone showed up at his place trying to collect he would kill them. Apparently he claimed he
was from Chicago and a member of the mob.

LeBell relayed the story to Blassie, who loved playing
a good angle when he could. Blassie came up with a concept to retrieve the cash, and "Judo" Gene went back to the
dealership asking for the tough guy's address. Blassie wanted
LeBell to show up on the gangster's doorstep holding a big
box of matches claiming to be a pyromaniac. LeBell didn't
know what that was and Blassie explained it was someone
who liked to watch houses burn.

The house in question was located in Hollywood, near
the Honda dealership just north of Santa Monica Blvd.
LeBell showed up and got into character like Blassie would.
As soon as the front door opened, the man inside tried to
shut it on LeBell, who quickly blocked it with his foot.

"Mr. Robertson told me I could burn your house
down," LeBell said, adding a speech impediment. "I'm a
pyromaniac."

He shoved the door open and observed how nice the
curtains were. "Oh, I'm happy," LeBell muttered. The man
asked what he wanted. "Bill says you're going to give me
$2,000, but I'm going to burn your house down," LeBell
said as he spilled matches onto the floor.

The man quickly walked to the back of his house, reap-
pearing with a thick wad of cash. He peeled off the balance of
the debt, which went directly into the pyromaniac's pocket.

Returning to Honda of Hollywood, feeling good about
himself, LeBell rolled out a beautiful motorcycle he had had
his eye on. "At that age most guys were looking at women,"
LeBell said. "I was looking at motorcycles, so you know

I was screwed up." He wheeled the bike out and sat on it while waiting for Robertson Sr. to show himself. It wasn't long before the owner walked downstairs carrying a ball-peen hammer. Robertson asked if the customer had been paid a visit. LeBell gave the bike some gas then handed over $2,000, which sixty years later was worth roughly $17,500.

Robertson asked LeBell if he liked the motorcycle. Yes, of course. LeBell wanted it but he said he didn't have the scratch. The next thing LeBell remembers is Robertson caving in the metal gas tank with the hammer.

"Write it up," Robertson told an employee. "It's his bike."

One of LeBell's friends in the service department used a screwdriver to remove the big dent. "You couldn't even tell," said LeBell, the new owner of a $320 machine, who was in heaven riding his first bike that "went really fast."

LeBell has never been a wrench—he broke things not fixed them—so he threw a lot of work towards the Hollywood Honda folks. Plus he offered free towing, often taking a judo belt, his obi, to tie his bike off to another. Over the years LeBell's friendship with the Robertsons grew, and he referred more than a few customers their way. The dealership still offers a 10 percent discount on parts and service to anyone carrying a "Don't Fight It, Ride It" preferred-customer discount card. The replica autographed card features a photo of LeBell corralling Ali in the heavyweight champion's corner during the Inoki fight.

Robertson Sr. took "Judo" Gene on flights with him aboard a single-engine Beechcraft Bonanza piloted out of Whiteman Airport in the San Fernando Valley. It was rare, but once in a while they flew as far south as Mexico. In

March of 1962, the same month Blassie dropped the WWA title to Rikidōzan at the Olympic Auditorium, Robertson Sr. made use of many hours logged over Baja California by navigating and copiloting a flight aiding a pair of motorcyclists, including his twenty-four-year-old son Bill Robertson Jr., on a first-of-its-kind 1,000-mile ride along the rugged Baja Peninsula. Telegrams were sent from the start and finish to document the thirty-nine-hour, fifty-six-minute trip. Honda went on to sell many bikes and the Mexico 1000 became a yearly tradition after 1967.

Robertson Sr. also helped inspire LeBell to become a successful stunt motorcycle rider. Already doing stunt work as a martial artist, LeBell added to his slate when productions began looking for riders who could get on a bike and lay it down or jump over obstacles if needed. It wasn't long before a third of LeBell's jobs were motorbike related. Soon he met the right folks and was approached with parts for character bits, leading to one of the most extensive résumés in Hollywood that continues to grow even as LeBell approaches his mid-eighties.

"Because of Freddie Blassie," LeBell said, "that changed my life."

When LeBell told Blassie the story of his pyromaniac adventure, the loud blond-haired wrestler loved every word, especially after hearing about the foot in the door. All Blassie wanted for LeBell was to remain in character, and accomplish the mission. The key for Blassie was simple: once a persona was created, never break that illusion.

LeBell obviously knew Blassie well and was mesmerized by his "Faces of Eve." In 1957 Nunnally Johnson wrote, directed, and produced *The Three Faces of Eve*, an adaptation of a book written by psychiatrists who identified dissociative identity disorder. Joanne Woodward won the Academy Award as best actress for portrayals of Eve White, Eve Black, and Jane. LeBell knew Blassie to be the sweetest guy or a wild man prone to "annihilate, mutilate, assassinate." For his part, Blassie considered LeBell a close friend, a far cry from Aileen Eaton's other son Mike, who was widely disliked by wrestlers as he helmed the box office at the Olympic Auditorium and became a power player with the National Wrestling Alliance.

"It still amazes me that a guy like Gene LeBell could have a brother like Mike," Blassie said in his 2003 book, *Listen, You Pencil Neck Geeks*. "There are times I'm sure one of them was adopted."

As long as Blassie made Mike LeBell money, they didn't have any problems. Meanwhile, his relationship with Gene had nothing to do with business. They genuinely enjoyed being around one another, sharing a sophomoric sense of humor, a love of practical jokes, and a reverence for all things wrestling.

"Not only was [Gene] one of the top martial artists in the country, he trained with some of the most vicious wrestlers and shooters in the business," Blassie said in his book. "When the family needed an enforcer to step in the ring with a wrestler who didn't want to go along with the program all they had to do was open Gene's bedroom door and tell him to get in his wrestling gear."

Bearcat Wright became the first African American to hold a major pro wrestling title when he took the WWA heavyweight belt off Blassie in 1963. Wright bought into being champion, and though he was supposed to give up the title in short order, that was the last thing he seemed to be willing to do. The wrestling power players at the Olympic— the Eatons, booker Jules Strongbow, and Mike LeBell— grew nervous that this six-foot-six, 270-pound guy with a legitimate boxing background didn't want to go along with the plan, so Gene was unleashed to stretch him. Blassie and LeBell confronted Wright in the Olympic Auditorium parking lot, right outside the door where the "locker room" interviews were conducted. LeBell moved as if he was going after Wright, who dropped the belt, got in his car, and wouldn't return to wrestle in L.A. until 1971.

In the early '60s, LeBell owned a boat with an inboard motor, a seven-foot dinghy really, that he liked to put in his swimming pool. One day LeBell and Blassie decided to take it with them to the beach. (Blassie, then a big-time television star in L.A., lived in Santa Monica and spent most afternoons tanning near the pier. He was ritualistic enough with his sun worship that some of his most ardent fans knew when and where they could find him on any given day.) Blassie brought a good-looking girl who couldn't swim and took her out in the boat even though there wasn't room for two. A wave turned the boat over and LeBell went running to retrieve it. "How about the girl?" LeBell yelled at Blassie. "She'll wash ashore," replied the wrestler. She did. They drained the boat and got it and the girl back into the car, the end of her lone trip to the beach with the boys.

Such is the deviousness among wrestlers that there are different categories of pranks and cons. The most basic are called ribs. It could be as simple as twisting off the top of a salt shaker, or replacing a glass of beer with urine, or dropping a turd in a cowboy hat, but sometimes they were much more involved—and dangerous. Blassie was considered a hard ribber, but not the worst like the first WWWF champion Buddy Rogers or Johnny Valentine.

Valentine undertook a notorious set of ribs with and against Jay "The Alaskan" York that stand the test of time. One freezing winter night in Calgary, according to Roddy Piper's version of events, Valentine filled York's car full of water with a garden hose and let it freeze so in the morning the interior was perfect for ice hockey. Valentine, of course, was long gone by then. York took revenge the next time they ran into one another in Manhattan by finding an arc welder to angle iron Valentine's vehicle to street posts and parking meters.

York suffered from asthma and after matches always went right for his inhaler. Valentine knew this and decided that instead of inhaling medicine to open up his airways, York should draw in lighter fluid. After doing so, vomiting, passing out, and coming to his senses, York pulled a sawed-off shotgun on Valentine while his assailant was in the shower. Valentine looked at York and smiled. York blew a hole in Valentine's Halliburton aluminum briefcase. When people calmed down, Valentine went to his car. It wouldn't start. He opened the hood and saw that York, a demolition man in the Marines, had wired the car to explode but hadn't plugged it into the distributor. Instead, a fiendish note made it clear how close Valentine was to death.

A few weeks later in Minneapolis, Minn., the scene repeated itself. York walked into a dressing room packing a .357 Magnum as Valentine exited the shower. York spoke up and promised if Valentine messed with him again he'd die. Boom, the gun went off. Valentine went down, clutching his chest. The room froze. Most of the wrestlers packed heat back then, and one of them, Harley Race, plainly told the wild-eyed York to put down the piece.

Race was about to shoot York when Valentine sprung to life. The blast had come from a blank, and blood was actually ketchup. As soon as the room realized what was underway, it sank in that this was just another classic rib.

Swerves are more involved than ribs. They typically emerge as part of a storyline presented to oblivious fans. The marks. Wrestling writers will also throw curveballs when smart fans, the snarks, think they know where a story is headed.

Most people assumed Ali's match with Inoki was going to be a work. That was the discussion behind the scenes and it went so far as Vince McMahon Sr. laying out the finish. The idea was to play off the sneaky Japanese stereotype, which is why Ali and Blassie both invoked Pearl Harbor in the lead-up to the match.

"The way Vince wrote it, Ali was supposed to come out and look like he was hitting Inoki with punches," Bob Arum told *Sports Illustrated* in 2012. "Now wrestlers, they use razors to cut themselves so Inoki was supposed to cut himself, and blood would be everywhere. Then Ali would turn to the ref and say, 'Hey, please stop the fight.' Then Inoki would jump on Ali's back and pin him. Ali would get up and say this was just like Pearl Harbor, then we'd all go home."

Before Ali met Inoki in Tokyo, while Vince McMahon Sr. promoted the WWWF closed-circuit locations in the U.S., his son, Vince McMahon Jr., was sent to Japan as an emissary. Junior presumed the Ali–Inoki contest would be worked, but soon realized that both sides of the bout had different plans.

Junior tells a story in which he attempts to persuade Ali to agree to stick with a scripted outcome. In Ali's hotel room, chairs and beds are pushed to the walls, making just enough space to wrestle. The story goes that McMahon took Ali down to the floor with ease, and made his case against participating in a legitimate fight.

"I certainly remember Vince being there and spending time around Ali," said publicist Bob Goodman. "But wrestling Ali to the ground would have been a little strange to me."

Publicly, of course, Blassie was all in for Ali. Privately he admitted rooting for the wrestler, though he disliked Inoki for several reasons, not the least of which was because to him Inoki had followed the path laid by Rikidōzan and jammed it down the throats of Japanese audiences. Blassie fully expected Inoki to twist Ali into a pretzel, but just in case the match went sideways, McMahon Jr. claimed a plan was concocted between himself, Blassie, and LeBell for everyone involved to save face.

In Blassie's 2003 biography, McMahon Jr., the promotional face of modern-day wrestling, laid out the scheme. According to the story, LeBell would sneak a blade with him into the ring. Some wrestlers were like surgeons with blades, and they could be very sneaky in terms of how it was used. As soon as there was any contact that made it look like Inoki was in trouble, LeBell was allegedly going to put himself in the middle of the combatants and figure out a way to knick Ali across the tip of his hairline. It wouldn't need to be a big cut, just large enough for sweat to take over and make it look bad.

"A lot of times it's the referee that does the gimmick," said Dan Madigan, the former WWE writer.

"Even Ali wouldn't know what the fuck was happening," McMahon is quoted as saying in Blassie's book. "We had the deal where Ali wouldn't get hurt, but he would bleed profusely because Gene would do a damn good job, and Gene would have to stop the fight because of the blood. Thus, the fans would want to see a return match or some damn thing."

For his part, LeBell said he doesn't even recall McMahon being in Japan. LeBell knew McMahon Sr. and spoke with him, but said he never got on well with Junior. "Vince McMahon Jr. didn't mean much to me at the time," he said. "Just Freddie," his old dear friend from Los Angeles.

Over the years LeBell heard the McMahons wanted the Ali–Inoki contest to be pro wrestling, "but it's just hearsay," he said. "I thought Vince Jr. wanted to see Ali win and go against Andre the Giant. Shoot or work, either way, Junior wanted to make it happen." LeBell asked Blassie in Japan before the match if Ali–Inoki was going to be a shoot or a work, and Blassie responded, "Sounds like it'll be a shoot to me."

LeBell thought that was nice. "I heard every story about that in the world, but I didn't get it from the *jefe*, the boss. Nobody told me anything. If the promoter said, 'Hey, we're going to work,' I would have said, 'Fine.' I'll referee a work or referee a shoot. It doesn't make any difference to me."

Asked if as part of a work he would have taken a razor to Ali, LeBell said he wouldn't. The WWE did not reply when asked if the quote from McMahon Jr. was accurate.

"You have a better chance of reaching the president or the pope," Madigan said. "Vince is protecting the business, as he should."

McMahon Jr. learned many lessons from the Ali–Inoki promotion that shaped his opinion of mixed martial arts contests as being a far riskier proposition than wrestling. Even with the rules stacked against Inoki, there was a tremendous amount of uncertainty on all sides because of lack of control. For a pro wrestling production, it was a unique feel. And Junior, an adventurous guy with vision, felt what it was like to operate on the world stage.

The soon-to-be-dominant pro wrestling impresario didn't know how his dad found out about the plan, "but he knew I was up to no good over there," McMahon Jr. explained for Blassie's book. "He said, 'Goddammit, you're dealing with Muhammad Ali, and you're going to get into trouble legally in Japan. Get your ass back here now.'"

Madigan, who was privy to the company's versions of the Ali–Inoki stories, noted that Senior had placed great faith in Blassie.

"How can Vince not trust and respect a guy like that?" Madigan said. "No matter what, with Freddie over there Vince Sr. knew he had *the* set of eyeballs."

McMahon Jr. returned to New York by the time the official weigh-in began in Tokyo on Friday. The weight tally was to be shown on live local TV but Inoki materialized a half hour behind schedule and, not to be outdone, Ali followed him with nearly forty of his entourage in tow. Andrew Malcolm, the *New York Times* Tokyo bureau chief, shadowed Ali as he made his way to the scale. There was plenty of cheering and yelling to accompany the moment. Inoki stood waiting on the stage and Ali bounced down the aisle, acting as if he wanted to get at the Japanese rassler.

"Save it for the fight, champ," said one member of the entourage. "Save it for the fight."

Ali looked at Malcolm and winked a knowing wink, like *you know this is just show business, right?*

"I don't want Inoki," he told the reporter. "I want that redhead over there."

"There really was a redhead," Malcolm recalled. "There was a thing in his eyes. Because I happened to be close in that moment you could see that."

After the experience of the stage falling in Munich, Goodman tested the platform to make sure it was stable. He smiled knowing it was. Soon it filled with people from both camps, and Ali started up with his act.

"I will dee-stroy Inoki," he yelled. "I want Inoki . . . Inoki . . . Inoki . . . you are in trouble."

Ranting and raving, Ali finally pushed Inoki towards losing his cool. The broad-shouldered Inoki stood, arms crossed, staring at Ali. Then put his hands on his hips. He had held fast but finally . . . Enough.

Inoki's personal physician claimed he was in fine shape. There was some concern with his left shoulder but it wouldn't be an issue. Inoki looked strong at 100.5 kg (221.6 lbs). When he stepped off the scale Ali jabbed in his direction.

"I hit you and it's all over," Ali said. "Just don't get hit."

Ali weighed 99 kg. "How much is that in English?" he asked. The answer: a fit 218.3 lbs.

Before leaving the stage Ali grabbed Inoki behind the neck. Inoki bristled and Ali went theatrical. Dundee and the rest of the entourage stepped between them.

Kilroy, Brown, and Rhee all stood close by. Kilroy looked concerned as he sized up Inoki.

"You wait until I let go for real," Ali said. "I'm joking now."

Inoki stuck a finger in Ali's face and Ali swatted it away.

"I'll see you tomorrow," Ali shouted, wagging his finger at the wrestler's nose. "Be serious tomorrow. Be serious. You're meeting Muhammad Ali. The gloves will be small and I will be dancing. I will be dancing. I don't like you. I don't like you. Tell him I don't like him. You're ugly. I will destroy you. Tomorrow. I want you tomorrow. I'll see you tomorrow. *Sayonara. Sayonara* motherfu . . ."

ROUND TEN

Pitting a heavyweight world champion boxer against the top Japanese heavyweight wrestler was professional wrestling's way of saluting the American bicentennial. That's what it said on the cover of the program that sold at arenas where live wrestling supported the American closed-circuit broadcast. The photo-heavy souvenir was clear about the night ahead. Under the simple headline "WRESTLER Vs. BOXER," the program explained that the broadcast was promoted by Top Rank, Inc., Video Techniques, and Capitol Wrestling Corporation (unmentioned were New Japan Pro Wrestling and Lincoln National Productions, Ltd.).

"Your local wrestling promoter has arranged this exclusive showing for this area," it said.

Fans at Shea Stadium in Queens had the chance to see one half of the closed-circuit feed in person. As an appetizer to Ali vs. Inoki, thanks to Vince McMahon Sr. and the World Wide Wrestling Federation, boxer Chuck Wepner would meet iconic pro wrestler Andre the Giant. Meanwhile, WWWF heavyweight champion Bruno Sammartino's emotional return from a broken neck got top billing at Shea.

Running the evening's production and promotion, pro wrestling folks were in the midst of making a major statement about the future of their business.

The "WRESTLER VS. BOXER" program included images and quotes from the contract signing at the Plaza Hotel in Manhattan in March, laying out the expectations and relevance of the live pictures being beamed from inside the stifling Budokan Hall, and a ring above the Mets' pitcher's mound on the first Friday night of summer in Flushing, Queens. Ali vs. Inoki and Andre the Giant vs. Wepner "are the culmination of an effort to decide which sport has the superior fighters. Both will be seen here live tonight through the magic of television" the program promised in advance of a "history-making presentation."

The technology that allowed audiences to view back-to-back events as they happened on opposite sides of the globe came courtesy of Henry A. Schwartz. His Brooklyn-based Video Techniques was basically alone in pulling the strings on major heavyweight closed-circuit fights since Ali–Frazier I in 1971. According to a piece published in *New York Magazine* ahead of the "Rumble in the Jungle," Schwartz made money in more than a few ways as cable television penetrated American homes.

Forerunner to the pay-per-view business—which generated grotesque wealth in 2015 because of the promotion of Floyd Mayweather's fight with Manny Pacquiao and a record setting year for the Ultimate Fighting Championship—Video Techniques monetized the lease and sale of projection equipment and technical services for satellite broadcasts, and Schwartz worked with Don King and Bob Arum to do all of Ali's fights on closed circuit.

In 1974, Schwartz found the money to put on Ali–Foreman in Zaire, and joined with King to sell the fight. The "Rumble in the Jungle" was seen perfectly in 390 closed-circuit locations in North America and in nearly one hundred countries worldwide. At Madison Square Garden, seats to watch ranged from twenty to thirty dollars. Ali and Foreman were set to split a $10 million purse, double Ali's take versus Frazier three years earlier, and the bout was projected to bring in twice the revenue, too, increasing from $20 to $40 million.

In addition to the group-watching experiences, the bout was available live in about 50 million homes, mostly in Central and South America and Japan. The rest of the world except China, India, the Soviet Union, and other Communist-bloc countries saw the fight live or tape-delayed over free home television.

On the road to Ali, Foreman trashed Joe Frazier and Ken Norton in the second round each. Hundreds of millions of people around the world watched live as Ali's brilliant rope-a-dope strategy unfolded against a man who hadn't needed more than four rounds to put away any of his previous twelve opponents.

A new kind of megastardom was bestowed upon Ali as the spread of communications technology netted him a much larger audience. And Schwartz was the guy creating the conditions for record purses to go to Ali, whose incredible feats were shared with the world in innovative and exciting ways.

Even if the mixed-ruled contest failed as an event—and
there was a chance of that because some of the regional
promoters weren't 100 percent on board—wrestling would
likely benefit in the long run from being attached to The
Greatest. On the night Ali–Inoki was broadcast in the U.S.,
there were significantly more closed-circuit locations in place
than for the first Wrestlemania in 1985.

The WWWF delivered for promoters across the country
both with press attention and satellite access. This was a rare
spotlight moment for wrestling, which had been relegated to
near backwater status by the mid-1970s. The pro wrestling
business was split into little fiefdoms across the U.S. Each
promoter intended to protect his enclave since it wasn't to
anyone's benefit for fans to learn about different regions and
champions.

Though action was live at Shea Stadium, and Jeff
Wagenheim had on many occasions made the trip from
New Jersey to see the Mets play, he and a friend felt it was
too much trouble to make the trip for Ali vs. Inoki.

"Our interest level was enough to go to the next town
over and go to a theater," Wagenheim said. "But our interest
level was not so high that we were gonna hop on a bus or a
train into New York and then take a subway out to Queens
and see it there."

The open-air spectacle played out on a hot and muggy
New York summer night. Other cities featuring live wrestling
to go with the satellite show included Chicago, Houston,
San Francisco, Atlanta, Indianapolis, Dallas, Miami, Los
Angeles, Detroit, Calgary, Tallahassee, St. Louis, and Tokyo.

Depending on what part of the country the feed was
coming from, star pro wrestlers from their territories were

shown in addition to the two matches everyone saw. Wrestling pulled out its biggest names and matches during the nationwide festival.

"This wasn't the NWA that did it," said Dan Madigan. "This was the WWWF at the time. The country was still divided up at the time. That was huge."

The WWWF, under an increasingly influential Vince McMahon Jr., held over four hundred dates across the Northeast in 1976.

"Superstar" Billy Graham was the first WWWF champion to take the belt outside the territory, and in 1978 he wrestled NWA heavyweight champion Harley Race in a bigtime crossover bout on a rainy night at the Orange Bowl in Miami. Other than slipping on the wet canvas once in a while, neither champion was allowed to look weak. After an hour the match ended in a draw, each wrestler scoring a fall apiece.

The "Superbowl of Wrestling" again showed the McMahon family's ambition to grow their brand beyond its current confines. Respected by everyone in the business, Senior was old school and wanted Junior to honor the traditional boundaries.

However, when Senior stepped down and Junior formed the WWF—World Wrestling Federation—with his wife Linda in February 1980, all bets were off. NWA-affiliated or not, promotions across the country soon struggled and many of their popular wrestlers found safe harbor under the WWF banner.

"This is a business. The Ali–Inoki match was business. How can we generate revenue?" Madigan said. "It was also the seeds of Vince's expansion into other territories."

In Los Angeles, where the LeBells dominated after the Daros, strong local wrestling promotion ended when Worldwide Wrestling Associates, whose title was on the line during the Blassie–Rikidōzan trilogy, closed the day after Christmas in 1982. By shuttering his NWA promotion, Mike LeBell, the first North American promoter to make closed-circuit television locations available to fans who couldn't get into the arena, ceded the territory rights to Vince McMahon.

"Cable guaranteed the end of the territories," Dave Meltzer said. "It was just obvious because once you had national exposure you could promote in more places and offer the guys more money to work major cities. The local promoters couldn't afford to keep up."

Speaking in a famous article from 1983 that blew up kayfabe, Bay Area wrestling promoter Roy Shire told the *Los Angeles Times* the truth behind wrestling, in and out of the ring. *What you thought you saw, you didn't. And this is how it all really happened.* Shire left the wrestling business two years earlier after a long stretch as the dominant promoter out of San Francisco's Cow Palace, but in reality he was out of the game well before that.

Approaching retirement, Shire's last partnership was with Eddie Graham, a promoter out of Florida who served as the NWA president in the 1970s. Graham was the one who approached McMahon Sr. with the idea of a WWWF vs. NWA title match in '78, and though Florida is a long ways from San Francisco, he and Shire pulled off three shows.

Shire hosted his last eighteen-man "Battle Royal" at the Cow Palace, which had a reputation for its share of knife fights on wrestling nights, on January 24, 1981. Fans did not know they were witnessing the final wrestling event

Shire would promote after decades of selling seats to Bay Area crowds. Without a TV partner he was only able to draw 6,000 fans for his last show. Lacking good TV exposure, which he lost in the early 1970s, he simply could not promote.

Speaking with the *Los Angeles Times*, Shire tabbed the rise of the WWF and Vince McMahon to the promotion's national television exposure, and longstanding connection to Madison Square Garden.

"He's not that great a promoter," Shire said. "But if you've got TV, and you go national, you know, and people are seeing those wrestlers, week in and week out, then you come along—that's the scenario of our business—you put a guy on TV and you get people to like him or hate him, then you put him in a town, and the people that have seen him on TV for seven, eight, ten weeks or months or ten weeks—or whatever, long enough to either you really like him, or really hate him, you bring him in the people'll pay their money at the box office to see him. That is the essence of our business. Has been."

Starting on December 5, 1982, Joe Blanchard's *Southwest Championship Wrestling* became the first weekly wrestling program on cable, airing its regional stars to the country Sunday mornings on the USA Network. As a result of the new national exposure, SWCW staged a one-night tournament in Austin, Tex., to determine an "undisputed world heavyweight champion." Lou Thesz even presented Adrian Adonis with the oldest existing pro rasslin' championship belt, which is on display at the National Wrestling Hall of Fame Dan Gable Museum in Waterloo, Iowa.

USA canceled the program (in spite of the high ratings the show was garnering for the network) and turned the time slot over to the WWF when SWCW couldn't pay the bills to keep up the time buy. The promotion soon disappeared.

McMahon Jr. was the one that made the move but some people, especially those immersed in the Japanese side of the business, like Dave Meltzer, who spoke a lot to Terry Funk, saw it coming.

"Terry Funk was the booker of All-Japan Pro Wrestling, so he was living in the Japanese world," said Meltzer, who started printing the *Wrestling Observer Newsletter* in 1982. "He knew, because Japan was way ahead of the U.S. in every aspect of pro wrestling, that cable would be the equivalent of network. And he knew that Japan is all over the country because you're on TV all over the country. And the small guys can't compete with the big guys."

This hit Meltzer while he watched wrestling from Georgia. All of a sudden, his interest in the California stuff waned because there was better professional wrestling below the Mason–Dixon Line.

McMahon figured it out and implemented a broader vision before anyone else. Whatever competition he had along the way went belly-up, and the wide territory system consolidated into super groups.

Both the business of American pro wrestling and its reach around the world greatly expanded under McMahon Jr., who became known as an innovator and more enterprising than his father. They lived apart for much of Junior's childhood, reuniting when the son was twelve. Following college, to the displeasure of his dad, Vince quickly moved into the family business and concocted gimmicks like slicing Ali with a razor blade.

Junior had returned to New York by the night of June 25 so the voice of the WWWF could call the matches from Shea Stadium. Publicly McMahon was just the announcer, but behind the scenes he was starting to build the third-generation business. Sitting at the precipice of control of a solid pro wrestling kingdom, McMahon surveyed what was in front of him and asked how he could push the business. He wanted to be the world's biggest promoter, not necessarily of just pro wrestling, though that was the priority.

"I believe that no matter how outlandish it is, knowing Vince to be the risk taker that he is, that he's out there trying to push," said Madigan, who left the WWE in 2010 and writes screenplays in Los Angeles. "He's always tried to elevate wrestling outside of its parameters. This is another way of opening up the world. At the time it was still territorial. WWWF, which came from the Capitol Wrestling Corporation, was territorial and you're still trying to carve out who you are.

"You could walk in a room and see the potential of something from Point A to Point B. Vince sees it from Point A to Point D. To Point E. Vince sees the potential going off until he can't see it anymore. I've been in meetings when Vince will talk about something. He'll look up and all of a sudden his eyes will look off. You can see where Vince sees this going. This is amazing foresight. Sometimes it works, sometimes it doesn't. Without Vince's foresight, wrestling would still be territorial. It would be in the dark ages, and no matter who you had wrestling for you—you could have the greatest guys in your promotion—but you are still watching

the promotion. Vince knocked the walls down. He was like
the Romans and spread the empire.

"Vince doesn't push the envelope. Vince knocks over the
post office. That's what I love about him. He's always said
no matter what you do you learn from it. I think he learned
from it. What to do. What not to do. And never put yourself
in a position to look weak.

"Vince puts it on the line every time. Whether you agree
or disagree you can't fault the guy for trying to be the best.
It's his vision and if you don't like it get the fuck out of the
way. You're either in or in the way. I think this just spurred
him on to bigger things. For the first time, in a way, even
though it's Japan, it's giving the WWWF a bigger spotlight."

Ambition could be heard in McMahon's voice when he
called Ali's skirmish with Gorilla Monsoon in Philadelphia.
The seeds had been planted for expansion. After "Toots"
Mondt and Jess McMahon formed the Capitol Wrestling
Corporation, which begat the WWWF, the WWF, and eventually the WWE, pro wrestling was fit for Saturday morning cartoons. Merchandising became a big deal. The more
McMahon pushed, the larger his wrestling empire's sphere
of influence grew.

Less than a decade after creating the WWF, Vince K.
McMahon described the style of his professional wrestling
league as "sports entertainment." Though the term dates
back to February 1935, when *Toronto Star* sports editor Lou
Marsh described professional wrestling as "sportive entertainment," in 1989 McMahon used the phrase before the
New Jersey Senate as he spoke about reclassifying professional wrestling to "sports entertainment"—and thus not
fall subject to regulation or taxation like a competitive sport.

The death rattle over pro wrestling's sporting legitimacy, as it was widely regarded two generations ago, finally stopped. Business, though, was just picking up.

Wrestling is a funny thing in that it works off the zeitgeist of the time—sometimes as embarrassing entertainment unafraid to latch on to whatever holds attention. At the highest level, once you know where you can take an angle or a story, you stay there. Then you're forced to push or swerve and find new ways to hold the crowd. One of the wrestlers Madigan worked with at the WWE was Kenzo Suzuki, a wrestler from New Japan Pro Wrestling. Suzuki had some good size to him, and Madigan didn't want to touch the old characters. They had done the samurai. The ninja. The cliché.

Then Madigan pitched McMahon on "Hirohito," the great-grandson of the Emperor Hirohito, coming back to avenge his family honor and cultural heritage.

"God knows why," Madigan laughed. "I said, 'Imagine this. You're watching the screen. All of a sudden you see an atomic explosion. Out of the mushroom cloud two Asian eyes peer out.'

"Vince went crazy. He loved it. He loved it. He goes, 'That's great.'"

McMahon purchased archival footage of a devastated Hiroshima after the U.S. dropped an atomic weapon on Japan, and WWE showed two eyes peering out from behind a mushroom cloud during a presentation in the arena. Someone went so far as to toss a bucket of "blood" onto the screen and it ran down over the eyes as the angle played out.

"Hirohito is coming," the screen read.

This was shown on television live just once, on Raw, WWE's flagship Monday night program that debuted on the USA Network in 1993. Wrestlers backstage wondered what the hell it meant. McMahon was very happy.

"I'm walking around on cloud nine," Madigan said. "Two days later we're back at the home office and Vince comes in. 'We don't talk about Hirohito,' he said. 'We don't mention Hirohito. It never happened.'"

The Japanese Imperial Family was very upset with the promo and its implications, and according to Madigan they threatened to kick out WWE from Japan.

"I didn't know there was a Japanese royal family," he replied to McMahon.

"Well neither did I. Apparently they watch wrestling."

Madigan once pitched a Nazi gimmick to McMahon. Baron Von Bobbin, the goose-stepping Nazi found frozen in the Swiss Alps. McMahon apparently stood up, didn't say a word, and walked out of their meeting. That one didn't fly, but others did and Madigan was responsible for sparking complaints from high ground. The Canadian government was upset over a character named Eugene because it portrayed a mentally challenged person. He also felt heat over the character "Mordecai," a religious zealot who was banned by the Church of England.

"If you can't get in trouble with the Church of England and the Japanese royal family you're not doing your job," Madigan quipped.

McMahon retrofitted the WWF into a unique brand that reached out to family audiences while attracting fans who had never before paid attention to pro wrestling. By directing his story lines towards highly publicized supercards, McMahon capitalized on a fledgling revenue stream by promoting these events live on pay-per-view television, a concept initiated by then-rival Jim Crockett Promotions. In 1987, the WWF reportedly drew 93,173 fans to the Pontiac Silverdome (the "biggest crowd in sports entertainment history") for WrestleMania III, which featured the main event of Hulk Hogan versus Andre the Giant.

For many fans it was the moment Andre got slammed, and WWF played it up that way even though in the old territory structure Hogan had done so many times. YouTube compilation videos of Hogan repeatedly lifting and dropping the Giant onto wrestling canvases across America are highly amusing.

Pro wrestling touches people in funny ways. The emotion of sport wrapped in a hippodrome. The formula obviously works and from time to time can serve as base social commentary. Muhammad Ali, a poet and philosopher, didn't need a low-brow way to express such things; however, he loved wrestling and grabbed a chance to play in that world when he could.

"He's got the same blood," said Ali's doctor, Ferdie Pacheco. "They had the blood of a con artist. Wrestling is con. It's just a con. And if they went and wrestled and did crazy things it's because they were doing stunts. So Ali liked that. He liked the idea of jumping off the top rope and landing on a guy."

Because people don't take it seriously, sports entertainment can touch issues—more to the point: play off current events and stereotypes—that more serious spaces might shy away from for fear of paying a public relations price. In the wrestling business there's no such thing.

McMahon relied on the "sports entertainment" tag to help navigate his company through a steroid scandal, and is doing the same as wrestlers file lawsuits against WWE regarding concussion-related problems such as chronic traumatic encephalopathy, known as CTE, a degenerative brain disease found in people with a history of repeated head trauma.

Hardly anyone made much noise about concussions as the calender turned to 1970, when, for instance, Chuck Wepner went down to George Foreman and Sonny Liston ten months apart. His main talent was taking as much punishment as an opponent could give.

At Madison Square Garden, a snappy left jab, stinging left hooks, and solid rights helped Foreman, in his fourth pro fight, stagger Wepner in the second round. Cut over his left eye heading to the third, Wepner needed to be saved after Foreman split the gash wide open with a series of punches. Big George wouldn't lose until his forty-first bout half a decade later against Ali in Kinshasa, Zaire.

Liston's final fight took place six months before he died at the age of 40 from "natural causes." Many people believe he was murdered. One theory is that Liston was supposed to take a dive against Wepner, and killing him was payback for his failure to do so. (Others suggested he died from injecting heroin.) Among Wepner's people in Jersey City, N.J., at the Armory on June 29, 1970, the fight was stopped after the ninth round due to severe cuts over both of Wepner's eyes. He required seventy-two stitches and also suffered a broken nose and a cracked left cheekbone.

Wepner got a taste of the big time when he fought Ali in 1975. He inspired Sylvester Stallone to create Rocky Balboa after knocking down Ali with a clubbing shot under the heart in Round 9—one of four times in The Greatest's career that he went down, although the other three came off clean punches, while Wepner clearly stepped on Ali's foot when he connected.

"It wasn't a great punch," admitted Wepner. "But when he went down and the referee started counting, I went back to my corner. I walked back and I remember saying to my manager Al Braverman, 'Start the car. We're going to the bank. We're millionaires.' And he said 'Chuck, you better turn around. He looks pissed off.' And he was."

The tall, bruising liquor salesman made it to Round 15 before Ali stopped him. Wepner wasn't long for boxing at that point anyhow, and he already considered himself "best friends" with the WWWF people when Vince McMahon Sr. called with an offer in the spring of 1976. "I was asked if I would do this 'mixed martial arts' thing with someone," Wepner recalled, "I said, 'Who was the someone?' He said, 'Andre the Giant.' I said, 'Why not? What the fuck. I fought a bear twice.'"

Andre the Giant stood and weighed, according to the most impressive estimates, seven foot five and 525 pounds at the time Wepner faced him. The bear, closer to eight feet tall, had another 725 pounds on the famous Frenchman.

"I got the shit beat out of me and I got mauled twice, but it was for charity," Wepner said. "They told me I wasn't supposed to hit the bear in the nose. It was a trained bear. But nobody told me that. So I'm moving around popping this bear in the nose, and he flipped out. And threw me off the mat and jumped on me. Thank God I was able to get my hands out to wave so the trainer could whistle him off. He blows a whistle and the bear stops."

A year and a half later, to Wepner's detriment, the mauling boxer was again matched with the bear.

"This bear remembered me when I fought him in Asbury Park and was hitting him in the nose," he said. "And I told my manager when we were sitting in the ring that this bear remembers me and he don't like me. And Al's like, 'He's fought a hundred guys since you. He's not gonna remember you.' Bears get your scent. They're like elephants, another animal with a strong memory. He remembered me and I remembered him."

When the bear charged, Wepner sidestepped and tried to jump out of the ring, but he got tangled in the ropes and the bear slung the 225-pounder by the leg.

"I went out into the crowd on the table, knocked over all the dishes," Wepner said. "There was 160 people in the place. My friend picked me up and said, 'Come on Chuck, get up, go get 'em.' This bear's standing. You can imagine, it's eight feet tall and 1,250 pounds. He's roaring. And then they said, 'Go get 'em.' And I said, 'Go get my ass.' And the referee's counting, he's up to four. And I said, 'five, six, seven, eight, nine, ten, good-bye.' So it won by default. We raised almost $28,000 that night for the Make-A-Wish Foundation. Tickets were $350 apiece, plus the drinks, and they had a thing before that. Anyways, we did a good job."

Wepner had a month's notice for Andre the Giant. Since he was in shape anyway and in the gym all the time it was an easy yes.

"Of course it was show business so nobody was going to get seriously hurt," he said. "Unless there was a mistake. They wanted Andre in the fourth round to body slam me to win the fight. I said are you out of your mind? He's 525 pounds. We weighed in with Brent Musburger from CBS. They had to bring in a meat scale to weigh in. I was 228; he was 525. We took some pictures. He had a hand two and a half times the size of mine. He was just a huge man."

The atmosphere at Shea Stadium was tremendous as both men made their way to a ring situated in the center of the baseball diamond. Most estimates pegged attendance for the second WWWF promoted "Showdown at Shea" at over 32,000. Wepner said it seemed like half that to him. It was still a big crowd and fans were getting two attractions for the price of one, featuring Andre the Giant, the most popular wrestler in the world, and Muhammad Ali, the greatest fighter in the world.

A precursor to Wrestlemania, the "Showdown at Shea" took place in 1972, 1976, and 1980. Bruno Sammartino headlined all three events, though he probably should not have in '76. Two and a half months earlier at Madison Square Garden, Stan Hansen slipped while executing a basic body slam and dropped Sammartino on his head, resulting in a broken neck. Nothing like that had happened before to Sammartino and the big wrestling hero wasn't in condition to do anything athletic as the bicentennial approached.

Doctors told Vince McMahon Sr. not to, but Shea Stadium was booked, and so were major arenas in the WWWF's territory throughout the Northeast. McMahon rang Sammartino, his long-reigning heavyweight champion, and told him that because of all the money locked up in this thing, if the promotion failed it meant they could be out of business. So Sammartino had to show up, especially since most of the people who turned up at Shea were there to see him.

Sammartino reluctantly agreed to take 3 precent of all the closed-circuit money but never saw a penny. McMahon eventually told him that Bob Arum, the boxing guy in the equation, messed up the deal. Regardless, the promoters got what they wanted. Sammartino sold some tickets and Wepner and the Giant romped on closed circuit.

It started out with putting on a show, then Wepner began belting Andre. He sidestepped the mammoth wrestler once, and hit him with a couple of rabbit punches. The Giant grew mad and threw a backhand that struck Wepner across the chest and the side of his face.

"Christ, it was like getting hit with a bat," Wepner said. "He was such a strong man. And then we picked it up a little bit. We gave them their money's worth. When he threw me outta the ring, I landed almost directly on the pitcher's mound in Shea Stadium because it was right there in the middle of the field."

When Andre the Giant faced Jersey's own Chuck Wepner, the crowd across the river at the Liberty Theater started buzzing. "Even though the Bayonne Bleeder was one of our own, my recollection was that the crowd was very heavily Andre," recalled Jeff Wagenheim. "And when the moment came when he picked up Wepner and threw him out of the ring, the whole theater went crazy."

"Every time Andre would wrap his hands around Wepner, the boxer would grab the ring rope, and that would prompt the ref to break them up. So not much was happening. So there was a little restlessness in the air, and the crowd's energy would kind of dip, and then Andre would grab hold of him and the crowd would rise and get all excited. But generally speaking it was not, it was kind of up and down. If that had been the main event, fans would have walked out of there feeling maybe a little disappointed there wasn't more action, but generally satisfied by the finish. Picking him up and throwing him out. Wepner was a big dude and he looked like a midget out there, so it was something exciting."

Gorilla Monsoon came over to Wepner and put his hand out. Monsoon was playing Andre the Giant's "manager" and a few weeks earlier, at 419 pounds, he had twirled Muhammad Ali in the air before tossing him to the canvas. Now Wepner thought Monsoon was going to help him back into the ring, but instead the bully wrestler pinned down the boxer on the infield with a size twenty boot to the chest. Needless to say, Wepner wasn't going to make it into the ring by the count of ten. Then, according to Wepner, the show turned real. Wepner's cornermen, easy to spot in their white satin jackets with "Don King" written in black lettering across the back, hustled to Wepner's aid, shoving ensued, and that's about all it took for a melee to break out.

In the ring in the middle of the fracas one of Wepner's seconds threw a punch that hit Andre the Giant in the shoulder. He broke his pinky and the next finger over on his right hand. A jaw was rearranged. Someone got knocked down. It was wild.

"I was like what the hell is going on here?" Wepner said. "It got very heated. Some of the wrestlers were jumping into the ring. Gorilla Monsoon was throwing guys around like rag dolls. It got heated and was finally broken up. I didn't want to get involved. We were in there to put on a show and give them a good time. A real fight over this? It was crazy."

More than two decades later, on March 28, 1999, Wepner appeared as the chief judge for a shoot fight at Wrestlemania XV.

"This was going to be another mixed martial arts bout," he said. "Well, Butterbean was gonna fight Tommy Gunn, one of their top wrestlers. It was in Philadelphia. They picked me up by limo and drove me and my wife down there. Before the bout I went in the dressing room. And I said to The Rock and, oh, the other champion, Steve Austin, I said, 'Butterbean is gonna knock your guy dead.' And they said, 'Get the fuck out of here. He'll take that fat bastard down and break his arm.'

"Vinny Pazienza was the referee for Wrestlemania XV. They come out and right away Butterbean, who weighed 330 pounds, by the way, came out and hit him about three shots and dropped Gunn. He staggered up at the count of five and Vinny is looking at me to wave the fight off. And I said *don't stop it.* Vinny's looking at me. He said the guy's defenseless. I said *no, don't worry about it.* Butterbean hit Gunn with an overhand right that picked him up off the ground, drove him through the ropes and out on to the scorer's table. And now he's absolutely unconscious.

"Butterbean destroyed him in half a minute. Now I go back into the dressing room. Vince is sitting there with The Rock. I grabbed myself on my crotch and said, 'Here's your gun!'

"The Rock had some shoes in there that were taken off. They were put out into the hallway. So I was standing by the door and I grabbed two—one from each pair—and I jumped into the limo and said to the driver *let's get outta here.* I ended up raffling off the shoes at a charity event in New York about a month later."

Between the end of the Wepner–Andre the Giant bout and the start of Ali–Inoki, Sammartino–Hansen went off for ten minutes at Shea, just enough time to lead up to the match in Japan. Sammartino was given a chance to beat up and bloody

Hansen, and he did. After Sammartino's New York faithful got to cheer for their guy, the lights dimmed as the projection of Ali–Inoki began on big screens inside the ballpark.

Sammartino had always wanted to fight Ali, and made several challenges in the 1960s. Despite his efforts, boxing people passed and Vince McMahon Sr. had no desire to do it either. Bruno resented Inoki for getting the opportunity and called the match with Ali "hogwash."

Standing along a guardrail near the pitcher's mound at Shea, Sammartino waited for the fight from Tokyo to start. Inoki's reputation among most pro wrestlers put him in the class of a tough guy, and he was thought capable of hurting someone if he had to. But Sammartino had been vocal in the media about calling Inoki a "third rater"—a fairly large insult to the Japanese wrestler—pining, some said, for the fight himself.

"It's absolutely ridiculous," Inoki responded through a spokesman. "Obviously Sammartino is envious that I'm fighting Ali and not him."

As the program for the closed circuit emphasized, the night was about boxer versus wrestler. And the main event was set to start.

Regarding the match, Inoki declared: "Ali may be the greatest boxer, but not the greatest in the martial arts, and that is what this bout is all about. Ali has been making a lot of derogatory comments about me and is not treating this fight seriously. Some of my fans are beginning to think this isn't a serious fight so now I must go out there and dispose of him in a manner that will show he is finished. I know I can break his leg or arm, whatever's necessary to win. And he's insulted me so much I will do that."

And Ali: "I'll whip Inoki bad. I've always wanted to take on a wrestler and now I'll be able to do it. Mark my words, Inoki will fall. One good right hand and it will be all over for him. I've stopped George Foreman, paralyzed Joe Frazier, and now I'm gonna use my explosive right-left combination on the chin of Inoki. When you can beat the toughest of the boxers in the world you can beat anybody and Inoki will fall like the rest."

Against Andre the Giant, Wepner knew what was coming. He also figured that the Ali–Inoki match would be show business.

"Come on, this guy Inoki is a legitimately tough guy," he said. "You're not gonna put him in there with the most famous man in the world and look for him to break his arm or legs."

Two weeks before Ali faced Inoki in Tokyo, "Toots" Mondt, who played a large role in innovating much of what Ali loved about wrestling, passed away at the age of eighty-two. Ahead of one of wrestling's biggest showcases, a boxer versus wrestler clash at that, the timing is worth noting.

ROUND ELEVEN

The Japanese tradition of handing out floral bouquets to combatants prior to an important bout is a tribute to the Rikidōzan era. Around noon on June 26, 1976, inside a steamy Nippon Budokan Hall, this practice was in full effect. In some sense the ceremony offered a sweet-smelling salve for the destruction that was potentially about to unfold—to the dead man walking, a bed of roses.

Following all the talk and hype, there remained a distinct unease as to what might happen between Muhammad Ali and Antonio Inoki. Crowds in venues throughout North America were buzzing, and the predominantly Japanese Budokan Hall audience, most of which had spent quite a lot of money to attend, was atypically noisy.

"It wasn't as loud as a Yomiuri Giants game, but it was loud," recalled Andrew Malcolm, the *New York Times* Tokyo bureau chief who sat fifteen rows from the ring. "I was worried whether they could hear me on the dictation machine in New York."

Despite the heat, neither heavyweight noticeably perspired as they left their respective locker rooms.

Wearing a brilliant purple robe trimmed in orange around the collar, Inoki strode through the crowd. The back of the robe was festooned with a mythological creature, the phoenix, giving an indication perhaps that there would be no giving up today no matter how many times Inoki went down. Flanked by coaches and seconds all wearing white shirts trimmed in red that had been tucked neatly into red pants, Inoki stepped into the ring, raised his right hand, and offered a 360-degree twirl for the crowd, which returned a warm applause. The Belgian catch wrestler Karl Gotch, former Olympic judo coach Seiji Sakaguchi, teacher of New Japan Pro Wrestling's "young boys" Kotetsu Yamamoto, and Kantaro Hoshino, an early star of the junior division, calmly stood by Inoki as he waited for Ali to appear.

Coming out second is generally reserved for champions or more established fighters, and thus it was appropriate for Ali to follow. Also wearing red and white in the form of a satin robe with ALI emblazoned above his heart and the Everlast logo, the boxer was surrounded by his entourage and handlers while smooth funk music greeted him inside the arena. "Classy" Freddie Blassie, the famous wrestler, donned a mustard-yellow shirt and brown cravat around his neck, almost a Western formal look. He was joined by Top Rank's Butch Lewis, Ali's manager Herbert Muhammad, the taekwondo man Jhoon Rhee, and, of course, the boxer's typical corner: trainer Angelo Dundee, Dr. Ferdie Pacheco, hypeman Drew "Bundini" Brown, and trainer Wali Muhammad.

Ali entered the ring gloveless, and gave a smile and a wink to a beautiful black woman who handed him flowers. Meanwhile, "Bundini" Brown, holding a bucket, moved to the middle of the ring and glared at Inoki. Visible on the back of Brown's white satin jacket, in red lettering:

**FLOAT LIKE A
BUTTERFLY
STING LIKE A
BEE**

ALI

Soon Dundee laced up Ali's specially made four-ounce Everlast gloves. First the left, then the right. All the while Ali stared across the ring and mimicked punching the wrestler.

"Trouble," he mouthed. "Trouble."

Inoki stood stoic in his corner, that pelican chin hanging so temptingly high.

The crowd grew louder as Ali, reveling in the speed his light gloves might afford him, unfurled punches in a neutral corner. Gotch, expressionless, joined Inoki in watching. A loud cheer boomed throughout the Budokan when Ali's name was announced. At the moment of his introduction, Inoki snapped off his robe, as was his typical prefight routine. He shared a knowing smile with Gotch while being wiped off with a red towel that had been hidden beneath his robe.

Referee "Judo" Gene LeBell brought the men to the center of the ring and made quick inspections of both. "You both know the rules, OK," LeBell said without a hint of irony since he would later admit to not really knowing them himself. "Shake hands and go back to your corners." Gotch stepped forward to examine Ali's gloves and the boxer responded by putting a fist near the mean catch wrestler's face. "It's fine," said Dundee, and Gotch mumbled something that made the veteran boxing man smile. Ali was less amused, and exchanged a few words and glances with Gotch, who surely would have loved a chance to get sadistic on the boxer.

"I'm going to send you back to your ancestors," Ali told Inoki.

LeBell said the wrestler was psyched out. "It seemed he got a little scared then," noted the referee.

They stared at one another before retreating to their corners. Ali kept jawing and Dundee did a fairly poor job of faking a need to restrain his charge. Inoki stood still as Gotch, who exited the ring last, patted him on the shoulder. Ali moved once more to the center as his corner filed out, but LeBell cut him off.

It was time—yet again—to see what might happen when a boxer fights a wrestler.

ROUND 1

Before Ali's cornermen could find their seats, Inoki hurled himself with a swinging kick towards the champ's left thigh. Ali absorbed the attack and made faces as he danced away. The most famous man on the planet ran to Inoki's corner and, like any American pro wrestler might, bounced back-first off the ropes.

Ali's inclination was to skirt around Inoki, who assumed a position on the canvas that would forever be derided as "crab-like." Brazilian jiu-jitsu competitors termed it the "butt-scoot," a boring but admittedly useful tool for any grappler with an aversion to taking punches from a standing opponent.

"When the fight first started, to see Inoki almost immediately get down in this crab position and start leg sweeping and kicking Ali's legs, the style of the fight was determined then," recalled Bobby Goodman, Ali's publicist for the fight, who also provided minimal analysis on the closed-circuit broadcast. "He didn't want to get hit by Ali, of course, and Ali didn't want this guy getting his hands on him."

Standing above Inoki, unsure what to do, Ali experimented by kicking Inoki's legs. Accomplishing little, the boxer leaned forward and gestured for Inoki to come at him—the first of many times he tried to goad Inoki into a mistake. Instead, the Japanese wrestler landed a solid kick that ruffled Ali's balance and drew cheers from the crowd.

Ali shuffled his feet and Inoki stood. "Now," Ali said as his eyes opened wide. "Now . . . Now." He wouldn't find what he was looking for because Inoki scored flush with a kick to Ali's left thigh. Moments later, after several swings and misses, Inoki scored with a strong side kick, which play-by-play man Frank Bannister acknowledged. So did Ali's corner. "Move away from him champ!" yelled "Bundini" Brown.

Ali asked Inoki to stand but the pro wrestler slammed home another kick, bringing a roar from the crowd and a shake of the head from the boxer, who raised his right arm as if to say, "No, I didn't feel nothing."

The bell tolled for the end of the opening period, and neither man looked at the other as they headed back to their teams.

"Well it's obvious to me, Frank, forget the rules, forget the prefight publicity, forget the ballyhoo. The gentleman from Japan is not fooling around," said Jerry Lisker, sports editor of the New York *Daily News*, who provided color commentary during the fight. "He's playing for keeps. Take a look at Muhammad's shins. They've been bloodied already. Now I don't know if Muhammad had anticipated the intensity of Mr. Inoki in the ring, however he realizes that he's not playing with a dead cobra. This is the mongoose and the cobra and everyone should watch out."

In San Jose, it was clear to Dave Meltzer and his pals "that this was not a pro wrestling match." Meanwhile at Monzo's Howard Johnson's outside of Pittsburgh, Kevin Iole wasn't sure what to make of it: "Like when you saw Inoki do that crab thing or whatever you want to call what he did, it was like, this guy seems to be doing some kind of strategy, but is it really true?"

A call came for the seconds to exit the ring and Ali jawed at Inoki: "You coward. Don't let the Japanese see you're a coward." Inoki dismissively waved his left hand and Gotch gave Ali a hard look out of the corner of his eye.

ROUND 2

"Ali's legs are in very much danger," Bannister noted after Inoki leapt forward with a side kick. Inoki swung, missed, and flopped to the floor. Dancing clockwise, Ali moved near the ropes when someone from the boxer's entourage screamed for Inoki to "get up." He did, leaning and crouching to the right, doing everything he could to remain out of range of Ali's punches.

"I just need to hit you once," Ali said in the ring. "One time."

Inoki missed with a kick and Ali mocked him, leaning forward, hands down at his thighs, sticking his tongue out.

"Muhammad Ali is joking and Antonio Inoki is serious," Bannister said.

Range is a notable factor in fights, and Ali played with range more than most fighters. At various stages of his career he could dance on the outside, keeping opponents on the ends of his punches, and move away while making them look amateurish. Other times, like 1974 in Zaire against George Foreman, he enticed them to work on the inside. It didn't take long before Ali thought he had figured out Inoki's kicking range, like he saw the attacks coming from a million miles away. Ali jumped to the side, mocked Inoki, and got a laugh from the crowd. Inoki stood, wound up, and missed big again. Ali, mouth agape, let out a yell and backed away.

"As the second round started to unfold, and it was the same as the first round, the boos started up," recalled Jeff Wagenheim, who watched the closed-circuit feed at the Liberty Theater in Elizabeth, New Jersey. "It was deafening and constant. People were beside themselves hating on this event that was happening. Even as it was happening in front of our eyes. But as much as people hated it, people stuck around in case something happened."

Inoki swung and missed and Ali made fun of him for it, producing the first confident words from Dundee: "Let him blow his stack, Muhammad."

"No more tonight," Ali said to Inoki. "No more tonight. Getting tired? Are you tired?"

Inoki headed to his corner after the period closed, and LeBell stepped in front of Ali, who kept coming at his opponent. It was more for show than anything else.

"It's very obvious that Muhammad Ali will not be sucked into Inoki's tactics," Goodman said on the broadcast. "He will not get on the canvas and he's trying to stay away from the center of the ring."

Said Bannister: "Muhammad Ali knows what he has to do and he's confident now."

Between rounds Ali shook his fist in the air and berated Inoki: "He's afraid. He's a coward. A coward. Coward in Tokyo. All your people see you, coward on the floor."

Dundee asked LeBell to inspect Inoki's shoes. He did, and everyone was satisfied for the moment.

ROUND 3

"A coward in Tokyo!"

That's how Ali greeted Inoki to begin the third. *No one wants to see this! Get up off the floor and fight like a man!* This was the gist of what Ali was getting at. "It's the same every time," Ali said after Inoki missed a kick and dropped into a heap on the canvas. "We can do this all night."

From a sideways stance, leaning to the right, his right hand shaking a bit, Inoki didn't care and continued with his plan of attack.

"He can't understand you," yelled "Bundini" Brown, who scolded Ali for getting too close to the ropes—this despite the fact that touching the ropes was a lifesaver requiring LeBell to separate the fighters.

"Don't worry about it!" Ali snapped back.

Brown: "Give yourself room to move."

Ali: "Don't worry about it!"

A half-hearted flop by Inoki ramped up Ali's frustration. "Ah, you're tired, huh?" said the boxer, who moved forward against the advice of his camp and took a kick to the inside of his left leg.

"One lick. One lick," Ali crowed. "I gotta get one. I gotta get one."

From Ali's corner came advice to take his time and leave the hard work to Inoki, who responded with kicks to the right side of Ali's hip and the inside of his left leg. Again "Bundini" Brown raised his voice.

Ali turned vicious.

"Shut up motherfucker," Ali yelled. "Shut up motherfucker. I got this sucker. I got this faggot. I got this homosexual faggot."

If Brown was correct and Inoki couldn't understand what was being said—by most accounts he could have because his English was more than suitable at the time—he, like any lucid person, would have recognized the tension in the boxer's voice. While Ali may have been clowning around before, his tone now was of someone not to be trifled with.

"You could see the frustration in Ali when he acted out of character," Goodman said as he recalled the event years later. "There were some times in fights when Ali would turn his mean switch on, like when he fought Ernie Terrell and he meant to do some damage. And he did."

A member of Ali's entourage seated ringside meekly tried to placate the champ: "Kick him in the thigh, Ali." Inoki was the one doing the kicking, though, and after several swings and misses he dug a shin into Ali's rapidly tenderizing left quadriceps. Another hard shot followed, eliciting "oohs" from a crowd begging for action. Ali danced to close the third.

"It's very difficult to score this match against a completely unorthodox combatant," Lisker said. "However if we watch closely at Muhammad's shins, this is Inoki's obvious plan. To slow down Ali's legs by kicking him, which is illegal under the rules unless the kicks are made with the side of the foot soccer style. Now he has not adhered to this. He has also kicked low in the groin area more than once."

Lisker was calling it very tight, as there had not been any obvious low blows to that point. Regarding kicks, both men had landed with the points of their shoes. Ali's corner became disgruntled, and Dundee shouted to LeBell that he failed to start a count whenever Inoki hit the floor.

"You gotta count, Gene," yelled the trainer. "What's he gonna do, jerk off all night? It's ridiculous."

"Only if the shoulders are on the canvas," responded LeBell.

In the opposite corner, Karl Gotch was dying to respond but kept quiet.

Meanwhile Ali kept up his verbal attack. To that point he hadn't mustered a physical one, throwing exactly zero punches. This fight, though, wasn't going to be won or lost based on punch output.

"One punch. One punch. I want one punch," Ali said. "I'll slap you, coward. You slack-bellied coward."

ROUND 4

Ali walked to the center of the ring shaking a fist in the air. Inoki greeted him. Action had been slow to materialize, with no real sense that a fight was about to break out, but it was still early. That unexpected moment people expected remained lurking in the shadows.

Inoki missed on a jumping side kick, then crab-walked towards Ali. "Get out of that corner!" yelled Brown. But this is where Ali wanted to be. He placed his glove-covered hands on the ropes, pressed up as if doing body-weight exercises, and flailed his legs like Quint had against Jaws, the killer great white shark that terrified audiences in movie houses the previous summer.

LeBell jumped between the fighters. "Break, break, break, break! Break!" he roared.

Inoki delivered a cheap low kick between LeBell's legs that connected to Ali's right shin, causing LeBell to raise his voice. "Wait! Wait!" shouted the referee. Ali made like he was going to go after Inoki and turn it into a street fight. He stuck out his tongue and rammed his chest into LeBell's back. "Hold it!" demanded the 180-pound official, who was seemingly capable of beating either fighter in a one-on-one contest. LeBell swiveled towards Ali, turned 180 degrees to face Inoki, then restarted the action after the boxer extracted himself from the corner.

"OK," LeBell said, "wrestle!" Instead, Inoki swung and missed with this right leg. Ali's frustration boiled over. "I thought Inoki could wrestle!" he screamed. "I thought Inoki could wrestle! I thought Inoki could wrestle! I thought Inoki could wrestle!" Inoki followed with a kick that nearly reached Ali's chin, drawing complaints from the boxer's corner. "That's a foul, Gene," said Dundee. Color commentator Jerry Lisker agreed. In broken English, Ali decided to make his case to the crowd: "Inoki cannot wrestle. No wrestle. No wrestle." With that Inoki stood and Ali smiled. "Now," said Ali, waving on the Japanese fighter. "Inoki cannot wrestle. Inoki sissy. Inoki girl. Inoki girl. Inoki girl lady. Lady fight on floor. Man stand up and fight! Man fight."

Inoki made a windmill motion with his hands. Ali sized him up, stepping side to side.

"Crack him and pack him, Ali," yelled "Bundini" Brown. "Knock him out. Knock him out!"

Again Ali started in on Inoki, calling him a girl just as the thirty-three-year-old face of Japanese professional wrestling thumped another kick off Ali's left thigh. Inoki followed with a push kick to the same leg, and then a double push kick. Ali didn't like any of this, so he supported his weight in a neutral corner and his legs dangled off the floor. The boxer's team, including his advisor Gene Kilroy, went mad as Ali pressed himself into the air. LeBell stepped between them and sat on Inoki's knees. Ali's mouth opened as wide as it could, and he stepped off the ropes. The crowd loved this.

At the sound of the bell ending the fourth, Ali stood up straight and stared at his opponent: "Inoki girl. On the floor. Fight on floor like girl." With that LeBell walked the heavyweight champion to his corner. Ali turned and raised his glove. "Inoki girl," he repeated before pointing to the floor and waving his glove. "On the floor. No man." To the Japanese crowd, Ali hammered home his point. "Fight on floor like sissy," he said. "Man stand up. Man stand up. Man stand up. Inoki girl. Man stand up. Inoki afraid. Inoki afraid. Inoki afraid."

Ali paced around his side of the ring. Meanwhile, Inoki stood quietly in his corner getting toweled off.

"Well it seems to me that the referee is allowing Inoki to get away with more than just a casual breaking of the rules," Lisker said. "Now I have counted seven times where Ali's been kicked to the groin area. It is absolutely essential for the referee to watch those kicks to the groin. Ali's ploy to call him a sissy, an old man, an affront to the masculine gender has obviously [not worked]. He wants Inoki on his feet."

Ali continued with his histrionics in the center of the ring, and LeBell stepped between them before the commencement of the next round.

ROUND 5

"Muhammad Ali has not thrown a punch," Bannister told audiences back in the U.S., who needed no reminder as they grew increasingly restless. "This is about the longest he's gone in his boxing career without throwing a punch. But this is different."

Indeed.

Inoki launched himself towards Ali and slammed a kick into the boxer's lead leg. That's "lead" as in "forward," not the bluish-gray soft metal listed on the periodic table, although as the kicks added up and Ali's capillaries began to burst, the champ's puffed-up thigh must have felt heavier than normal. The hard blow knocked Ali off his feet, propelling the crowd to life. Ali bolted off the canvas and Inoki lurched forward, wildly taking an illegal bare-fisted swing with his left hand that nearly connected. Inoki picked up his aggression. Ali responded by dancing away and making him miss. The crowd roared "Ali! Ali! Ali!" and the boxer raised his right arm asking for more. Following another leg salvo, Bannister made mention of the accumulating welts and blood on Ali's shins.

When a kick or a punch really stings, some fighters act like it didn't hurt at all. Almost an involuntary response, like blinking. The next kick Inoki landed made Ali dance to his left and wave away the strike as if it were a gnat. But he felt that one and responded by talking again.

"Inoki fight like coward tonight," he said. "The Japanese people see Inoki not so great."

Inoki wasn't necessarily happy with the fight to this point. How could he be? He was being berated in front of his people and made to look ineffectual when in fact he found some success in a situation that was designed to hamstring him against the greatest boxer on the planet. "Bundini" Brown called for Ali to hit Inoki on that big chin, but another solid kick, this time to the back of Ali's left thigh, forced the man from Louisville to dance out of a corner. Brown stood, not liking what he saw, and placed a hand on Dundee's right shoulder. Inoki crawled towards Ali, kicking the inside of his left calf until the boxer grabbed the Japanese wrestler and dragged him a few inches before the bell sounded.

For the first time at the conclusion of a round, Budokan Hall offered some appreciation with applause.

"Now I think the trainer is going to have to start looking at the blood on Muhammad Ali's legs," Bannister suggested, "and Angelo Dundee is checking that right now."

From his seat at ringside, Jerry Lisker didn't like the looks of Ali's leg either: "It is badly bruised. It is red. It is raw. And I don't know how long those beautiful legs of Muhammad are going to be able to take these kicks."

ROUND 6

The first third of the fifteen-round affair had, so far, been a dud, which is why Ali could say things like the "Japanese see a coward" and come off reasonably fair.

Ali predicted an eighth-round finish of Inoki, yet thus far he gave no indication of how that might happen. To find his finishing punch he needed to actually throw one. Meanwhile, Inoki kept to what was working and began the most interesting stretch of the fight with a side kick that concluded with him crawling on the canvas again. The wrestler wasn't wrestling much, nor was he standing and striking, but he was safe from everything save Ali's words.

A kick to Ali's groin prompted LeBell to remind Inoki that he could not connect with his toe, only the top of a foot that was wrapped in a wrestling boot laced up to the middle of his shins. From the stands someone yelled, "That's a foul," to which Ali offered encouragement. "Every time he fouls you tell them," said the boxer, whose front thigh absorbed another heavy shot, fair and square, causing him to dance the cha-cha.

From Ali's corner came a call to move to the right, to move away. Inoki, however, had his range dialed in, and as Ali heeded the advice another kick cut into the boxer's thigh. Ali pursed his lips and made a face as if to say no, that hadn't hurt. Of course, it did.

With Ali standing directly over him, Inoki took hold of the back of the boxer's left shoe while thrusting his hips up and forward. As if he was a child Ali tumbled to the canvas, showing just how little balance he possessed when a man his size wished to sweep him off his feet. The crowd screamed because Ali was on his back and Inoki was sitting on him.

"This is what the people have been waiting for," Bannister said.

So excited was a white-and-red clad member of Inoki's team that he nearly jumped into the ring. Well aware of the danger, Ali grabbed around Inoki's waist and slung his right leg over the bottom rope, a prudent play that was all LeBell needed to break the fighters apart and restart them on their feet. However Inoki wasn't going to let Ali get away without taking at least one good shot. Facing the boxer's feet, Inoki uncorked a blatantly illegal backwards elbow that bounced off Ali's forehead. Dundee and Brown jumped onto the apron, yelling obscenities while pointing at Inoki.

"That's illegal! That's illegal!" Dundee screamed. He mimicked the elbow and called Inoki a "son of a bitch."

Rescued by the rules and the referee, Ali stood with a look on his face that gave every indication of how pissed he really was. LeBell took a double take as Ali expressed his displeasure. The boxer touched the right side of his head with his right glove and noted, for the record, "it was an elbow." From ringside, members of Ali's entourage howled: "That's a foul, you son of a bitch. That's a foul."

Inoki was unfazed. The ropes saved Ali, and he knew that. He couldn't have locked in a submission even if he wanted—and there were several available to him. So he enjoyed his cheap shot and strolled to the center of the ring.

LeBell called for action to resume but Ali protested. "You gotta take a point off," Ali said. LeBell walked to Inoki, explained that elbows are a no-no and attempted to restart again. Ali didn't budge. He stared at Inoki and made a downward elbow motion with his right arm while shaking his head "no." For clarification, LeBell touched his tricep as if to say that's fine, then did the same with the point of his elbow and said this is not.

In Inoki's corner, the big Belgian Karl Gotch was as animated as he'd been all fight. "Make him come down!" he bellowed. "Make him come down!" Gotch wanted nothing more than to twist Ali into an assortment of knots, and it was unfathomable to him that in more than fifteen minutes of action Inoki had not yet done so. As the bout resumed, Ali looked intent on hurting Inoki. They mixed it up in one of the corners and were separated again when Ali used the ropes for offense as he kicked down at Inoki. "Hold it! Hold it!" said LeBell. "You can't do this when you attack." Ali didn't move from his spot and waved Inoki forward. His expression changed. "I'm a nigga," he said, before uttering something about black people.

The sixth and most eventful round of the fight came to a close.

"Ali wanted Inoki to stand up," Bannister said. "Now a lot of people know how hard it is to get to the head of the wrestler, especially when he's able to lay down on his back and score points."

For the illegal elbow, LeBell notified both judges scoring with him that he deducted a point.

"Ali has not thrown a single punch all evening," Jerry Lisker said. "Inoki seems to be getting stronger. The back of Muhammad's left leg is so damn livid and angry. If he would only go to the left and receive the brunt of the kick on the other leg, which he hasn't done. Inoki seems much more confident now. He seems to be able to reach Ali with his kicks better and better. And more and more each round. Ali has got to land a punch."

Ali yelled once from his corner: "Coward!"

ROUND 7

Ali was a magical boxer, smooth and graceful, effortless in his speed and power. As a kicker, not so much. What he hoped most to do during the fight was hit a man while he was down. That's what he said leading up to the bout, at least. Yet when the seventh frame began, to the relief of Kilroy, Ali ignored Inoki's requests to join him on the ground. "Don't go down into his game," Kilroy screamed from his seat at ringside. "Make him come up to your game." He can't be blamed considering Inoki's reputation as an arm and leg twister. Instead, Ali offloaded ineffectual silly kicks that brought groans and grumbles from fans who spent their time and money to participate.

Then it happened.

Ali produced a punch, a long jab that came from too far to carry much pop. But it was what his supporters desperately wanted to see. "That's good," came a yell from the crowd. "That's good, Ali. That's it!" Inoki refused to allow Ali to gain any punching momentum and sent a message with a heavy sweeping kick that knocked the champ clean off his feet. This produced a big cheer from the crowd and looks of concern among Ali's cornermen. Dr. Ferdie Pacheco, in particular, perked up and appeared disgusted. Ali seemed as if he wanted to jab again, but after being swept to the floor he didn't fully commit. Chants of "Ali! Ali! Ali!" once again rose in the crowd. Inoki put an end to that with a strong forward burst and a hard kick that produced a loud smack.

"Muhammad Ali has a lot of welts, blood, and scratches on his left leg," Bannister noted. "That is the leg Inoki is working on with Muhammad Ali. Ali has to find some kind of way to make some kind of range to hit Inoki."

Between rounds Pacheco got to work rubbing down Ali's left thigh with ice and ointment.

"Dr. Pacheco is keeping very close watch on it," Lisker said. "He just asked Ali if he was getting much pain."

Then Angelo Dundee slid through the ropes and walked over to Inoki's corner. Speaking with Karl Gotch, Dundee wanted the toe of Inoki's right shoe covered with tape. Frank Bannister said on the broadcast that there was concern over a "foreign substance," but that was wrong. Inoki's constant kicking had detached the top of the sole on his left boot from the leather, making it protrude and create a razor-blade effect.

"There is a brass eyelet missing from one of the laces on Inoki's shoes," Lisker also indicated. "Angelo Dundee wants the open eyelet to be closed so it can't cut and scratch into Ali's legs, which it evidently has done. Now they're going to tape it. Score one for Angelo."

ROUND 8

By the midway point of the bout, its pattern was all too familiar. As was a restlessness among fans watching on screens across the U.S. Inoki continued to throw himself towards Ali's left leg. If he connected, fine. If not, he remained relatively safe.

"My uncle was a real sports fan," recalled William Viola Sr., the martial artist out of Pittsburgh. "After the seventh round he said to me, 'If you wanna go anytime early, let me know.' Everyone knew. It was bad. Really bad. Even the people in the crowd, this is strange, imagine this. When you boo, you boo someone live. They were booing closed-circuit. I couldn't believe that."

Ali predicted Round 8 was when he would put an end to the Japanese wrestler, but by the looks of things a lightning strike would be needed to make that happen. Inoki feinted as action got underway, then launched a kick with the toe of his left boot that dug into Ali's thigh. Another kick below the inside of the boxer's left knee cost Ali his balance, though he quickly popped up and mocked the man on the floor.

Out of position, LeBell missed that it was a clean kick and cautioned Inoki "not in the balls." A missed high kick to Ali's chin prompted another warning. "You can't do that," LeBell said, wildly shaking his head no, making his ginger hair dance, as Ali watched from his corner.

"It's hard for these fighters to adjust to these rules because these rules are new to them," Bannister said. "You can believe Muhammad Ali, being the heavyweight champion of the world, has already signed a contract to defend his title at Yankee Stadium on the 28th of September with Ken Norton; his corner is going to be watching every move that he makes. And they do not want Muhammad Ali to get hurt."

The boot issue also became a nuisance. LeBell was forced to halt the fight several times to apply tape to Inoki's sole. Inoki waved his arms in frustration. "Oh Gene!" he said. Bannister suggested he wouldn't be surprised if the match was stopped so Inoki could change boots, but that didn't happen. Any delay would have turned what was an unbearable contest to most observers into an unmitigated disaster. The tedious eighth ended with a disgusted Ali saying, "Nothing. Inoki nothing!"

Angelo Dundee and the rest of Ali's corner were obviously concerned as they inspected the fighter's banged-up wheel. That mattered much more than, as Bannister put it, the possibility "at this point Inoki—Inoki!—may just be ahead of Muhammad Ali on points as we go into Round number 9." Meanwhile, Ali berated Inoki from across the ring. "Stand up like man," he yelled. "Fight! Stand up like man. Fight! Inoki don't fight like man. Inoki fight like cripple. Coward! Inoki coward! Fight on floor like girl."

ROUND 9

Ali's left thigh, never before feeling the wrath kicks can bring, was swollen and sweating and just a mess as the fight resumed. Most people watching around the world may not have understood the impact of Inoki's strategy, but that didn't mean it was ineffective.

"Ali now has to be on the defense and wait to land a punch," Bannister said as the fighters squared off. "One man, fast, quick and strong with his feet. The other man, fast, quick and strong with his hands."

Crouched low, Ali feinted with jabs and danced. The familiar chant of "Ali! Ali! Ali!" rekindled when a group of women made their presence known. Ali danced and moved, finding life in the rhythmic chanting of his name. The arena sensed this. Ali moved back and to his left while Inoki remained stationary in the center of the ring. Ali traced the ropes like hands on a clock, prompting Inoki to hop to his right to cut off the boxer's path.

Ali "is trying to get Inoki to follow him so that he can get him into hitting range," noted Bannister. No luck. Inoki plowed forward with a hard leg kick that knocked Ali off kilter and sent him tumbling towards his corner. The crowd roared as Dundee, Pacheco, Brown, and others watched in silence while their man struggled in unfamiliar territory. Ali slid to the ropes, felt another kick coming but couldn't scurry out of the way. It slammed into the rear of his left leg, connecting more to the hamstring than quadriceps. Ali stumbled once more and Budokan Hall reacted as if that one must have hurt.

"Inoki is sticking to the Japanese principle: Wait for his best chance," surmised Bannister. "Inoki has kept his head out of range from Muhammad Ali for the entire match."

Despite the repeated attacks, Ali danced to the bell. He danced after the bell, too, then strolled to his corner upset at what was unfolding.

ROUND 10

Ali's corner massaged and iced their man's screaming thigh. Everyone knew what was coming and Inoki initiated more of the same at the start of the tenth.

Then Ali popped off a stiff jab and quickly moved away.

"Oh, Inoki was hit!" cheered Bannister. "A good smash by Ali."

Lisker confirmed: "A good smash to the mouth."

Inoki froze for a brief moment. This is what Ali felt he could accomplish against a wrestler. Dance. Pop off a jab or a right cross. Use his speed to exit. It had not, to this point, happened often enough to make a difference in the fight. Moving to the left meant exposing his front leg to more hits, which Inoki took advantage of as he dug in a hard one a few feet from Karl Gotch. Ali made off as if he didn't feel it, shook his head, and waved Inoki towards him. As Inoki rose to his feet, Ali, again, shook his head.

"Now the fans are yelling to Inoki, 'Be fair. Fight on your feet,'" Bannister indicated. "So the fans here in Tokyo want to see a good fight."

Perhaps Inoki had not heard them. Perhaps he didn't care. Perhaps no one in Tokyo other than Ali's minions wanted the Japanese fighter to stand in front of the best heavyweight boxer on the planet. So Inoki lunged in, landed low to the left thigh, scooted forward and kicked to the inside of Ali's same leg. Swollen, lumped up, and only getting worse, Ali was knocked around. He wrapped his right arm over the top rope to regain sure footing and Inoki picked this moment to surge forward. Finally, the rassler wanted to grapple. Ali launched a sneaky left hook underneath Inoki's right arm that just missed, and since the boxer was tangled in the ropes it was, beyond charging up the crowd, a useless takedown effort. Gotch reached up to touch Ali's gloved right hand, as if to gently shoo away a fly.

There were brief respites from the monotony of Inoki's leg attack, and this ranked among the notable ones. The round ended as Inoki walked the boxer into a corner and scored again. Ali appeared to be bored by the whole thing. From the crowd came a demand: "Inoki you sissy, get up off the floor!" Someone, presumably Ali or LeBell, would need to make him, and that seemed highly unlikely through the thirty-minute mark.

Dundee closely inspected Ali's left leg as he rubbed it down with ice and a salve before passing off that duty to Pacheco. "Bundini" Brown, meanwhile, gingerly took a sponge to Ali's right leg, which was far less damaged but had felt the brunt of Inoki's kicks as well.

"There are a lot of worried faces in that corner," Lisker pointed out.

ROUND 11

The swelling around Ali's left thigh was as severe as it would get, so much so that he finally attempted more than simply sidestepping Inoki's kicks or relying on the ropes for an escape.

A thudding strike from Inoki was partially blocked when Ali dropped his left hand into its path. The tactic, a suggestion in the corner from Ali's taekwondo instructor Jhoon Rhee, didn't come without its own dangers. "I didn't say anything before that because I didn't know what to expect," Rhee said. "I wanted to see how they fight and then I'd give them advice. My advice was to block." Saving his bursting blood vessels from painful leg kicks meant exposing his hand, wrist, and elbow to the full force of a heavy boot.

"When Inoki was throwing kicks, Jhoon Rhee said, 'Block them like you'd block a punch,'" remembered Gene Kilroy. "So Ali started putting his elbow and hand down."

The self-defense technique also allowed Ali a chance to grab and twist Inoki's foot nearly 180 degrees. By itself the move accomplished nothing, and it was clear that Ali wasn't aware that for twisting leg locks to work the knee had to be isolated so pressure on the joints wouldn't be released.

A camera zoomed in tight to Ali's left thigh, which appeared lumped, scratched, and bloody. Inoki slammed another unblocked kick into Ali, who flinched and didn't commit to blocking. The tally was running high and Bannister noted discoloration in Ali's leg. Next time he did get his hand in the path of the kick, and Ali was pleased that it worked. Like a golfer taking practice swings, he mimicked the move while Inoki scooted towards him. Ali decided against blocking the next time, throwing a swift counter jab instead that missed. For the price of a counter attack, Ali felt the full impact of Inoki's boot.

That was it for Round 11. Pacheco, Dundee, and Brown attempted to soothe Ali's left leg as best they could, immediately applying ice to the raised, damaged skin.

Jerry Lisker picked up on a conversation in Inoki's corner. Karl Gotch, who was as frustrated as anyone that the match had not concluded on the mat yet, told Inoki "to go in for the kill," Lisker said. "He feels Muhammad's legs can't stand the battering anymore and if he can get him down this round with a kick, with a crescent kick, and stay on top of him then he can finish it this round."

Inoki nodded.

ROUND 12

"I saw Inoki, and Karl Gotch was in his corner, and Karl said, 'Tackle him and take him down and it's in your backyard,'" LeBell remembered. "Ali's corner said to knock him out."

Ali deflected the first kick, posed, and practiced the downward block. He followed with another strong chop that intersected an Inoki kick. The boxer's confidence was brewing. "That's right!" yelled a member of the champ's camp. "That's right!" Ali backed away and blocked the next one as Inoki rushed at him—perfect defense. Ali quickly became cocky, as if he'd discovered a secret and everything would work itself out in his favor.

After Ali waved Inoki forward, the wrestler altered his rhythm and fired off a kick that connected. Ali had mistimed the deflection. "You can see these kicks are hurting

Muhammad Ali just a little bit," Bannister noted. "You can see his facial expressions when the kick is coming." Inoki walked towards Ali giving the boxer hope that the wrestler might stand in front of him for a moment and provide a window to punch. "Come on," mouthed Ali. "Come on." The boxer's left arm hung low just off his thigh, and he blocked down as Inoki attacked. The defense worked and Ali was pleased with himself. Again he practiced the motion, but this time Inoki switched it up and scored to the inside of Ali's left leg.

From a standing position, Inoki connected on a rare shin-to-thigh kick, drawing immediate objections from Ali's corner. "Hey, hey, hey!" someone yelled. "He's standing on his feet. No kicking!" Bannister noted that according to the rules, Inoki was barred from doing this. But if Inoki was going to anyhow, Dundee realized right away that it opened him up to getting countered so he called for Ali to throw a right hand over the top. Inoki refused to give him the chance and dove in low, as he had most of the contest. The hard kick was blocked, Inoki butt-scooted towards Ali, and the boxer waved at him.

As the round came to its conclusion, Ali stood straight and square to Inoki, put his gloves on his hips, and moved his mouth while shaking his head side to side, like a child on the verge of a tantrum. Beyond that, neither fighter acknowledged the other as they headed back to their corners sans the finish Gotch hoped for.

Ali's early talking had quieted down, and his left leg appeared to be double the size of his right.

"Inoki is landing some very hard shots," Bannister said. "This has to hurt Muhammad Ali some. I know they're totally concerned about this because once any fighter, or any athlete, loses the use and flexibility of his legs he slows down quite a bit. Ali cannot afford an injury, a mysterious injury, at this point in his career."

ROUND 13

Inoki established himself as the aggressor off the top of Round 13, taking the center of the ring while Ali hung tight in his corner. Angelo Dundee and "Bundini" Brown stood on the apron until Ali finally strolled to his right. Ali travelled to a neutral corner, and Inoki assumed a low stance.

Rather than doing what he'd done all night, Inoki just sort of rushed forward and grabbed hold of Ali. It would be wrong to call this a takedown attempt in any real sense of the word. Inoki's technique was terrible and Ali was already against the ropes, so there wasn't much to be accomplished as LeBell rushed in to separate them. The de-clinching didn't happen right away. Ali turned his head towards the crowd, amused, and stuck out his tongue. Pushing Ali's left hand away, Inoki backed out slowly, like he had managed to navigate and exit a maze.

Ali leaned forward, touched his left elbow with his right glove, and made it clear that he was prepared to block Inoki's next kick. He wouldn't have to, as the Japanese wrestler swung and missed. Herbert Muhammad began yelling from the corner. Dundee rested his elbows against the apron, pensively gripping his hands together. The rest of the team shared a mix of concern and irritation that they even had to be in this position.

Then, again, this time from the center of the ring, Inoki faked a kick and charged at Ali, clasping his hands around the boxer's waist as if he was ready to toss the champ Greco-Roman style. Ali adeptly backpedalled near Inoki's corner and wrapped his right arm around the top rope while his left covered the wrestler's neck.

"Inoki tries to take him out with another body slam and Ali holds onto the ropes," Bannister shouted into his microphone. "The referee is trying to break them apart."

For the first time since before the opening bell, when both camps met in the center of the ring for LeBell's instructions, Ali and Gotch made eye contact. The boxer raised his right fist like he might strike down at Gotch, which certainly would have made things more interesting.

"It's a fair break," said LeBell.

In boxing, a clinch often results in the bigger man putting his weight on the smaller man. Over the course of several rounds, this can be an effective strategy because it's incredibly taxing. Ali had few occasions to work inside the clinch with Inoki, but this time he decided to lean onto the neck of Inoki, who was hardly pleased, and responded with an illegal knee to the groin. Like the elbow in Round 6, it was blatantly illegal. Since knees and groin strikes were prohibited, LeBell gave Inoki a long look as Ali walked to his corner and pointed low. LeBell called time and spoke to Inoki about the cheap shot. Dundee was livid, wagging his finger at Inoki. Brown was also worked up. Ali, meanwhile, relaxed among his cornermen, that damaged leg propped up on the bottom rope. He shook his head at the sudden foul play.

"He kicked below the belt, to the groin!" Brown howled as LeBell walked towards the Ali corner. "He kicked to the groin! He kicked to the groin!"

Ali had his own thoughts, telling LeBell the low blow was "bullshit, motherfucker. That's horrible."

All the referee could do—or all he decided to do—was ask if Ali could continue. The fighter looked incredulous and ducked under the ropes, making it seem like he was done for the night. The crowd screamed. "Ali is gonna leave the ring," Bannister said. "Ali refuses to keep fighting with the action going the way it is." Jerry Lisker said Ali wanted assurances he would not be kneed in the groin again, as if such a thing were possible.

LeBell then pulled Ali back into the ring: "Get back in here," said the stuntman, "I've got money on you." It was a joke and Ali didn't laugh. Dundee and Brown sat as Pacheco talked to them. Gotch stood on the ring apron, waiting just in case all hell broke loose and he would get to twist someone into a knot.

Soon the fighters met in the center of the ring, and Inoki rekindled the action by offering a standing low kick that Ali blocked. The boxer, still angry, popped off a glancing jab. Then he tossed out a better one, which got the crowd going. Inoki flopped to the ground on a missed low kick, and scooted towards the champ as the bell closed a wild three minutes.

Ali immediately targeted LeBell, who walked over to the other officials and deducted a point from Inoki.

"Low blow," he yelled. "One point. Down."

Ali's team—the boxing folks plus Freddie Blassie and Jhoon Rhee—closed ranks around their man. Inoki and his crew, especially Gotch, stared in Ali's direction.

ROUND 14

Though the damage to his leg was severe, it didn't prevent Ali from moving on his toes at the start of the penultimate round. Half-hearted jabs, or rather the hint of jabs, came from Inoki before he dropped levels, kicked, and fell to the floor. Ali acted as if he didn't feel the strike and reiterated that by patting his left thigh with his left glove, waving "no" with his right glove, and shaking his head to the effect of "nah." The swelling in Ali's left leg moved from his thigh to above and below his knee; meanwhile, those jabs that Ali had tossed out in the thirteenth round prompted a bit of swelling around Inoki's left eye.

Ali hadn't thrown his right hand all night, yet a call came from his corner to toss one out. He wouldn't. Instead, after a couple of missed kicks by Inoki the boxer moved to the ropes, prompting the wrestler to complain. Pointing to the ropes then the floor, Inoki communicated with LeBell. Ali stood straight up, mocking Inoki by pointing to the floor as well.

"I'm the boxer," Ali said, suggesting that he was free to do as he pleased along the ropes.

"Yeah, tell 'em," Brown chimed in. "You tell 'em."

Inoki's late frustration was odd considering the opportunities he didn't make for himself or capitalize on, but nonetheless the Japanese fighter stood and gestured with his hands before pointing to the ground. Ali, wide-eyed, hands low, was quick to respond. "You lay down," he said before squaring up and letting out a yell that made "Bundini" Brown hop up and down in the corner. Both men postured, asking the other to go where they did not want.

"Lots of people would have thought that Inoki would have thrown Ali out of the ring by now," Bannister said.

At that moment Ali snapped off a stiff jab, and the second-to-last round came to an end.

"That was an excellent left smash," Lisker said, "the best punch that Ali's thrown all night . . . and it took a little of the starch out of Inoki. Evidently Ali is believing that Inoki is going to abandon all caution, get up off his back, and try to go wrestle and fight and throw Ali out of the ring. This is what Ali wants him to do. To fight on his feet where Ali can hit him."

Said Bannister: "And the crowd is also hollering, Jerry. 'Inoki, fight like a man. Inoki, don't be cheap.' So they're saying they don't want Inoki to cheat them. I still see they're working on Muhammad Ali's leg. There's lots of swelling in that left knee there. They've put ice packs on it ever since the second round, and it's continued to swell. So this is the fifteenth and final round."

ROUND 15

Sportsmen that they were, Ali and Inoki walked to the center and exchanged a handshake before the bell for Round 15. The crowd, still waiting for that magical moment, roared in anticipation that something, anything, might happen. Then

Inoki lunged in with a low kick to Ali's thigh. Ali didn't react outside of reminding Inoki that this was it.

"Last round," he said. "Fight."

Bannister managed to get out another promo for the Norton affair at Yankee Stadium on September 28, and offered this thought: "Ali has surprised a lot of people going fifteen rounds with the heavyweight champion of the world in wrestling, Antonio Inoki."

Ali began talking, then the wrestler continued with what was working, plowing a hard low kick to Ali's left leg.

"Come on, last round," yelled LeBell. "Make it go, go, go!"

Ali nearly smiled at the suggestion, looked at LeBell, and pointed: "You go."

"It's been a bizarre night," suggested Jerry Lisker. "It's been a night Ali will never forget. Certainly the fans in attendance here will never forget. And maybe it wasn't what they expected. But perhaps they're seeing something that they've never seen before and will probably never see again."

(Of course they would, and two decades later the tale of mixed-style fighting in America through the Ultimate Fighting Championship would just be getting underway.)

"Inoki is teeing off like an American football kicker, Garo Yepremian, putting his leg into a forty-five-yard field try," Lisker continued.

One last time Inoki plunged forward with a kick, but Ali managed to pick him off with a perfectly timed counter jab that halted the wrestler and dropped him on the canvas. The punch drew cheers from Ali's camp, though Inoki sprang to his feet ahead of the final bell.

An hour after it began, it was done.

★ ★ ★ ★ ★

Punch totals were Inoki, 0–3, and Ali, 4–7. Every other strike landed was a kick, except for a dirty knee by Inoki from the clinch in Round 13. Only one takedown was attempted, also by Inoki in the eventful thirteenth.

Inoki scored once to the head and three times to the body. Ali connected with four punches to the head and none to the body.

Nearly all strikes landed were to the legs. Ali took 107 kicks, and Inoki felt 49 from the boxer.

According to FightMetric, pioneers in MMA statistics and analysis and the first to take a comprehensive, analytical approach in combat sports, only six of Ali's nine strikes are considered "significant," in that they came with power. Inoki, meanwhile, is credited with landing 78 of 123 significant attacks.

ROUND TWELVE

Muhammad Ali extended his right hand.

During fifteen rounds with Antonio Inoki, not once had Ali thrown a proper power punch. Yet in the immediate aftermath of an event that failed to impress anyone, the heavyweight boxing champion of the world offered up the right.

Inoki's frustration over what had transpired during the last forty-five minutes was equally apparent when, as fighters often do, the pair shook hands and embraced. An even mix of jeers and cheers inside Budokan Hall greeted their postfight exchange. Soon the ring was inundated with people entering from all sides as both men awaited the official decisions from their respective corners.

Inoki casually leaned against the ropes, his team wiping him down as he cooled off. The dormant volcano Karl Gotch took in the scene. His man had let a tremendous opportunity slip away—not just for himself but for the grappling community. Gotch wanted to beat the hell out of both guys. Inoki had brought him to Japan and paid him $60,000 per season so he could teach prospects how to hook and shoot, and whatever it was Inoki had just done hadn't been wrestling. Gotch knew.

Freddie Blassie knew just the same and said as much to his friend Gene LeBell.

"I didn't think in that fight either one of them actually got to show their true ability," LeBell said. "They were both a lot better competitors than they showed that night. But it was the first big mixed martial arts fight. It'll go down in history as that."

Ali's camp wasn't concerned about history. Their man had engineered enough of that already, and this sideshow didn't seem destined to go down in the annals of his most important moments. More than anything they were glad Ali had finished the fight on his feet and made it through without having been broken or twisted. Sure, his leg was a mess, but Ali was a freak of nature who always seemed to recover no matter what kind of battering he took. The hard-fought win in Manila eight months earlier and the hectic schedule leading to the Inoki match was proof enough of that.

On the English closed-circuit broadcast Dr. Pacheco told Jerry Lisker that Ali's left leg "was angry" but "two weeks of rest would be enough for a person of his recuperative capacity." Any risk to the fight with Norton at Yankee Stadium was minimal, he suggested, and training wouldn't begin for that trilogy-making bout for another four weeks. Ali was due a much-deserved rest anyhow.

One by one members of Ali's entourage visited Inoki's corner to shake hands with the rassler. Blassie took his turn and, despite their shared experiences, received a lukewarm reception. He tried again later to meet with Inoki but was turned away from the Japanese wrestler's locker room.

Blassie wanted Inoki to win, but based on the bout he came to the conclusion that Inoki couldn't tie his shoes—either Inoki wasn't very skilled, or, perhaps, he wasn't interested in toppling Ali.

As people milled about the ring and awards, including a giant trophy, were put on display, Dundee untied and removed the sparingly used gloves John Toms from Everlast had created for Ali. Herbert Muhammad passed the heavyweight a comb so he could make sure he felt good about his hair during the TV interview. Unlike other fights, there was no need to concern himself with damage to his handsome face. Ali hadn't even worn a mouthpiece, such was their expectation that he wouldn't be touched—and other than Inoki's illegal elbow in the sixth round he hadn't been.

Frank Bannister, the play-by-play man who three months later became the first person of color to call a major sporting event in the U.S. when Ali met Norton on a wild evening in New York City, made his way over to Ali. The boxer first thanked Allah, then mentioned civil-rights activist Dick Gregory, who was some seventy-five miles outside of Harrisburg, Penn., en route to New York, where Ali said they planned to meet on July 4 for the final leg of the former comedian's cross-country "Dick Gregory Bicentennial Run Against Hunger in America."

As for Inoki's tactics, Ali had expected the Japanese man to "try to rassle." He said based on the experience, a rassler would not stand a chance with a boxer. The fact that Inoki gave him no opportunity to throw a punch told Ali that a rassler was scared to get knocked out by him, and if that's how they felt then that's likely how it would have happened.

"I wish the fight was better but I did my best according to the conditions," Ali said. "I've never fought a man who fought on the floor, and I can't fight my style with a man who stays on the floor. He showed fear respecting my punching ability. He showed all rasslers who want to try me, I don't think no Americans fighters are like these Orientals that good on the floor. But I never expected him to fight on the floor."

The great boxer explained that it made no difference to him who won. It meant nothing to his boxing status, wouldn't impact his prestige, and, in the end, he had had fun.

"I think I won, just the mere fact of him not fighting," Ali said. "I stood up and I tried to fight. I was the aggressor. He wasn't. He fought like a coward."

Then scores were announced. Kokichi Endo, who wrestled as a tag-team partner with Rikidōzan and was well connected inside Japan's pro wrestling establishment, saw it 74–72 for Ali. Boxing judge Kou Toyama went the other way, tallying a 72–68 scorecard for Inoki. The decision came down to LeBell, who, as referee, deducted points in the sixth, eighth, and thirteenth rounds—LeBell recalled taking only two points away and nearly four decades after the fact couldn't pinpoint the penalty in Round 8. His final tally registered 71–71.

"It's a draw!" he yelled. Well, technically, a split draw.

"I had the best seat in the house, right in the middle of the ring," LeBell recalled years later. "A lot of people thought Inoki had more kicks. I judged the fight not based on how many jabs or kicks were thrown. I judged based on damage done. I could throw one hook and throw a guy into the nickel seats. And throw seventeen jabs and not do any damage. What and who did the most damage? I called it a tie. Both of them did the same amount of damage, which is nothing."

From the Budokan Hall cheap seats rained trash and cries of "Money back! Money back!" Made worse by the fact that few people had a frame of reference for what went down in the ring, the disappointment of an event that failed to live up to a hyped spectacle permeated everyone everywhere. "It was stupid," said Pacheco, who hated the idea from the jump, and nearly forty years later denied even being there before admitting to blocking the trip from his stroke-stricken mind. "How could you have a match against a wrestler and a boxer? Someone is going to get fucked. And it ain't going to be the boxer because the boxer was Muhammad Ali."

In San Jose, Calif., where Dave Meltzer watched with friends, people threw chairs after the decision was announced. They turned unruly around the eleventh round, "almost like a riot," because few enjoyed or understood what was happening. Said Meltzer: "I think they were expecting something like a cross between a boxing match and a pro wrestling match and got nothing resembling either."

On the other side of the country, The Liberty Theater in Elizabeth, New Jersey, remained full until the end. Full of paying customers and boos. Jeff Wagenheim and his friend filed out in relative silence, hearing only a few lingering complaints. "I feel like covering my face in case anyone on the street recognizes me," said Wagenheim's buddy Rob. They still share a laugh about the night it felt like "somewhere between being spotted walking out of an X-rated movie house and walking away from a three-card monte game with your wallet twenty dollars lighter."

As confused as he was disappointed, Kevin Iole needed answers. And after the match there were more questions than before. "What did I just see?" he wondered while leaving Monzo's Howard Johnson's near Pittsburgh. "Was this true or phony?"

The legitimacy of the fight had been up for debate since it had been first announced in March. Behind the scenes there was plenty of discussion about whether or not it would turn out to be legitimate, and in the end the outcome looked nowhere near predetermined.

"People walked out of the Liberty Theater not too gratified that they had witnessed something that was real," Wagenheim said. "They were more pissed off. I think they would have been happier to see a scripted-out but exciting event."

Most spectators figured if it had been worked, like the match at Shea Stadium between Andre the Giant and Chuck Wepner, it would have been far more entertaining.

The *New York Times* certainly treated Ali–Inoki as sport, which is why Andrew Malcolm spent the first Saturday of summer 1976 at Budokan Hall. Considering the people involved, especially Inoki and the pro wrestling side, the bout's authenticity was worth contemplating, but after it was done Malcolm found no reason to suspect something so shady.

"The punches I saw, they looked real to me," Malcolm said. "The fact that Inoki didn't want any more of them tells me they were. The badly bruised legs on Ali, there wasn't anything fake about that. I was disappointed as a spectator that there wasn't any of this real boxing, or wrestling, or tying up and then flipping Ali over. I remember being tired of saying, 'And he kicks the backs of Ali's legs again.' I felt like a goof. All these people around me cheering and I'm saying, 'Now a left. Now a right. Now he's kicking.' There's nobody at the other end. Every fifteen or twenty minutes they would take off what I said and started typing it. They had someone write a story based on my talking notes. I knew there was unhappiness but I wrote it off as everyone is unhappy with an athletic event. I didn't have to pay a lot of money to see it. If I had paid a significant sum of money I would have been very unhappy. I never covered enough of them to know how often you're really disappointed. It wasn't a fight but it was a sports phenomenon."

More than anything, for Malcolm, who was admittedly in awe of a boxer he had first heard of going back to his days at Northwestern University, the assignment was an opportunity to see Ali up close and personal. Japan was one of the few places Malcolm worked where he felt like a large man, so the *New York Times* Tokyo bureau chief didn't have much trouble moving his way to the front of the press mob gathered outside Ali's locker room door after the bout.

Malcolm knocked and the door cracked open, prompting the throng of reporters holding small microphones and cameras to coalesce. "Is Angelo there?" he asked above the din. Dundee walked to the door and vouched for Malcolm, who slid inside and immediately noticed Ali, in obvious pain, straddling a locker room bench. After the bout in the ring, Ali played coy about his left leg. It's a "little sore, naturally," he said. "A few welts and blood veins popping but nothing real serious." The champ sweated profusely as he took in fluids.

"You could see the backs of his legs. I mean, they had the shit kicked out of them," Malcolm recalled.

From Ali's left quad and hamstring down through the midway point of his calf, it looked like he had dumped a motorcycle and slid along the pavement. They were red and bruised, and the worst spots were puffed up by at least half an inch. Despite Ali's discomfort he remained in good spirits while members of his entourage decided it was time to clear the room.

"There was some reference to white people to get out of the room. Only 'brothers,'" Malcolm said. "Dundee looked at me and winked. He took me and literally shoved me in a locker. Like a high school locker. He says, 'Wait here a minute,' and shuts the door. You hear all this yelling and the bros are clearing the room. Maybe two minutes later Angelo opens the door, I come out and get an interview with Ali."

Gracious with his time and forthcoming with his answers, Ali winced as he reiterated his frustration over not having much of a fight. The boxer felt his $6.1 million purse was well earned—many fighters have said over the years that the money they're paid is for training and prefight promotional work, not the actual bout, which is the fun part; or the consequences thereof, which sometimes aren't—but had he known it was going to be a "dead show" he wouldn't have gone through with it.

If the production accomplished anything, Ali myopically argued to Malcolm, it proved boxers are "so superior to rasslers. Inoki didn't stand up and fight like a man. If he had gotten into hittin' range I'd a burned him but good."

Malcolm interviewed many famous folks for the *New York Times* and other news organizations over the years.

People in public life fascinated him and one of the things he enjoyed most about being a reporter was getting close enough to see how they operated. The two most impressive public personalities Malcolm ever encountered, he said, were Ali and Diana, Princess of Wales. Having spent time around Ali before and after the bout, Malcolm sensed Ali's innate ability to connect with anyone he wished. He enjoyed meeting new people and making them feel good. There weren't many people who disliked Ali, and if you were anywhere close to him, Pacheco said, you succumbed to his talent. If Ali wanted you to love him, you did. This is what Malcolm experienced during his brief exchanges with the boxer. He also observed just how many people operated around Ali in what was tantamount to an "SNL skit of suck up." The "bros" tried hard to prove their street cred to the champ. "I was like, really, does he need to hear this?" Malcolm said. "It was more that they needed to show it. I hate to think he needed that but I don't think he minded."

Unaware of Inoki until the contest with Ali materialized, Malcolm's quick impression of him settled on the notion that the wrestler was very easy to like. Malcolm considered him an Arnold Schwarzenegger type, a big guy perfectly comfortable in his own skin, the result of which generally garners attention from Japanese crowds.

For the most part that easygoing sense of self was on display as Inoki spoke with the media in his locker room after the fight. He did the best he could, he said, and was content with a draw. Inoki expected that holding his spot on the marquee alongside a luminary like Ali would provide a big boost for his celebrity at home and abroad. Still, he needed to explain his tactics.

"I was handicapped by the rules that said no tackling, no karate chops, no punching on the mat," he told reporters. "I kept my distance to stay away from Ali's punches. I resorted to that tactic when I found out that Ali's hands were taped to dish out a knockout punch."

Inoki's attempt to frame the contest this way did not go over with the Japanese press, which was in a maelstrom over the result. That night during the 9:00 P.M. news on NHK, commentators treated the match as a farce, remembered Hideki Yamamoto, who watched half of the contest with his junior high teammates and coaches before growing bored and returning to the baseball diamond.

"That ended up being my thoughts on the show as well," he said.

In fact, though Inoki was correct about Ali's wraps—smaller gloves prompted the boxer's team to encase his multimillion dollar fists in extra layers of tape and gauze that should have allowed him to punch as hard and as often as he wished without damaging hands known to be brittle—the wrestler's game plan was set in motion weeks before.

At his dojo Inoki practiced kicking his sparring partners' thighs, which were protected by a rubber pad bound by rope and wrapped with a towel. Now he'd have to live with the consequences.

The next day newspapers trashed Inoki to the point that he didn't want to go outside. One headline called the bout "the rip-off of the century." But it didn't take long to see that regardless of the outcome, Inoki's participation had an impact. People from Asian countries seemed to appreciate him representing them.

After nine days in Tokyo, most of Ali's American entourage were slated to return to the States in plenty of time for the bicentennial celebrations on July 4. The champ, however, had other business to attend to.

The South Korean government contacted Jhoon Rhee weeks before the fight, hoping that, if invited, Ali would accept a trip to Seoul. The key, Rhee thought, would be to catch the champ when he was in a "good mood." During their flight to Japan the man instrumental in popularizing taekwondo throughout the United States, who settled in Washington, D.C., and opened the Jhoon Rhee Taekwondo School in 1962, took his shot.

"I really almost begged him to go to Korea," Rhee said.

The government offered free trips for up to fifteen people if Ali said yes, which he did. Ninety-nine percent of the time if Ali agreed to something he followed through. "He did things that normal champions wouldn't even consider doing," said Bobby Goodman, who worked alongside Ali for many fights starting with the decision over Doug Jones in 1963.

In this instance that meant traveling against the advice of his doctor and closest advisors a day after suffering significant damage to an area of his body that had not been targeted before. "I don't think anyone thought it was a good idea, but he had made a commitment," said Goodman, who never saw Ali banged up like he was following fifteen rounds with Inoki—not even the previous October's grueling third fight with Frazier in Manila. "His legs were so swollen he couldn't put pants on. It was awful. It was just grotesque. I think Inoki broke every vessel in Ali's legs. He was in such pain. Ali tried to minimize everything. 'I'll be OK. I'll be fine.' But it was definitely not fine. It was ugly. I saw him just for a little while before I had to go back to the U.S. the next day. It was hard to look at. All the different colors. Black and blue wasn't a fair description."

Dundee was extremely concerned—the Norton fight was closing in fast. Kilroy, who claimed he wrapped Ali's legs in ice, said to hell with Korea, let's head home. Pacheco made an impassioned plea and suggested Ali's legs were "filled with hand grenades." He advised the man he treasured to remain in bed for three days before even considering stepping foot on a plane. Then he made Ali aware of the dangers: "If any of those clots get loose and go up into your head you're dead. You can die from this. Those knots that are in your leg can get infected and can travel. And when they travel they'll go right to the lungs, right to the heart, right to the brain."

Addressing members of the team including Herbert Muhammad, who seemed fine with the pugilist continuing his Asian adventure, Pacheco said, "You guys are brutal. You're absolutely dumb. You can't do that with this guy."

It didn't matter. Ali's mind was already made up, and whatever he said went.

Later that night in Ali's palatial hotel room Rhee massaged the champ's legs with ice. "He was taking it pretty well," Rhee said. "I know it was painful." Among the concerned and disappointed fight watchers in Tokyo the diminutive forty-five-year-old Korean felt the match was shameful, a disappointment for himself, the crowd, the whole world. "I think Antonio Inoki was scared," said Rhee, who, like Ali, expected a standup fight.

The pall cast over the bout was short-lived, and Rhee shifted from a fight advisor to the man who would bring the great Muhammad Ali to Korea. Many Koreans saw Ali fight Inoki, and, like Rhee, they weren't pleased. But they were happy to have a chance to see the man himself in person during a three-day visit.

On Sunday, they departed Tokyo. Following a planeside ceremony three hours later, hundreds of thousands of people waving American and Korean flags lined the streets as Ali enjoyed a motorcade from Kimpo Airport to downtown Seoul's City Hall plaza. Rhee put the number at a million, though most news reports at the time had it about half of that.

"It was also the biggest day of my life," Rhee said. "I had many expectations for the trip. To many people who didn't know me I became known as the man who brought Muhammad Ali to Korea."

At a news conference, Ali credited his "deadly" taekwondo punches, an obvious nod to Rhee and the Korean people, for scaring Inoki into fighting off his back. Behind the scenes, both men remained worried about those damaged legs but Ali's pain subsided during the trip. He made twelve personal appearances and attended several special events, including boxing exhibitions with American troops a half marathon away from the demilitarized zone. Ali bragged to 2,500 soldiers assigned to the U.S. 2nd Infantry Division that he earned "one million dollars a punch. And you are going to see hundreds of punches for nothing." Ali's swollen leg didn't keep him from dancing and peppering soft shots into two would-be contenders during a pair of five-minute exhibitions, according to an Associated Press report.

Ali was able-bodied for more than boxing. During one car ride with Rhee, Ali shared that he thought all Korean women were beautiful. "Can you fix me up with one tonight?" he asked. The man who brought Ali to Korea didn't respond; he pretended not to hear the question. A few beats later Ali tapped Rhee and asked if he heard him.

"I will do anything but that," Rhee told the champ. "I will not introduce a woman to you. That's one thing I will never do for anybody."

Many people over the years had answered yes to Ali's request. Though Ali claimed he was a "single man," Rhee explained he doesn't "believe in sex before marriage, so I wouldn't cooperate." A minute later Ali tapped Rhee again and, according to the taekwondo man, said, "Master Rhee, I really respect you."

Ali still found a woman to pal around with.

Indeed, Ali enjoyed the Korean people. Wherever he and Rhee went their meals were paid for. Kimchi was a bit too spicy, but the kegogi—dog meat—suited Ali fine.

The day Ali departed Korea, the country's authoritarian president, Park Chung Hee, asked to meet with him. Due to a conflict with the boxer's flight time it never happened. Park assumed control of South Korea following a military coup in 1961, and three years after Ali's visit was assassinated. The great boxer had bumped into his share of military strongmen over the course of his well-travelled career. Unsavory characters and sordid affairs were just part of the boxing business. And as Ali returned to the U.S., bad financial dealings around the Inoki bout began to surface. The $6 million Ali was guaranteed turned out to be $1.8 million, insofar as that is what he received in the aftermath of the bout.

"It confirms my principle," Ali's manager Herbert Muhammad told Dave Anderson of the *New York Times*, "of getting all the money in the bank ahead of time. I didn't do it this time."

The financial details were prickly. "The $3 million from Japan," Muhammad told Anderson, "was split up—$1.8 million in a letter of credit that's in the bank and $1.2 million in a dollar-for-dollar tax credit" that was held up pending an accounting by Top Rank of Ali's share. (Top Rank boss Bob Arum ignored several requests to participate in this book.) Anderson cited closed-circuit TV sources that projected Top Rank's gross at $2.5 million, less than a $1 million net. "So far Ali hasn't got a quarter," Muhammad told the *Times*. "Nobody's got paid."

Even more concerning, Ali's left leg started killing him as soon as he departed Korea. After dedicating the Ali Mall in Manila—the first major shopping center in the Philippines—Ali returned to Los Angeles on the first of July and Gene Kilroy took him posthaste to St. John's Hospital in Santa Monica, where X-rays revealed blood clots. He was admitted for a three-day stay.

Tests showed superficial clotting near the surface of both knees, according to a report by United Press International, which noted, "Ali also suffered from severe muscle damage in his left leg; anemia produced by bleeding into the leg from the injury to blood vessels in the muscle of the leg; vein damage; and an accumulation of both fluid and blood in the entire leg." Doctors administered blood thinners to Ali, Kilroy said, and within a couple days it was reported that he had made "substantial progress."

Once again, Ali seemed to have dodged a bullet, though Pacheco remained angered over how things had played out in Japan. "You're fucking lucky those lumps didn't travel," Pacheco told him.

Six weeks after the match with Inoki, Ali was back to running three miles a day as he began preparing for the third fight with Ken Norton.

ROUND THIRTEEN

In all athletic endeavors, energy is best transferred from the ground to the feet to the legs to the hips and so on; power loads before it can be unleashed. The more efficient the transition, the more force is created. This process helped refine martial arts to a feat of literal human engineering. The body is designed to do certain things in certain ways, and special martial artists, like other talented athletes, can appear smooth and rhythmic generating tremendous acceleration and damage.

Antonio Inoki didn't make it look smooth and rhythmic against a man who was the smoothest and most rhythmic of all time. That fight—that's the correct word for what happened—was ugly, and that's another reason fans and media sneered at it at the time. Watching Inoki launch himself to the floor while swinging a boot wasn't the best, but it served him well by keeping that "pelican" chin clear of Ali's punches.

Aesthetics aside, Inoki's lack of connection to the ground while kicking reduced the attack's venom. So it was that an accumulation of kicks did in Muhammad Ali. Had Inoki consistently thrown kicks with proper technique—it was against the rules, plus he tried but didn't trust himself—it's highly unlikely Ali would have survived the full fifteen rounds.

In 1976, hardly anyone in the mainstream grasped the true devastation of a well-timed, well-placed leg kick. That's one of the reasons Inoki's effort was widely panned. Some reporters wondered afterwards about the point of throwing kicks to a guy's leg in a fight. Few people had any inkling that, done right, a leg kick could actually debilitate an adversary. There was hardly any kickboxing happening in the States at the time, and only a select few hardcore martial artists fully understood the implications of shins meeting thighs.

"If you think about it Inoki was smart," said Maurice Smith, who watched the contest as a budding fourteen-year-old karate and taekwondo student in Seattle, Wash., the adopted city of Bruce Lee. "He did something Ali wasn't unaccustomed to: those low kicks. We weren't covering low kicks in my training, but I understood that getting kicked didn't feel good. Not to the level that we know now, but definitely to a point. It had a big significance in diminishing Ali's skill set, his abilities."

Inoki may have peppered a great boxer's legs, yet Smith is rightly considered mixed martial arts' godfather of leg kicking.

Two decades after Ali was hospitalized for taking Louisville Sluggers, Smith neutralized UFC heavyweight champion Mark Coleman, a powerhouse grappler, partly because he could bludgeon the wrestler's lead leg. The outcome served as a wakeup call to the wider martial arts world because four years after the debut of the UFC, grappling was the dominant combat style. An onslaught of big, strong Olympic-caliber wrestlers, many of whom freely used steroids to boost their training and physical advantages, dominated mixed-style contests—adding to the perception that fighters who had to stay on their feet to have a chance almost never did.

For all of Smith's success in kickboxing (he retired with a 53–13–5 record) and foresight adapting striking to MMA, he closed out a decade of mixed-rules bouts having twenty-eight fights. Nowadays, thanks in no small part to Smith, the leg kick is a mandatory MMA tool. Fighters must know how to throw or defend one if they want a chance of winning at an elite level.

The sport's most effective low kicker, it could be argued, is the first man to hold the UFC 145-pound belt, Brazilian Jose Aldo, whose dynamism made him among the game's most devastating offensive fighters. His classically brutal victory over Urijah Faber in April 2010 is the gold standard of leg-kick effectiveness and devastation. Missing once in twenty-six attempts, Aldo debilitated Faber, a terrific fighter, en route to a lopsided win that went the distance due to the Californian's conditioning, desire, and ability to endure pain.

Aldo kicked Faber much more effectively than Inoki kicked Ali, but the Japanese fighter connected four times as many kicks against an opponent who had never been hit in that spot before. Afterwards Faber's left leg resembled a massive elephant trunk more than any part of the human body, and it took over a month for the purplish hue and swelling to subside.

Beyond his kicking ability, Smith is remembered as being one of the first true mixed martial artists because he melded unique styles to boost his strengths. He incorporated the groundwork of Brazilian jiu-jitsu, which had been derived from judo. Known as the guard, or in catch wrestling lore "leg-and-hip control," Smith essentially learned how to defend himself from the bottom in the likely case that a grappler secured top position over him. There's a lot that can happen both ways from this spot, but it certainly wasn't where a fighter like Smith wanted to be.

Alongside pioneering UFC champion and submission fighter Frank Shamrock, Smith embraced the full spectrum of martial arts. His important affiliation with Shamrock and Tsuyoshi Kohsaka in the late 1990s, during MMA's media-starved days in the U.S., subsequently changed the way fighters prepared and fought by highlighting the wisdom of training everything all the time. Smith learned a wrestler's sprawl in hopes of shutting down lower body takedown attempts, and if that didn't work he revolutionized control from the bottom with his grappling half-guard. The trio called themselves "The Alliance" and described their style as "cross training."

This way of thinking would have been rare in the 1970s, a result of the mainstream drive at the time to represent pure martial arts styles. There were practitioners who sought to remove themselves from this dogma. Smith turned out to be one. Gene LeBell, a misfit of his day, was always willing to use whatever worked. Exposure in his earliest brushes with martial arts to the anything-goes grappling ideology of Ed "Strangler" Lewis played a large part in shaping his open thought process.

"If you don't know something you usually don't like it," LeBell said. "That's why a lot of us argue with our neighbors.

In the martial arts, it was the mystic, the secrets of the martial arts. They come from the Orient."

A two-time national and overall judo champion—the sporting equivalent of best in show—LeBell ran headfirst into the limiting principle associated with my-way-or-the-highway martial arts practice. Thrown out of more dojos than he cared to remember because he wouldn't do things the way they wanted, LeBell recalled one time in particular when a stodgy Japanese Rokudan, or sixth-degree black belt, challenged his credentials.

"The guy comes up to me and says, 'I'm Rokudan,'" said LeBell, who was asked to share his rank. That meant it was time to goof around. Now in his eighties, LeBell features an assortment of belts, accolades, and awards on the walls of his San Fernando Valley home office. He swears they don't mean a thing. To the Rokudan, LeBell simply stated that he was a teacher. Systems vary, explained LeBell, so different degrees meant different standards. The Rokudan didn't appreciate the answer and was more direct. "How good are you?" he asked. LeBell told him he won the nationals a couple of times, back when it took eighteen matches over two days to do so. The Rokudan did an about-face and walked away unconvinced the red-haired loudmouth who wore a pink *gi* was an actual champion. But, that he was. Not only did LeBell represent grappling, particularly judo, to great effect against Milo Savage in 1963, he challenged the linear thinking that permeated media and popular culture, which positioned flashy television and film-friendly styles like karate, taekwondo, and gung fu as worthwhile to watch and practice because, supposedly, they were the most dangerous.

The best-known martial artist of his day, of course, was the legendary Bruce Lee. He epitomized the karate flash audiences craved yet worked to outmode that paradigm by promoting concepts that updated and modernized martial arts. That is why, despite never fighting professionally, Lee is regarded as a forefather of mixed martial arts.

If LeBell is thought of in similar lines, and he should be—quite a bit more than Lee to be fair—it would be because he was a let-me-see-what-you-got kind of guy.

LeBell knew Lee very well. They met on the set of the classic television show *The Green Hornet*. Lee starred as Kato for twenty-six episodes, and from 1966 to 1967 LeBell worked as a stuntman under prolific stunt coordinator Bennie Dobbins.

Lee moved so fast that people didn't know how to react, though the camera loved him. During their first interaction, LeBell, who outweighed Lee by fifty pounds, lifted the little guy over his head, eager to show off the kettlebell work he put in with Karl Gotch. In strength, fitness, and flexibility exercises, the Belgian killer routinely tossed around the equivalent of ninety-pound cannonballs affixed with a handle. LeBell was good for half of that, and the judoka claims he ran around the set dangling Lee in the air before locking him in a reverse nelson.

The world-famous Chinese-American threatened LeBell.

"Put me down or I'll kill you," Lee said.

Typical LeBell mouthed off: "I can't put you down. You'll kill me."

"I demand respect," Lee shouted, and LeBell let him loose. "OK, you're the boss."

They chatted and Lee invited LeBell to train with him. "I'll teach you gung fu," he said.

"I don't know if I'm allergic to it," the stuntman replied, "but I'll do it."

Lee felt LeBell disrespected him and that was unacceptable, but as their communication improved LeBell said Lee realized that the son of Hollywood was "brain dead." Soon Lee called LeBell, who knew how to fall and make Lee look good, to work on various shows.

"Bruce Lee was the man for what he did," LeBell said. "I loved Bruce because a lot of the gung fu guys didn't like him because he showed other things that were practical but weren't traditional in his art. I weighed 180, he weighed 135. A guy like that, I don't care how good he is, you're going to have him for lunch. That doesn't make me any better. If we were the same weight he might've done some gung fu to me. At that time he got very interested in wrestling."

This was right before *Enter the Dragon*, which was released in 1973 and became one of the most famous martial arts movies of all time. Perhaps the most famous. Lee had offered LeBell a chance to work on the movie in Hong Kong for $200 a week. The American judoka was pocketing five times that doing stunt work on cowboy movies, and passed.

In the opening sequence of *Enter the Dragon*, Lee showcased an armbar technique that gave grappling a prominence it was unfamiliar with among the flash and dash of recent martial arts pop-culture treatment. "As a competitor he was a hell of a salesman," LeBell said. "He convinced everybody he could do this or that. He did parlor tricks, but he was good at what he did." Lee's impact was enormous nonetheless, and many people defend his status as a superior martial artist and fighter. Lee touched countless lives, including Muhammad Ali, his taekwondo coach Jhoon Rhee, who exchanged techniques with Lee starting in 1964, and future UFC heavyweight champion Maurice Smith.

Smith grew up in Seattle, where Lee attended the University of Washington and was buried at Lakeview Cemetery following his sudden death at the age of thirty-two from brain swelling while working in Hong Kong in 1973. Smith's life in martial arts was born out of Lee's role in the 1972 film *The Chinese Connection*. "That was my first martial arts movie ever," Smith said. "And that became the impetus to being who I am now. There's no question that he had a profound effect on me to become a martial artist. And not because he was from Seattle. It's because of who he was. Everybody in my generation, they were all influenced by him."

Smith decided he wanted to fight around his eighteenth birthday. He didn't have a goal of becoming a champion, he simply wanted to compete at something he was good at.

"It wasn't racial," said the African American fighter, "but I looked at the people teaching me martial arts at the time and I thought, 'Why can't I beat this old guy? He was thirty years old. I was a teenager. Why can't I beat him?' I looked at it as a compliment. Not a negative thing. He did a great job teaching me. Why can't I beat him?"

Fighting took Smith all over the world, and in Amsterdam in 1984 he discovered the virtues of the low kick—otherwise Dutch kickboxers, with their power strikes, would have eaten him alive. The Dutch used a class system that developed kickboxers and allowed them to rise through the ranks. Smith paid close attention to their progression.

"You had to low kick," he said. "I had the good fortune of being one of the guys to use it at the time—and I was American and they didn't use the low kick. I thought that was a great technique. When I would fight against the Dutch, whether I beat them or not, I understood the low kick game."

Another example of recognizing what the opposition was doing, adopting and adapting it for your own means, and becoming a more dangerous martial artist. "You're not using your foot to low kick," he said. "You're using your shin. If you're getting kicked in the leg enough times, it's not going to feel good. Your whole game changes." Low kicks prompt respect even if they don't really "hurt," and "it changes the offense of the guy being kicked. It's a different strategy if you become proficient at it and know how to do it. If you take a fighter that's never experienced low kicks, they won't know how to deal with it."

Without the proper defense of a leg check, which essentially comes down to raising a shin into the path of an oncoming kick, fighting becomes a game of pain tolerance, a lesson Ali learned the hard way. As uncomfortable as the response can be—think about the last time one of your shins hit a hard edge—it beats eating a flush kick to the thigh, and is generally worse for the attacker. "You can toughen your shins but there's no way to toughen up yourself to get kicked," Smith said.

All-time great UFC middleweight Anderson Silva lost by technical knockout on December 8, 2013, at UFC 168 when his left leg fractured below the knee because Chris Weidman timed an inside leg kick with a perfect counter check. That sort of thing is not unheard of.

As he progressed as a martial artist and a pro fighter, Smith added tools to his arsenal. Kickboxers have eight weapons at their disposal—both hands, both feet, both elbows, and both knees—compared to boxers who use just two. Mixed martial artists, understandably, have many more. Smith labeled Ali a "specialized fighter" because, despite an expanding knowledge base, he had been called one himself. The businesses of mixed-style fights and their interpretive dance, *puroresu*, have boomed in Japan during the years since Inoki drew Ali. In that way, the bout in 1976 was a big success and influence. During a bus ride around Kobe City ahead of Smith's first mixed bout on November 8, 1993, for the nascent Pancrase organization, which was built from the legacy of Ali–Inoki, the one and only Ken Shamrock turned to the kickboxer and shared a thought.

"Maurice," Shamrock said, "you're not a fighter."

Smith looked back at Shamrock, who less than a week later would be in Denver to participate in UFC 1, and thought, *I've been a champion for two years. What's that mean, not a fighter?* Smith had stepped into the ring to kickbox more than thirty times before Pancrase gave him a shot at MMA. Fighting with hands and feet is incredibly difficult to do at a high level over a period of several years, so Smith, perturbed, asked Shamrock what he meant.

"Because you're a specialized fighter," Shamrock replied. "You only fight kickboxing."

"What the hell you talking about?" Smith shot back.

It took guts on Ali's part to get in the ring against a grappler, even though he stacked the deck against Inoki as far as the rules went. And it took guts for Smith to move beyond his comfort zone of kickboxing into the MMA realm. "No matter what, it's a business decision to keep your name going," Smith said. "But it's a big gamble." As far as Ali's foray, "obviously they didn't practice against low kicks and this kind of fighting. They knew they were fighting a wrestler but they didn't know what he was going to do."

Smith thought about what Shamrock said and conceded he had a point. A specialized fighter only competes a certain way. And at that moment, the description fit him, as it had Ali in 1976.

Ali was "kind of, sort of afraid of martial artists," said his taekwondo coach, Jhoon Rhee. "Martial artists kick and punch. He didn't know how to kick." They grapple, too, but the point remains the same: what you don't know can be scary if you're forced to face it head-on.

When Rhee was a kid in Seoul, Korea, where he was born in 1932 during the Japanese occupation, he was enamored with martial arts. By the time he was fourteen, having realized the value of taekwondo, he opened his own school and had visions of bringing an art reliant on flexibility, speed, and kicking to the United States.

"I fell in love with American blondes and thought I would find one when I come here, but I found a black-haired Korean woman," he joked. "When I made taekwondo famous in America it became famous all over the world, and soon it became an Olympic sport. I am very proud of that."

Rhee has been profusely honored throughout his life. The same year as the Ali–Inoki contest, the Washington Touchdown Sports Club, as part of its selection of five sports figures for the Bicentennial Sports Awards, named Rhee its "Martial Arts Man of the Century." Also honored were Ali as "Boxer of the Century," Wilt Chamberlain as "Basketball Man of the Century," Joe DiMaggio as "Baseball Man of the Century," and Jim Brown as "Football Man of the Century."

Over 2,000 people attended the black-tie awards dinner. Bob Hope served as the master of ceremonies, and the then secretary of state Henry Kissinger received an award for "Man of the Century." These were the circles Rhee moved in as he created a taekwondo empire. In the year 2000, the National Immigrant Forum, in conjunction with the Immigration and Naturalization Service, named Rhee as the only Korean among the two hundred most famous American immigrants of all time.

Rhee's prominence led him to many opportunities, including a deep friendship with Bruce Lee that furthered the expansion of both their martial arts repertoires. Nine months after stoking Gene LeBell to fight Milo Savage in Salt Lake City in December 1963, Ed Parker debuted his famous International Karate Championships in Long Beach, Calif. Both Lee, making his introduction to the martial arts world, and Rhee offered demonstrations. Lee was not an easy person to get close to, but Rhee's bond with him quickly became strong. They made sure to visit at least once a year, either in Washington, D.C., or at Lee's home in Los Angeles. Lee's Hong Kong film producer, Raymond Chow, cast Rhee in the leading role of *When Taekwondo Strikes*, based on a synopsis Rhee wrote about Koreans fighting for independence from the Japanese occupation. On July 19, 1973, Lee called Rhee from Hong Kong with news that the movie was ready to be released. The following day, Lee tragically passed away.

"People realize today that there is no one great martial art," Smith said. "Everything combined is the one great martial art. MMA, you could say. Mixed martial arts. But back at that time, in the '70s, they were all separated. You had karate, gung fu, you had taekwondo, boxing, judo. You didn't hear much about jiu-jitsu or judo too much, but they were there."

For the first time the term "mixed martial arts" was readily used in conjunction with a fight. Vince McMahon Sr. sold pro wrestling events all over the U.S. as "mixed martial arts," and called it that while offering Chuck Wepner a chance to meet Andre the Giant at Shea Stadium for $25,000.

"Me boxing and Andre wrestling," Wepner said. "They were gonna try it. Years later, Donald Trump called me. He wanted to do the first MMA cage match in Atlantic City. I was gonna fight Tex Cobb. It was one of those first MMA fights when I'd saw the cage matches. And I turned it down. It wasn't a fight. I was fifty-two years old. I thought I could've beat Tex Cobb. Even in a mixed match. Even though I lost 14 out of 147 amateur and pro bouts in the ring, I was a good street fighter. But they didn't want to pay us no money."

McMahon's mixed martial arts concept was driven by Inoki's mission that had been inspired by Rikidōzan's success—to prove pro wrestlers could and should fight, and be the best in the world at doing so. In Japan, this was one of the most appealing elements of Ali–Inoki. Headlines built up the clash as boxing versus wrestling, but the layers were far more textured than that. The sport was rooted in barroom brawling and refined, scientific, well-reputed disciplines. Seeing how they meshed, and elevating the methods that prevailed, initiated a renaissance for martial arts.

"You have to be familiar with another person's sport to be competitive," Smith said, pinpointing the thinking that put him in position to defeat Mark Coleman at UFC 14 in 1997, a feat informed by revelations about martial arts that manifested from the Ali–Inoki contest.

Ali knew by agreeing to fight Inoki, a seed could be planted. He was aware Milo Savage had been choked cold by the grappler Gene LeBell fought. The question about what happens when a boxer fights a wrestler had been asked and answered enough times. Yet Ali still had to know.

"When you're talking history it's bullshit," Pacheco said. "Who was the boxer? Who was the wrestler? The fact is an equal boxer with an equal wrestler, the wrestler gets killed."

This is what Ali thought, too. It didn't matter what rasslers had done to boxers in the past because they hadn't done it to him. If you didn't have Ali no one would have cared. But Ali fighting Inoki, that's different. Ali opened the door and he knew he was going to open the door. Ali was incredibly competitive, and the appeal of testing himself was an easy yes.

More than a year before the bout, when he began training with Jhoon Rhee at the Deer Lake compound ahead of the third Frazier bout, Ali sent a clear signal that his interest rested in more than the potential of boxing's richest purses.

During that time Ali credited Rhee with teaching him to punch as fast as he could think. Ultimately Ali fought Inoki to prove to himself that he was the greatest fighter of all time. But if he could also pay for mosques in Chicago and London, why not? Ali expanded the reach of Islam perhaps like no person but the Prophet Mohammad himself. He wasn't the most famous Muslim on the planet. He was the most famous person on the planet.

ROUND
FOURTEEN

Four decades after Muhammad Ali and Antonio Inoki participated in the highest-profile example of mixed martial arts the world had seen, the professional sport that rose in part from their escapade sits in a well-formed, growing global niche. In some ways, this style of combat was always global, at least as long as human civilization existed. Unique peoples from disparate places somehow produced similar wrestling and fighting techniques, yet it wasn't until technology brought us together that methods were proven and honed, then shaped into big business.

The emergence of the Ultimate Fighting Championship was a watershed moment in martial arts. November 12, 1993, began a literal arms race that influenced how humans best knew to defend themselves. While the Octagon was not combat sport's first petri dish, it certainly cultured our notion of what functions best in a fight, which many people wrongly felt they already knew. Inside the UFC's fenced-in, trademarked area that was conceived with the help of legendary Hollywood producer John Milius, the styles that didn't work were crushed.

Much of the fundamental growth among MMA tactics and skill is owed to knowing what the hell to do when you're on the floor because some lessons, like Royce Gracie's four master classes on grappling, rebooted history and opened the world's eyes in a way Inoki totally did not. The expansion was rabid, and disparity in *newaza*—judo's word for ground-based fighting—closed fast. Others took from that and were inspired to innovate in distinct ways, like adapting boxers to deal with grapplers or kickers (stances and distances all repurposed from the sweet science Ali showed up with in '76). Any fighter who preferred to stay standing followed a sprawl-and-brawl mindset, a term Ali might have enjoyed. Ground-and-pound was built to foil everything, and it evolved as wrestlers learned to stymie the guards of jiu-jitsu men after Dan Severn tapped to Royce Gracie's triangle choke at the fourth UFC.

Art Davie didn't set out to change martial arts so much as make money from them, but because he wanted to do it in a way that respected truths of the past while resolving some of their failures, cage fighting—anything-goes one-on-one hand-to-hand combat—became more than packaged barbarism. Style versus style, maintaining lines; these were dogmatic and superficial boundaries, felt Davie. The rules and regulations for UFC were in keeping with "creating the best and fairest fights possible," Davie explained in his book. He claimed to seek an equal chance at victory for all fighters by removing limitations on their games. Whether they came from Gracie-branded Brazilian jiu-jitsu, gung fu, boxing, sumo, you name it, the intention was to promote fighters who felt they were being treated fairly. That was the only way that this thing was going to work.

Fight proposals fell apart all the time because of rules that made mixed-style bouts awkward even when they happened. A basic principle behind the UFC was removing any semblance of those hurdles. Sure, use your style if you want, but just be aware that the other guy is free to do whatever he wants.

Davie's original idea was to promote a one-night single-elimination tournament with "no rules." Well, that's how it was marketed but technically speaking there were plenty of rules and regulations, listed A to J, with subsections and notes. So what happened? The day before Davie was set to see four years of work come to fruition, an argument broke out between fighters about the rules—exactly what he'd aimed to avoid. In Davie's book, *Is This Legal?*, which was optioned for a feature film in 2015, the fighter's meeting is recounted as the pivotal point of the whole thing.

Men diffuse in styles, temperaments, and cultures found common ground in the notion that the "anything goes" UFC showcase was set up for the younger brother of the rules director to win. Tensions rose as Rorion Gracie didn't allay their concerns, and it wouldn't have taken much more for guys to pull out of their fights. The attitude in the room degenerated towards a brawl.

"Getting martial artists to agree to the details is like asking two pit bulls how to cut up a steak," Davie said.

Beyond eliminating the cruel stuff in D, Subsection 6, Note "a"—eye gouging, biting, and groin strikes were mentioned as fouls worthy of disqualification—the only rules that mattered were E, "all punches, kicks, knees and elbow strikes, joint locks and/or chokes are permitted," and F, they could be targeted everywhere but the eyes and the groin. That got kickboxer Zane Frazier to chime in. Kenpo karate allowed groin strikes, he argued, but Rorion quickly shot him down. (UFC rules allowed for groin strikes in later events, leading to some ridiculous outcomes.) Things began to boil over in regards to rule G, section 1, which stipulated in part, "taping of the wrist must end 1 inch away from the knuckle." Conversation heated up around the taping issue and nearly boiled over when 420-pound Hawaiian sumo wrestler Teila Tuli said his piece.

"I don't know about you guys," Tuli blurted out, "but I came to party. If anyone else came here to party, I'll see you tomorrow night at the arena."

Onto the table in front of him Tuli slammed a signed release form with his name at the bottom. The fighter's meeting agenda, which doubled as indemnification for the promoters, was dated November 11, 1993. The room broke into claps and cheers. It was on. As real as it gets.

Without interventions like this one, said Davie, when the martial artist had a determining role in setting up a challenge match, those opportunities often unraveled. Davie watched Ali–Inoki on tape in 1977 and kept its lessons in his mind as he built the UFC. Early discussions between Davie and Campbell McClaren, Semaphore Entertainment Group's Vice President of Original Programming, touched on what they did and didn't want the UFC to be.

Almost everything about Ali–Inoki, LeBell–Savage, and Andre the Giant–Wepner—"nothing more than oddball one-offs," Davie said—was on the no-thanks list. "What we did with the UFC was avoid that. That was the success of our event."

The previous night's camaraderie at the fighter meeting had evaporated and laughs were sparse inside the McNichol's Arena. And any audible ones emanated from nerves or shock. During the first televised UFC bout, the sumo wrestler who came to party absorbed a kick to the mouth from six-foot-five Dutch Kyokushin karate stylist Gerard Gordeau. In twenty-six seconds a tooth went flying into the crowd, a face had been rearranged, and Tuli's enthusiasm led him to the wrong side of history.

One fight in and no one could condemn the UFC to a reputation of not being action-packed or violent enough. Ali versus Inoki this was not. Inspired by pankration, Davie envisioned a portal to Olympia. With some luck an exalted fighter would emerge for Davie to promote. His own Polydamas, perhaps, one of the great pankrationists. If another emerged, a rival, then he would really be in business.

In some sense Davie was looking to revive a franchise through rebranding. The record shows that people watch this form of entertainment when given the chance—in Ancient Greece; in Paris at the turn of the twentieth century; through-out America before World War I; in packed Brazilian stadiums and living rooms; at venues around the world showing satellite images live from Tokyo—and that's what the UFC set out to claim on pay-per-view.

"That was seminal research for me in the years 1991, 1992, and 1993 when I was putting together the business plan for the Ultimate Fighting Championship," Davie said. "I knew that there was a long history in grapplers versus boxers, yes."

Making another nod to the past, Davie wanted Gene LeBell to referee UFC 1. He went to his partner, Rorion Gracie, and mentioned that LeBell had shared the ring with Ali and Inoki. But Gracie wasn't interested because he and LeBell had butted heads on the set of ABC's *Hart to Hart.* (The judo man did stunts and the jiu-jitsu man filled in as an extra on the mystery television series. The crux of their dispute stemmed from working with officers from the Los Angeles Police Department and quarreling over the best technique to teach for handgun-retention defense.)

As he made the rounds with television executives, Showtime's Jock McLean, HBO's Lou DiBella, and ESPN's Michael Aresco never brought up Ali–Inoki as a reason why they weren't interested in broadcasting UFC 1. "What they brought up was the demise of PKA Kickboxing and that martial arts, in their minds, was basically *Karate Kid* movies," said Davie. "Fantasy shit." The success and subsequent failure of PKA Karate on cable was something that was waved at Davie. "It had a high point. It sagged and faded. It's not selling today," the executives told him. "That martial arts shit, that karate shit don't sell."

With martial arts, like fashion, what's old is new and old again. The key to leaving a mark is the where and the when.

"I believe there was some spiritual forerunners to the UFC," McClaren said. "That match with Muhammad Ali really was a spiritual forerunner. Its effect on the UFC was limited except to say we didn't want it to be like that. It was more what we didn't want. People said we were crazy to do no rules. No! If you actually try to figure out how to make rules, martial art versus martial art—because that's what it was, it wasn't MMA when it launched—what rules do you use? I saw it more retroactively. But I was aware how convoluted the rules were, and that's what influenced me and the UFC. The only way we could do this was if we 'don't have rules.'"

In 1976, McClaren was making grades at Berkeley in an "elevated state." He didn't care much about it but was nonetheless aware of that summer's Ali–Inoki showdown, which is easy to understand considering all the press it received. Any major daily worth reading in the U.S. featured coverage of the match in the months leading up to the fight, and most sent reporters to Tokyo to report on it live during fight week. Because of how big Ali was at the time, and how many papers he sold, the match received global media coverage, the scope of which was more intense than any mixed-style bout before or after.

Forty years after the match, fighters during UFC's Zuffa-era of MMA dominance have grown accustomed to receiving plenty of headlines and being treated like any marketable mainstream athlete. Under the vision and resourcefulness of UFC's second ownership group, Las Vegas casino owners Frank and Lorenzo Fertitta, and their minority partner and face of the company Dana White, Zuffa made an American, Ronda Rousey, and Irishman, Conor McGregor, the most popular mixed martial artists on the planet in 2015.

Being the woman who brought women to the Octagon and quickly emerging as the first mixed martial artist, regardless of gender, to transcend the UFC brand into pop-culture stardom aren't comparable to Muhammad Ali's legacy, of course, but more people have heard of "Rowdy" Ronda Rousey than any mixed-style fighter before her—other than of Ali, of course—and that means something.

★ ★ ★ ★ ★

William Viola Sr., then a twenty-six-year-old martial artist and part-time kickboxing promoter out of Pittsburgh, was heavily invested in the Ali–Inoki media coverage. Before premium cable, pay-per-view, and the internet, Viola always found a way to stay up-to-date on the fights. For Ali, the superhero trained in the sweet science, to fight Inoki, a mystery martial artist with several disciplines to rely upon, well, Viola was enthralled.

On Wednesday nights Viola ran an open class out of his dojo, meaning anyone of any style could show up to train. Judo guys, jiu-jitsu guys, boxers, full-contact fighters. "We had the full gamut of all the different arts," he said. "We didn't call it mixed martial arts. We just called it combined martial arts. We just combined things." They figured knowing one style was good, but not nearly as good as knowing several, especially when that meant harmonizing striking and grappling skills.

This martial arts interplay added a great deal to Viola's Ali–Inoki intrigue.

"To me Ali was a hero," Viola said. "He was a champion of champions at that time. I remember Ali was shooting his mouth off about either a Japanese or Chinese man couldn't beat him. That really got the martial arts community excited. Since we trained all the different people the big question in my dojo was who would actually win: Muhammad Ali, Bruce Lee, or Bruno Sammartino?"

Then the match happened.

"It was a dog and pony show," Viola said bitterly. "The martial arts community, they knew it was a disgrace. For a great athlete of that stature to lower himself to do that, it was pitiful. It was humiliating. I actually felt humiliated for him myself. He was a great boxer. I don't know why he had to do that. I knew it was real but I couldn't believe it. Inoki had no chance to win. It's like a race car, but he wasn't allowed to get out of first gear. That's exactly how I look at that. How could you change the rules the day or night before the fight? And the loser was the people like me that bought tickets."

Three years after watching a wrestler literally and figuratively flop against a boxer—setting the stage for a rare moment when Ali made people feel like they didn't get their money's worth—Viola set out to do mixed fighting his way. Style versus style was dated, he thought. Viola wanted to pit competitors with varied skills against one another. It should be about the best fighter, not style, because one discipline wasn't going to make the cut. With Frank Caliguri, Viola established CV Productions, which they claim is the first MMA-based promotional company in American history. Viola took to codifying standards that aren't far from the Unified Rules governing MMA in 2016, and used them over 130 times under a sanctioning body they established, the World Martial Arts Fighting Association.

To make the matches mixed, they had to figure out a way to cover fighters' knuckles. This was supposed to be sport, not the bloody Brazilian variety of mixed fights called Vale Tudo, which translates from Portuguese as "anything goes."Among taekwondo grandmaster Jhoon Rhee's accomplishments, inventing, patenting, manufacturing, and selling a line of safety equipment— including a small hand pad he called the "knuckle punch" for use on a heavy bag—is right near the top of the list. In total the University of Texas engineering grad created over twelve U.S. patents. Rhee's Safety-Face, a soft helmet, was put on permanent display in New York City's Museum of Modern Art in 1998. Rhee says the inventions saved the martial arts industry because insurance companies soon wouldn't cover any school, dojo, or academy that did not use safety equipment.

"Jhoon Rhee's glove is what inspired me to do this," Viola said. "The very first martial arts movie he made, it covered his hands and only weighed about two ounces. It had a piece of string on the front of it you put your fingers in. It was absolutely perfect for what I wanted, because you could grapple with it. You had an open hand. This was an open-hand glove. This was perfect. We could not have been able to pull it off without Jhoon Rhee's gloves. A boxing glove, even an eight-ounce glove, you couldn't grab anybody. For the wrestlers and judo guys, this thing was perfect."

Their first try turned out a standing-room-only crowd of 2,500 to a Holiday Inn. Viola says boxing people were upset that mixed fighting was selling out venues while they couldn't bring out more than three hundred to four hundred people a show. MMA has never had trouble creating headlines, and CV Productions' Super Fighters League (SFL) quickly received local press. Events built momentum. Then Pennsylvanian politicians moved to shut them down. State Senate Bill 632 (Session of 1983 Act 1983-62) banned "any competition which involves any physical contact bout between two or more individuals, who attempt to knockout their opponent by employing boxing, wrestling, martial arts tactics or any combination thereof and by using techniques including, but not limited to, punches, kicks and choking."

"The boxing commission at that particular time were pudgy and punch-drunk. They didn't want to hear anything," Viola said. "The mob had a lot of control over boxing. They did a lot of the betting. We were plucking the hornet's nest. We were upsetting them. We were transparent. The athletic commission could not control, tax, or regulate us. They had no damn clue on what they ought to do with us. So what's the thing to do? Outlaw us. They put us out of business by legislation. Which is a travesty. The people who came after me, the boxing commissioner was arrested for corruption. Some legislators who passed the bill went to jail. They weren't the most stand-up citizens. They were corrupted and shady. It's just one of those things."

Pennsylvania became the first of many states in the U.S. to ban this form of combat sport. Most of that took place more than a decade later, after the UFC gained its initial popularity in the mid-1990s and critics such as John McCain, the Republican U.S. Senator from Arizona, equated the action in the cage to "human cockfighting." In 1997, McCain, whose wife, Cindy, is heir to Budweiser, which was heavily invested in boxing at the time, sat as the Chairman of the Commerce Commission and worked with cable operators to purge the UFC from pay-per-view.

Fans were relegated to commiserating in online chat rooms and forums in the early days of the internet, and "tape trading" took off in a burgeoning underground market for MMA videos as the sport went dark in the U.S.

History repeated itself as authorities tried to ban the action. But edicts from Roman emperors and laws passed by representative governments are entirely different things, so over time modern people, for good or for ill, demanded and received what they wanted.

The wall began to crack in April 2000 when California became the first state to produce rules and regulations for MMA. New Jersey literally followed their lead that day and used the same rules to start sanctioning events. The first regulated card in the U.S., promoted by the International Fighting Championship, took place at the Tropicana Casino and Resort in Atlantic City, September, 30, 2000. Two months later the UFC, still under the old SEG regime, promoted at the Trump Taj Mahal.

Pennsylvania eventually legalized the regulation of MMA in 2009, and the UFC, promoted by a riding-high Zuffa regime, drew 17,741 fans to the Wachovia Center in Philadelphia for a gate of $3.55 million.

★ ★ ★ ★ ★

A generation removed from Ali–Inoki, as opposition to MMA in the U.S. hit its fevered pitch, Japanese promoters, television executives, and organized crime bosses made moves towards expanding mixed-style fights in Japan.

Predicated on the work laid down by Inoki, whose desire to represent pro wrestling as the strongest style of fighting manifested in many ways, the Pride Fighting Championships sparked a new and hugely influential chapter in the history of modern MMA.

"I think the Ali–Inoki show was a successful event, except for the fight itself was failure," said Pride executive Hideki Yamamoto. "It was a fact that the show caught the minds of many boys. When we started Pride those boys were in their mid-thirties and in position to manage budgets and projects. The memory of the show motivated those boys to join or invest into Pride."

Drawing 47,869 fans to the Tokyo Dome, Pride's inaugural event in October 1997 was headlined by an Inoki disciple, Nobuhiko Takada, and Rickson Gracie, the supposed best fighter in the family, mythologized with a 200–0 record, who was passed over in favor of Royce Gracie at UFC 1. In several ways it was the perfect clash to animate the Japanese mixed fighting industry. Takada carried with him the mixed fighting tradition that was cultivated by Inoki and Karl Gotch—pro wrestling is a martial art rooted in catch-as-catch-can. Even if Takada wasn't much of a shooter he understood the value of lining himself up against legitimate fighters, a major theme of Inoki, Gotch, and the New Japan Pro Wrestling at that time.

"When it came to Inoki's wrestlers, the New Japan Pro Wrestling dojo training is hard, not just because they need tough wrestlers but because they expect them to be able to hold their own and take care of business and be physical and be in shape because that's what Gotch believed," said Josh Barnett, who trained with the sadistic Belgian legend and both wrestled and fought for Inoki in Japan. "Gotch said conditioning is your greatest hold, so you better be in shape. He revolutionized the way Japanese professional wrestling is by coming in and showing even more of the catch wrestling lineage, showing more of the real fighting lineage, which would eventually get them even interested in learning Thai boxing and boxing and all these things which became the shoot fighting of UWF and Pancrase."

In the years following Ali–Inoki, Japan continued playing with mixed styles. That mostly pertained to grappling and pro wrestling, which looked nothing like the stuff that emerged from the theatrical influence of America's Gold Dust Trio. Inoki's camp issued newspaper ads declaring pro wrestling the strongest fighting style and that all challenges were welcome. And that's what he and his team portrayed any time they stepped into the ring, shoot or work.

Including Ali, Inoki "fought" twenty mixed martial arts contests—that's what the wrestler, his manager Hasashi Shinma, and Vince McMahon Sr. called them starting in 1975. Inoki lost just once against sixteen wins and three draws until his retirement from these kinds of bouts in 1989. Three months after the Ali match, Inoki returned with another "martial arts" contest against Andre the Giant. Giant challenged Inoki by claiming that the man who went fifteen rounds with Muhammad Ali didn't really represent the sport of pro wrestling. It had always been Vince McMahon's hope to see Ali matched with Andre the Giant, but that wasn't going to happen. So if it was a tournament of sorts to crown a mixed martial arts champion, which McMahon Sr. did in 1978, Inoki versus Andre made sense. Inoki won by technical knockout in the twenty-fourth minute. It was probably all fake. Some contests were more gimmicky than real, but some were real.

Like Ali, Inoki had a way of elevating his opponents. Inoki's profile never busted out as he hoped in the West, but matches in the Asian part of the world went over huge.

In December of '76, Inoki visited Karachi National Stadium to take on the star of a famed Pakistani wrestling family, Akrum Pehlwan. The original plan was to execute a "Broadway," a draw where neither side loses face—like the Ali result, some might say. But the day of the event Pehlwan declared that he was going to have his hand raised. Inoki said no, he wouldn't lay down for Pehlwan and they could do it for real instead.

In the back before the match, Inoki turned to Osami Kito, a training partner, and asked him to hit him. After taking a few punches and slaps to the face, Inoki met Pehlwan in the ring and dominated what was essentially a submission wrestling contest, though the pro wrestler also used the sliding Ali kick and open-hand strikes from back control.

Two minutes into the third round, Inoki was declared the winner after he snatched a double wristlock (a Kimura), bridged, and snapped the Pakistani's shoulder.

"I broke it!" Inoki yelled as he stood.

Three years later, Akrum's nineteen-year-old cousin Zubair Alias Jhara was big, strong, and groomed for vengeance. Pakistan shut down on June 16, 1979, as the thirty-six-year-old Inoki and the boy who wished to slay him met at the Gaddafi Stadium for a fabled match. They wrestled to a five-round draw, but Inoki raised Jhara's hand at the end and the crowd in Lahore, Pakistan, went wild. This gesture endeared Inoki to the Pakistanis, as did his growing embrace of Islam.

In the fall of 1977, Inoki brought American Chuck Wepner to Tokyo.

Wepner enjoyed the experience with Andre the Giant at Shea Stadium. He had been paid very well, and when Vince McMahon Sr. asked him to go to Tokyo a year later, he accepted right away. The rangy Wepner soaked in his first-class ticket to the newly opened Narita Airport and spent sixteen days in a four-room penthouse hotel suite in the center of the city. "It was almost like being the friggin' emperor,"

said the "Bayonne Bleeder." In the mornings leading up to
the Inoki match, which was "all show business," meaning a
work, Wepner confirmed, an army of photographers waited
to take his picture.

"Like that scene with Stallone in the first *Rocky* where
everybody was with him and he wanted to get away," Wepner
said. "He picked up and really ran fast. I used to do that and
these guys would keep up with me. And they'd be taking
pictures. I mean, I'm trying to lose these guys. They'd keep
up and be taking pictures at the same time. Everywhere you
went. Dinner. Out on the street. Clubs. Martial arts clubs.
It was always forty to fifty photographers there. They loved
to take pictures."

During their match Wepner almost messed everything
up when an overhand right that was supposed to miss
slammed into Inoki's pelican jaw as the wrestler stood up
straight.

"He went down like a sack of potatoes," Wepner
recounted. "And I'm saying to myself, 'Jesus Christ I'm in
Japan and I beat this guy. I'm going to get killed before I
leave the country. I beat the undefeated karate and wrestling
champion.' We continued on and in the next round he got
me in the Boston crab—that's where they bend your legs
over backwards—and I tapped out," a surefire way of knowing the outcome had been scripted.

"Inoki was a legend in Japan. A legend," Wepner said.
"They had signs and billboards fifty feet high about the
match coming up. Everywhere you went there were signs
with Inoki. He was the most tremendously popular athlete
of all time. The karate and jiu-jitsu champion of the world.
He was . . . everybody Inoki, Inoki. He was six-three, about

225, he was a handsome Japanese guy. He had a beautiful wife. And he was at the peak of his career then.

"The people in Japan treated me tremendously. It was probably the best time I ever had in my life. Whatever I wanted, they gave me. They took a million pictures. And I made friends with Antonio Inoki, too.

"I enjoyed working with, he was such a dear man too, Vince McMahon Sr., I fought for the father, not for the son. Vince McMahon Sr. insisted more on wrestling and stuff. Junior made a lot of money. He's a brilliant guy, more into the theatric things and the makeup and the costumes and the flying through the air and all that other stuff. And he made a lot of money for the wrestlers. But I fought for his father, who was very friendly with Madison Square Garden. That's how I really got the gig. He told me I did a great job, and I was paid well. And I enjoyed myself."

By the end of 1978, after Inoki won matches in Frankfurt, Germany, and Philadelphia, Pa., McMahon Sr. created the World Wrestling Federation world martial arts heavyweight title. Inoki's manager, Shinma, served as the figurehead WWF president in Japan, and the belt was said to be awarded to Inoki based on his "achievements" representing pro wrestling versus martial arts. Inoki held onto the title for a decade and, real or not, there were some rides along the way.

Five months after American Willie Williams, a six-foot-seven Kyokushin karate competitor, placed third out of 187 competitors from 162 countries in the second world open karate championships in November 1979, he faced Inoki in the most heated contest of the wrestler's mixed martial arts series.

Kyokushin—a form of karate created by Mas Oyama, a Korean-born Japanese national regarded as one of the most fearsome fighters in history—is the art Gerard Gordeau, the long lanky striker who slammed a foot into Teila Tuli's face, represented at UFC 1. Years later Gordeau told sherdog.com that based on his experience, there wasn't one best martial art, but Kyokushin, contested in open-weight elimination tournaments, was where the "real motherfuckers" proved how tough they are. That was Williams, who clawed and scraped his way through the Inoki match.

If it was worked it was a hell of a work that featured hard strikes to the head and body. At the very least it was wild; Inoki and Williams tumbled out of the ring several times. The contest, ruled a draw, ended when Inoki apparently broke Williams' elbow with an armbar on the floor—not the canvas, the floor. Inoki's ribs were also said to be fractured.

A decade after Ali, Inoki took to the ring with Leon Spinks, who split a pair of boxing bouts with The Greatest. The Japanese hero won by pin to close another panned boxer versus wrestler affair. Inoki "fought" five times in the 1980s. His closing two contests in 1989 were especially memorable.

Chota Chochoshvili, a two-time Olympian from the Soviet republic of Georgia in the Russian Caucasus who won the gold medal at ninety-three kilos in the Munich Games, threw Inoki hard onto the canvas on April 24, 1989. It was an odd open setup inside the Tokyo Dome, basically four pillars without ropes for the New Japan Pro Wrestling–promoted event. To the shock of Japan, Inoki was counted out at 1:30 of Round 5 and relinquished the WWF martial arts title. Chochoshvili coughed up the belt back to Inoki a month later by submission, a tried-and-true Kimura, and

Inoki retired from mixed martial arts "competition" the same way he started: claiming victory over an Olympic-gold-medal-winning judoka.

Almost three decades years later, Japanese wrestler Shinsuke Nakamura, using his "Bomaye knee" named in honor of Inoki, who took the phrase from Ali, is the king of strong style seeking to expand his reach to America after signing a deal with the WWE.

Fueled by an embrace of shoot-style pro wrestling, the Universal Wrestling Federation formed in 1984 after New Japan–trained grapplers branched off to focus on matches that were essentially choreographed fights made to look legitimate. No jumping off the ropes. Punches and kicks and takedowns came at near full power. The wrestlers knew they were going to suffer in a match, and much of the time working came in the form of letting an opponent slip out of a submission hold.

UWF was very popular with fans, but behind the scenes it was plagued with problems and fell apart from the inside. In its place sprang up Shooto, UWF-International, RINGS, and Fujiwara Gumi, among other splinter groups, that brought a shoot style of wrestling back into the spotlight.

Structurally speaking, Fujiwara Gumi wasn't much better than UWF despite Yoshiaki Fujiwara, a top Gotch disciple, running the ship. Worked-shoot matches were *puroresu*, but some of the wrestlers were less than satisfied. Masakatsu Funaki and Minoru Suzuki, who idolized Inoki during their experience as young boys in NJPW, left Fujiwara to show what legitimate combat looked like under pro wrestling rules. With Gotch's blessing, Pancrase—a variant of pankration—began hosting real fights in a pro wrestling space, bridging old-time shooting to modern-day pro wrestling and MMA. Starting in 1993, a couple months before UFC, Pancrase represents an incredibly influential organization in the growth of organized mixed fighting.

"I had done my homework on Pancrase and was convinced it was 80 percent work and 20 percent shoot," said Art Davie. "It was a more sophisticated version of American pro wrestling, but there were shooters in Japan. Funaki, as an example. There were people who had some skills. The question with that early on was separating the wheat from the chaff, and I was pretty good at that. Who was bullshit? Who was real? That was one of the genres I investigated. Above and beyond Vale Tudo in Brazil, I began to look at the whole wrestling situation and shooting and working in Japan.

"I think that the Japanese were very sophisticated in understanding the nuances of these things and how to combine elements that would be something new."

Pancrase took off and brought legitimacy back into pro wrestling. It was a different experience for *puroresu* fans used to drawn-out drama. Matches in Pancrase often ended early. For the most part it was shoot fights, stiff style, with an emphasis on submission wrestling. This was high-level hooking. Hearkening back to the good old days of catch, wrestlers had to know what they were doing in order to survive. Foreign stars were brought in to build up the talent. Frank Shamrock, Ken Shamrock, Bas Rutten, and Maurice Smith—all future UFC champions—made Pancrase cosmopolitan and exciting to watch. Passed down through Suzuki and Funaki, Gotch's techniques helped groom a new generation of fighters who soon enough would have a chance to participate in the UFC, which lifted the veil off of everything.

Funny enough, it was a man in a mask who may have pulled pro wrestling as close to real fighting as it could get. New Japan's famous "Tiger Mask," Satoru Sayama, wanted to create a sport that focused on realistic and effective combat. That became Shooto, a seminal organization and sanctioning body known for developing some of the best welterweight-and-under Japanese talent of all time. In 1994, Sayama, notorious for his brutal training sessions, including whispers of canings, added closed-fist punches to the face of a grounded opponent for the first Japan Vale Tudo tournament. For five years the JVT produced excellent cards with legitimate contests under real fight conditions.

Rickson Gracie won the JVT tournaments in '94 and '95, and became the man everyone challenged. Gracie never even considered competing in the UWF because, as he saw it, they fix fights and he had no need to risk his reputation as a killer on an organization that went against what he was about. So UWF's Yoji Anjo, a pretty good fighter compared to his peers, tracked Gracie to the doorstep of the Brazilian's Los Angeles gym. After getting a call that there was a crew of Japanese folks looking for him, Gracie hopped in his car and wrapped his hands on the way. According to Gracie's telling of events on *The Joe Rogan Podcast*, when he arrived, a van full of photographers and reporters were waiting to document what happened.

The first thing Rickson did was bar them from the gym. Anjo wanted a fight and Gracie was willing, but he wasn't going to let the media get a glimpse. A few minutes later, Anjo walked outside after being beaten up and choked unconscious. His broken nose leaked blood onto his T-shirt, and the photos and story were reported all over Japan. A few days later, Anjo returned to Gracie's gym with a package. He apologized as he handed Gracie a samurai helmet. When Anjo returned to Japan, however, he claimed he had been jumped. Gracie smartly filmed the fight, and he was the only one with a copy. When he sent tape of the demolition to Japanese media it was obvious his version was accurate and his reputation exploded.

About a year before Anjo came knocking on Gracie's door, Hideki Yamamoto visited Rickson's gym in Los Angeles and began training there as a white belt. Yamamoto's wife, Yukino Kanda, worked in events and her company shared business ties with Nobuyuki Sakakibara. Sakakibara represented Tokai TV and was in charge of promoting UWF and K-1 in Nagoya. Takada, a UWF star who was backed by gangster Hiromichi Momose, confided in Sakakibara that he wanted to fight either Mike Tyson or Rickson Gracie before his retirement. Takada had already followed the Inoki playbook by taking on mixed-style challenges. In 1991, for instance, he expelled boxer Trevor Berbick from the ring with leg kicks—not the sliding Ali kick, but a heavier more traditional Dutch- or Thai-style hammer. Berbick, incidentally, was the last man to fight Muhammad Ali, scoring a unanimous decision after ten dreary rounds in Nassau, Bahamas, in 1981.

Sakakibara and Kanda flew to Los Angeles to begin negotiations with Rickson in 1996.

Japan's K-1 was the dominant martial arts promoter on the planet, hosting opulent, exciting events that brought strikers of any style into the ring for single-night elimination tournaments. Kazuyoshi Ishii, a Kyokushin black belt, was the powerful owner of K-1, and Sakakibara approached him because of their television ties to say that Tokai TV, which is a part of the Fuji TV network, was interested in promoting Rickson Gracie's match with Takada. According to Hideki Yamamoto, Master Ishii, as he was known, insisted on investing money in the event. As the project moved forward, Ishii had second thoughts about promoting mixed fighting, which could potentially threaten K-1's market share in Japan. He was never a fan of grappling-inclusive events anyhow.

Prior to UFC 1, Ishii sat down for an expensive breakfast with Art Davie and Rorion Gracie at the Beverly Wilshire Hotel in Beverly Hills on a fact-finding mission of sorts. Ishii told them he wasn't interested in events with grappling, and eventually that same feeling caused him to withdraw his money and support for the Gracie-Takada fight. By 1998, Davie had left the struggling UFC to work with K-1.

Sakakibara then went to a man who had apparently been betrayed by Ishii, a shadowy *yakuza* figure named Mr. Ishizaka (aka Korean-born Kim Dok Soo). The underworld in Japan involved itself with events. If something big was happening, they felt entitled to a piece. Whether Rikidōzan or Antonio Inoki brought the crowds, fight game politics and organized crime were easily intertwined.

Inoki was certainly a player in front of and behind the curtain for Pride. The alliance was practical in the beginning, said Yamamoto. Sakakibara needed talent from New Japan Pro Wrestling to fight for his promotional company, Dream Stage Entertainment, which usurped control of Pride when KRS vanished upon Naoto Morishita's apparent suicide on January 9, 2003. DSE hired Inoki as a contractor and ended up booking some fights that hurt the pro wrestling business in Japan. Inoki, however, seemed to be just fine.

Since Sakakibara had not dealt with NJPW before, "to have control over Inoki, DSE hired Mr. Momose," Yamamoto said. "So payment was made through Momose to Inoki. It was always cash so that Inoki did not have to file income."

In his 2002 autobiography, *The Phantom of Pride*, Momose described himself as a strategic planner for many companies, including DSE. Considering he was the person who came up with the first 50 million yen to start DSE, it's easy to understand how Momose, who always sat alongside Inoki at Pride events wearing a baseball cap with "Young at Heart" stitched into it, earned his ghostly sobriquet.

I saw them together many times while covering Pride in Japan as a reporter until the end of 2003, when Momose was pushed out by Ishizaka as *yakuza* gangsters faced down at the Tokyo Dome.

"That had started with Morishita's death and it continued for the whole year and it culminated at that November event and what happened was that Ishizaka and his group basically had the numbers to take control or take full control of Pride," Miro Mijatovic, a former fight manager credited with exposing Pride's *yakuza* ties following a lawsuit, told Spike TV in 2012.

Several years after Pride made its mark on the mixed-fighting world, Ishizaka (the Korean Kim Dok Soo) reportedly fled to South Korea as Japanese authorities sought him for questioning when his ties to Pride were elaborated upon in a series of articles by the weekly magazine *Shukan Gendai*. The blowback cost Pride support from Fuji TV in 2006, and without television backing, the promotion rapidly unraveled. Sakakibara, the public face of Pride, endured a tear-filled press conference in Las Vegas before officially selling the show to Zuffa in 2007, solidifying the Octagon as the center of the MMA universe.

ROUND

FIFTEEN

On page 310, located in the second-to-last paragraph of the Pulitzer Prize–winning biography *King of the World: Muhammad Ali and the Rise of an American Hero*, journalist David Remnick dedicates the work to his brother. Such was the depth of the Remnick boys' fascination with Ali, the author noted, that they *even* ventured to the Beacon Theater on Manhattan's Upper West Side, Friday, June 25, 1976, to watch Ali battle a professional wrestler live on closed circuit.

Used as an adverb, "even" stands out as dismissively revealing. For many reasons Ali was special, and one way or another he tended to leave an impression. There was a sense that whatever Ali did—be it box, protest, make movies, provide his voice and likeness for Saturday morning cartoons, or, yes, *even* engage in perceived carnival acts like mixed-rules fights with pro wrestlers—some redeeming virtue would emerge. What that looked like after the Inoki bout greatly depended on a viewer's sense of the situation.

Like most Americans who watched Ali take on Inoki, for the seventeen-year-old Remnick it rendered down to a strange spectacle the value of which, if such a thing existed, resided mainly in Ali's vibrant presence. Forty years after the fact, Remnick, now editor-in-chief of the *New Yorker*, offered no recollection of the night he watched Ali–Inoki at the Beacon—other than suggesting it was something worth forgetting. Otherwise, it was as the boxing and wrestling media framed: a fifteen-round farce. A money grab. A footnote. A dangerous waste of time. A disaster. It was Inoki crawling around the floor like a crab. It was the crowd failing to understand what they were watching. It was the West being utterly disdainful of the East.

The existence of Ali–Inoki was partly a result of the attitude that produced George Foreman pummeling five no-name boxers in under an hour on *Wide World of Sports*; Billie Jean King besting Bobby Riggs in The Battle of the Sexes inside the Eighth Wonder of the World, Houston's Astrodome; Bob Arum and Vince McMahon Jr. promoting a closed-circuit event featuring Evil Knievel's aborted jump on a rocket-powered cycle across the Snake River Canyon; *Superstars*, which matched athletes from various sports in a multitude of competitions; and *Battle of the Network Stars*, which did the same with actors and actresses.

These were the reality shows of their day. The genre became common in American pop culture during the 1970s, yet some events stood the test of time. Riggs versus King, for instance, came to represent an important cultural moment for the cause of feminism in the U.S.

Bucking conventional wisdom, Ali versus Inoki has also come to signify more than a sad money grab. The history associated with the world's greatest heavyweight boxer, perceived then as the world's greatest fighter, taking on a skilled opponent with divergent abilities, is reason enough for the match to be remembered. It took quite a lot of courage for Ali to do what he did. No one asked him to step outside his comfort zone to take on Inoki. Rather, most people with any sway wished he wouldn't. He did it for himself, at the zenith of his career and fame, months removed from perhaps his most impressive win in the most trying of circumstances.

This was, in spite of the rules, a legitimate contest. Nothing between the competitors was scripted or rehearsed, at least. Conceivably it would not have taken much for Ali to end up in a risky situation. He could have been made to look a fool. He could have, regardless of his public protestations in venues like *The Tonight Show*, brought disrepute to boxing.

"Ali was always willing to endure ridicule to enhance his name and create interest in him and his sport," said boxing writer Kevin Iole. "But it could have hurt his reputation and it had the ability to do so. I don't think Inoki took any risk. It was all upside for Inoki."

Discussion around the legacy of the Inoki match rarely centers on the true cost or benefit. Ali was, in fact, hurt in Tokyo.

Whether or not it was a result of the Frazier contest, the blows to his legs by Inoki, the normal physical price of a long boxing career, or simply how it worked out, Ali wouldn't put an opponent on the canvas again during his final seven fights over the next five years.

Following the third Frazier fight, Ali's reflexes were noticeably slower and his speech patterns had shifted. The

Inoki contest only exacerbated his decline because it sapped the heavyweight of whatever remaining mobility he could muster. Early in Ali's career his defense, offense, and everything else were predicated on the swiftness coming from his legs. Now the decline was obvious for everyone to see.

"This guy was dying with every fight he fights," Pacheco said. "Blood was coming out in his urine and eventually it'll be the end of the road. They just kept on going until the last fight. He had to quit because he couldn't walk up to the ring. For them to put him up to the ring was criminal. The poor guy couldn't even walk to the ring. This model, wonderful athlete just run down. Like a Model T running the Indianapolis 500. It shouldn't have happened but it did. I said it on television so much they asked me to shut up."

Ali's kidneys were not only allowing blood to pass, there was evidence that the lining of his kidney's cellular walls were disintegrating, Pacheco said. The great boxer was literally falling apart from the inside, but he didn't care. In Ali's mind, a fighter's mind, The Greatest's mind, he remained invincible and untouchable.

Three months after the match in Tokyo, Ali received a victory many people felt he should not have over Ken Norton in their third fight at Yankee Stadium. He managed two more wins before dropping his title to seven-fight "veteran" Leon Spinks in 1978.

"It's like somebody with a paintbrush walking up to the *Mona Lisa* saying I can make that better," said Pacheco, who had sounded the alarm bells and removed himself from the equation in September 1977 after Ali's unanimous decision over Earnie Shavers.

"It's the *Mona Lisa*, you can't touch it! Well, that's what Ali was. He was the *Mona Lisa*. He was a perfect specimen. He was a masterpiece. Don't touch him. Don't fool around with him. But everyone did and he let 'em. He let them all. I didn't want to be a part of that and I wasn't, and to this day I'm proud I wasn't. I stopped and stepped away from him when I wanted to."

After regaining the belt versus Spinks at the Superdome in New Orleans, Ali announced his retirement in September 1979, which he promptly broke thirteen months later against Larry Holmes.

"The press conference that they had at the Forum for him when he decided he was going to retire was very memorable," said newspaper columnist John Hall. "They had a circus going. Several bars on the floor. Chick Hearn was the MC and introduced a lot of people. Ali made a big speech that day and was the most charming I ever saw. He said, 'I fooled you all. You believed I was a bad guy. I fooled you all. I've enjoyed it and thank you for everything.' He was totally charming. The next time I saw him he was already starting to mumble and lost the personality. I think it was from the punches. Larry Holmes really beat him up both to the body and head. He hurt him a lot too."

Ali looked deceptively great ahead of that fight. He weighed under 218, and as far as his personal goals went this was good news. Ali hadn't been less than 220 pounds for a boxing bout since upending Foreman in 1974, but in 1980 this was smoke and mirrors as he suffered from the dehydrating effects of thyroid pills. Gene Kilroy said he took Ali to the Mayo Clinic for a checkup before meeting Holmes. The boxer passed, though Pacheco knocked those results.

Fourteen months later in a minor-league baseball park in Nassau, Bahamas, Ali, weighing 236.5 pounds, went down to Trevor Berbick in an ugly display. He seemed almost unable to make it into the ring on his own. This was undoubtedly the end. No more propping up an old master.

"One of the main differences between Ali and other fighters today, he never walked around thinking he was a god," said Rudy Hernández, who remembered the great boxer shadowboxing at the Main Street Gym in Los Angeles in 1981 like the rest of the guys. "He walked around being humble. He spoke to us. There was no catch. No cameras. No one around. He spoke to us like another human being. To me guys today feel like they're owed, and they haven't earned it. They weren't as humble as he was."

Up until Parkinson's disease overtook Ali's life, the man exuded a special sort of boundless energy. It was here that Ali and Antonio Inoki, whose famous "burning fighting spirit" mantra follows him wherever he goes, truly connected. An important piece of Inoki's persona focuses on transferring his energy to fans, fighters and other wrestlers. A believer in the supernatural, Inoki will literally slap people silly as a goodwill gesture, and most recipients accept the experience with reverence. More than saying hello, Inoki always asks how are their energy levels. Someone wondering that, then, needs to be spry most of the time.

Ali didn't need to slap someone cross the face to transfer energy. He only needed to walk in a room. I saw him once in person, in 1998 at a K-1 kickboxing event in Las Vegas. Pronounced physical ailments caused him to shake and slow his gait, but the room didn't care that Ali wasn't Ali. They loved him just the same. Everyone stood and looked before offering an equal mix of cheering, clapping, and respect. The feel of the place bumped up a few notches—even then he had that sort of presence about him.

A year after their draw in Tokyo, Inoki traveled with his wife to California to witness Ali's wedding to Veronica Porche at the Beverly Wilshire Hotel in Beverly Hills. Ali's divorce from Belinda had just finalized when he and Porche became official. Ahead of the fortieth anniversary of The Rumble in the Jungle, Porche, who provided Ali two more daughters, including famed female boxer Laila Ali, claimed she and Ali had married in a secret service in Zaire in 1974. By 1986, however, they were apart for good, as he married a fourth and final time that November, taking vows with Lonnie Williams, whom thirty years later he still lives with in Scottsdale, Ariz.

Ali's influence on Inoki was massive—all one needs to see is how the wrestler patterned himself after the great boxer. Ali allowed "Ali Bomaye," a catchy, upbeat track from the movie *The Greatest*, the 1977 biopic in which he played himself, to be used as the Japanese wrestler's theme song. Inoki treated it as his own from then on. And when Inoki moved into the fight promotion business, he named his traditional New Year's Eve events "Inoki Bom-Ba-Ye." Inoki has always treated wrestling as a vehicle to bring people together, and in this sense the mixed match with Ali served its purpose, even if he never found the fame he hoped for in America. The closest he got to enjoying notoriety in the U.S. outside of hardcore pro wrestling circles, beyond being the Japanese guy that Ali fought in the non-boxing bout, was appearing as himself in *The Bad News Bears Go to Japan*.

Inoki continued to build his wrestling career, getting in and out of trouble, and playing off the mixed-match theme until 1989, when he made the move into politics—a new sort of public life—through the "Sports and Peace" party and the Japanese House of Councillors.

The next year both he and Ali visited Iraq as the U.S.-led coalition ramped up for the Gulf War following Iraq's invasion of Kuwait. Both men attempted to negotiate the release of hostages taken by Saddam Hussein as bargaining chips to stave off attack. Ali sought freedom for fifteen Americans, while Inoki hoped to secure safe passage for over one hundred Japanese families.

As he had in Pakistan during the peak of his wrestling days in the 1970s, Inoki embraced Islam while he was in its midst. Whether or not this was a nod to Ali it surely seemed so, though Inoki generally took on the defining characteristics of the environment he operated in at any particular moment. In 1990, he became the first Japanese politician to be admitted to the mosque at Karbala. Standing in view of news cameras with his hands raised and palms facing skyward in prayer, Inoki underwent the process of becoming a Muslim. He was given the name "Muhammad Hussain," although that was not revealed publicly for twenty-two years.

Days later, an estimated 35,000 people attended a "peace festival" Inoki organized in Baghdad featuring Japanese professional wrestlers, traditional taiko drummers, a rock concert, soccer, basketball, karate, and judo exhibitions at Saddam Arena. Another area in which Inoki and Ali were similar: they had no problem operating in the backyards of despots.

As Inoki's return to Japan loomed, Saddam Hussein's son Uday, Iraq's minister of sport when he wasn't raping, murdering, or torturing, announced that according to a special order from his father, all remaining Japanese hostages would be released. Uday went so far as to apologize for holding them.

Within days of one another, Ali and Inoki departed Iraq in the company of their respective countrymen, and a month later, on January 17, 1991, the bombing commenced.

Neither Ali nor Inoki were prone to following rules. They operated as they wished in a world that was malleable to their needs. This is how truly pioneering people operate, and there's no question that Ali and Inoki qualify. Ali's strain of rebellion is a well-understood American quality. For the Japanese, however, Inoki's subversion in wrestling, politics, and life has served mostly to push firm boundaries. At certain moments he paid a price, including scoldings from the Japanese government, yet, like Ali, Inoki functions best when the lights are brightest.

In 1998, Inoki retired from active wrestling. Ali flew to Japan and sat ringside at the Tokyo Dome, joining over 65,000 fans (another 5,000 were turned away at the door) to honor the Japanese wrestler, statesman, salesman, and chameleon. Inoki walked away from participating in "strong style" matches by working over American tough guy Don Frye—just as Rikidōzan might have done if he had had the luxury of wrestling to a conclusive career arc.

As the celebration of Inoki continued, Ali had a turn to offer his thoughts on the man with whom he tested his status as the best fighter on the planet.

"It was 1976 when I fought Antonio Inoki at the Budokan," Ali said. "In the ring, we were tough opponents. After that, we built love and friendship with mutual respect.

So, I feel a little less lonely now that Antonio has retired. It is my honor to be standing on the ring with my good friend after twenty-two years. Our future is bright and has a clear vision. Antonio Inoki and I put our best efforts into making world peace through sports, to prove there is only one mankind beyond the sexual, ethnical, or cultural differences. It is my pleasure to come here today."

ACKNOWLEDGMENTS

This is my debut book and I want my first acknowledgment to be that it's taken too long to muster the courage to get this done. I'm glad I finally did. Diving into an important and misunderstood subject, around which I've dedicated myself as a reporter since the year 2000, made it considerably fun and worthwhile.

For introducing me to my terrific literary agent, Nena Madonia, who works under the legendary Jan Miller, my good friend Doug Melville earns the first nod. Doug is one of many friends whom I told this story to well before any publisher expressed interest, and I want to thank all the people in my life who listened to me babble on about it. Almost everyone I spoke with seemed genuinely interested in the tale of Muhammad Ali's forgotten fight with Antonio Inoki, and their piqued curiosity only strengthened my desire to get this done.

Thanks to Glenn Yeffeth at BenBella Books for understanding the depth of the Ali–Inoki tale and agreeing to put his team on this project. I hope I did right by the story.

Thanks to Jason Probst for being a sounding board, editor, and researcher. Thanks to my friend Michael Weber for putting together the book proposal.

A heartfelt tip of the cap to everyone who spoke to me. Quoted or not, the folks who allowed me to engage them were crucial to the story I could tell. Culling memories of great moments in fighting and pro wrestling history is one thing, but several people went above and beyond.

Jimmy Lennon Jr. opened up his childhood memories and family photo archive to me, and I still feel bad about arriving late for our first meeting.

Gene Kilroy, whose morning shave in Tokyo begins this book, was a tremendous asset on the Ali side of the story. Among others, the Ali confidant led me to Bobby Goodman, the hall of fame publicist, whose answers helped me piece together the events of 1976 as they happened. Bobby also passed along some tremendous press photos of Ali and Inoki.

Gene LeBell, whom I've known for many years, allowed me to join him in his office several times as we discussed his recollections of refereeing the match and growing up in Los Angeles. I love that in their bedroom closet, Gene's wife, Midge, still hangs the Keio Plaza Hotel robe that he brought back from Tokyo after that trip. A month after the Ali–Inoki fight they bought a duplex across the street from a park in the San Fernando Valley, and have lived there since. I should also thanks LeBell's right-hand woman, Kellie Cunningham, who puts up with more than she should but, if seeing is believing, wouldn't have it any other way.

Many thanks to Grand Master Jhoon Rhee for his graciousness. Thanks as well to his son, Chun W. Rhee.

I want to acknowledge a truth now. The story I told is close to the full tale but it's not. I scoured newspaper stories and attempted to re-create events as they happened, but it can't be the whole tale because some people connected to it chose not to participate.

Antonio Inoki wouldn't speak to me. Despite expressing through his son-in-law, Simon Inoki, that he would, the great wrestler never came through—a disappointment, but I want to still thank Simon, who passed along DVDs of the match, which I watched nearly thirty times, and shared several hours worth of stories about the most famous face in Japan. Thanks to former Pride executive Hideki Yamamoto, who offered many insights on Inoki, some of which may ring controversial. I was grateful for his perspective about the match, Inoki's history, and the intersection of organized crime and the Japanese fight world.

Unfortunately, boxing promoter Bob Arum decided against engaging with me. I still have lingering questions about the role of Ronald C. Holmes and Lincoln National Productions, Ltd. Hopefully someday we can chat.

The pro wrestling side of this story was not particularly interested in participating. Vince McMahon Jr. and the WWE declined to answer any questions, so I tried other ways to get inside. Dan Madigan, the former WWE writer, was extremely helpful and, as one might expect, a great storyteller. A friend, Yoshi Obayashi, was one of this book's biggest champions and he led me to Dan and others. I'm very grateful.

Dave Meltzer, the great wrestling writer, was instrumental in backfilling the wrestling history. Admittedly I'm not a wrestling fan, and some wondered why I would want to tell such a pro wrestling–heavy story. One of the great results of all this is

I've fostered a new respect for the business, and I'm happy to report that I'm not the snob about it that I used to be.

With that, let me single out media folks. My colleagues. Thanks to Meltzer, Dr. Mike Lano, Bobby Goodman, Kevin Iole, Jeff Wagenheim, Rich Marotta, Bill Caplan, John Hall, and Andrew Malcolm for all your recollections and analysis. I hope you enjoyed the chats as much as I did. Dr. Lano lived and breathed wrestling around the Olympic, and told me one of my favorite anecdotes in the book, about Freddie Blassie's false fangs. There were so many.

Thanks as well to John Nash, Bobby Razak, Bill Viola, Josh Barnett, Maurice Smith, Chuck Wepner, Don Chargin, Art Davie, Rudy Hernández, Ferdie Pacheco, Alan Swyer, Dave Sloane from Honda of Hollywood, Don Fraser, Bernie Yuman, Rami Genauer, the Cauliflower Alley Club, and Ronald A. DiNicola.

Party on and Godspeed to Bas Rutten. One of my earliest mixed martial arts teachers was kind enough to pen the book's great foreword.

Lastly, I want to acknowledge how lucky I was to find the Ali–Inoki story. Somehow, after traveling to Japan twelve times to cover the biggest MMA events in the world from 2000 to 2003, life brought me to a fantastic fight and pro wrestling souvenir shop near the Tokyo Dome. Hanging on my office wall today is the only piece of memorabilia I ever brought back from Japan: a replica poster of the Ali–Inoki match that advertised closed-circuit venues in Riverside, Calif. The poster sells "East Meets West" and features copies of both fighters' signatures. It fascinated me on the spot and I told myself then that someday I'd write a book about this.

—*Josh Gross, 2016*

INDEX

Page numbers in italics refer to photographs

ABOUT THE AUTHOR

 **Josh Gross** is considered a pioneer of mixed martial arts journalism. Beginning in April 2000, his career spans MMA's evolution from an underground, counterculture free-for-all into a mainstream multibillion-dollar industry. While MMA earned a reputation as one of the world's fastest-growing sports, Gross covered action in and out of the cage for *Sports Illustrated* and ESPN. He is co-owner of Side Control Media, a fight world–focused production company. For more information on the author, please follow him on twitter, @yay_yee.